£2

CALL ME BY MY
FIRST NAME

CALL ME BY MY FIRST NAME

by

REGINE

with the collaboration of
Gilbert Maurin
translated by Alison Carter

ANDRE DEUTSCH

First published 1988 by
André Deutsch Limited
105–106 Great Russell Street London WC1B 3LJ

ISBN 0 233 97996 4

Printed in Great Britain by
St Edmundsbury Press Limited, Bury St Edmunds, Suffolk

To Lionel — to Roger

Become what you are

NIETZSCHE

Contents

Illustrations: between pages 70–71 and 198–199

1

Before the War

25 December 1929. Women's voices calling in the night: 'Joseph! Joseph! Where's Joseph? ...' No, not Bethlehem, but Belgium. A young mother, a neighbour and the midwife are looking for the father of a new-born baby. My father: Joseph. My life (night-life, already) had just begun, above a bakery in Anderlecht, and my father still hadn't been found. A message came back: he'd be there as soon as the game was over. Of course, I arrived well before he did. After the warmest congratulations to my mother (her name wasn't Mary either, it was Toba), he went straight back to his game at the café. Cards: he played while I was being born, and he carried on playing while I grew up, the one constant thing in his life. Here one minute and gone the next, Joseph was to blow hot and cold right through my childhood, always deadly serious about cards, but playing at everything else.

He was a baker by trade, when he wasn't at the card table, and he and my mother lived in a tiny flat connected to the bakery by a spiral staircase. What he called 'living above his means'. I knew nothing about him until much later: until his death in fact. He was born in a Polish town, and brought up, along with eight brothers and sisters, by his mother. He was the black sheep of the family, and had always been more interested in girls and cards than in school. He was as strong as an ox, but the only financial contribution he made to the family budget came from delivering a few bars of chocolate ... However, he came to have quite a reputation in the ghetto, and was one of its most faithful sons. During pogroms or police raids he didn't think twice about joining in the fighting, even though he was only young.

1

He refused to do his military service, deciding to leave the country instead. He and my mother had just got married — but only the religious part of the ceremony — when they first came to Belgium, and they left almost immediately for Argentina, where they stayed for several years. Exactly what they did there is still a mystery to me. But I do know that's where I was conceived. So I was Polish at birth, became stateless later on, and only became French in 1969.

I don't remember much about my mother; she's really more of a silhouette than a face. And a name, Rodstein. A surname she and I shared for seven years, because Joseph didn't get around to registering me as his daughter, just as he didn't get around to marrying my mother in a civil ceremony. So she and I were Rodsteins, and he was a Zylberberg. His main excuse was that he couldn't write, and that in any case the town hall had been closed the day I was born.

My first real memories start when I was two. I can remember Joseph coming down the stairs in his vest. He was a big, strong, handsome man with black curly hair — when it wasn't covered in flour. He weighed a good sixteen stone, and could hoist flour sacks the same weight straight up onto his shoulders. It was his party piece. Very soon I had a sort of crush on him: he did amazingly impressive things, but I don't remember loving him deeply. Though I may have called him 'papa' when I was small, for me he will always be 'Joseph'. I found him bizarre, and didn't really understand him, but I did like him. With all that flour around he didn't as yet have any pretensions to elegance. And he would keep on kissing me on the mouth all the time. Horrible sloppy kisses — wet and tobacco-smelling. I had to wipe my mouth dry afterwards.

I've tried hard to remember things about my mother, but it's not easy. I remember her shouting a lot; so did Joseph. Sometimes they hit each other. The atmosphere was pretty explosive. I soon got used to their violence, and luckily they patched up their quarrels almost as fiercely as they fought them. It seemed the tension dated back from even before I was born, and very early on I got the impression that that's what life was all about.

Then one day I noticed something different. Another, very small, figure appeared with the silhouette that was my mother. It was Maurice, my brother, born on 1 April. After a Christmas baby came a little April fool. And Joseph couldn't write any better than he could that Christmas day; and it was another public holiday, so the town hall was shut again. Joseph was happy enough to feed us both, but not to register us as his. Dates and birthdays, time

2

generally, meant nothing to him — so why bother registering births? And bits of paper were such a nuisance. Time, and red tape, out of the window! I sang much later about 'papiers frivoles ou sérieux, d'azur ou d'Arménie'. Joseph kept time to his own idiosyncratic calendar.

By the time I was three or four, Joseph, and the bakery he had bit by bit played poker for and lost, had disappeared from my life. Maurice, my mother and I were in Antwerp, living in a run-down, dirty part of town. We played out on the street. For several weeks, different men would appear from time to time at the door of the basement flat we lived in. Then one morning my mother started packing; we were going to Paris. I remember how much that word set me dreaming even then.

Gare du Nord. And who should we find waiting for us at the end of the platform by the engine, but Joseph. Joking and smiling, and very full of himself. It was he who'd brought us to Paris! He'd got a job in a bakery in Belleville, and started telling us all about his wonderful new delivery bike. When we got there, we found the bakery all right, but no flat for us. He and my mother moved into a nearby hotel, and we were looked after by people who boarded children. All within a stone's throw of the bakery. During the day Joseph sat us on sacks of flour or sugar in the back room of the bakery, and we watched him work. So, for us, Paris was really no different from Anderlecht, Belgium. We just watched the same man, doing the same job, telling the same stories, yelling the same insults. We had to sit there on our sacks for hours on end, while he paid absolutely no attention to us. We didn't even know where to go when we needed the toilet, so we cried. Since Joseph threatened to clout us, we just had to shut up and go right there on the flour and sugar. I was five and Maurice was three. Our mother, meanwhile, must have had other fish to fry.

Then one morning, or perhaps it was evening, I remember all of us being at one of the big Paris railway stations. There was Joseph, and also this woman, wearing a hat, her face in shadow, and just a shadow in my memory. I remember her fox-fur stole, her suit, and most clearly the steam hissing from the train close by. She and Joseph are face to face — with me in the middle. They've got an arm each, and they're pulling, which hurts. They're talking heatedly, but not shouting at each other. This restrained sort of violence frightened me. There were none of the usual screams or blows, so what was going on? I gathered that my mother was going away somewhere, far away, for a very long time. I realized that she wanted to take me too, and that Joseph was refusing to let me go. So for a long while they both just pulled ... In the end Joseph promised her that he would come out soon and join her with the two of us. She calmed down and they let go of me.

We never saw her again — that woman who was leaving for far-away Argentina. My father always maintained that she had abandoned us. In fact, what happened was that she clearly had to go, alone, but at the last minute she thought she'd take me too, like a bit of luggage she'd very nearly forgotten. But the papers she had (false ones obtained by my father) didn't mention either me or my brother. I still don't know whether it was some personal drama that forced her to leave, or whether I should have blamed her or felt sorry for her. Either way, I started to hate the woman who left us there in all the noise and bustle of that dreary, dirty station. She did write several times asking Joseph to let me join her. But he refused to be separated from 'half of his children'. Later, he referred to it as his 'sense of family'.

Joseph had no idea what to do with us, and occasionally, if we were getting too bored, he'd take us on his rounds with him, on the bike. He delivered margarine to the Jewish bakeries in the quartier Saint-Paul: a small wholesale business. So we got to know the three big Jewish quarters of between-the-wars Paris quite well. There was Belleville, between the nineteenth and twentieth arrondissements, with its artisans, labourers and sloping streets ... the quartier Saint-Paul, the 'Pletzl', which I loved for its tiny narrow streets full of homely smells. Through ground-floor windows you could see women bent over their shabby little sewing jobs, and consumptives pressing threadbare trousers. In the courtyards, stagnating pools of water seemed to complete the transformation from one-time aristocratic quarter to over-crowded ghetto full of the poorest and least integrated Jews. Lastly, the area between Bastille and Place de la République, extending westwards as far as Sentier, was the hub of the rag trade, full of workshops and boutiques; East-European Jews had taken over every available room in response to the demands of the booming clothing industry.

But what we saw most of were the bistros where Joseph endlessly played cards. As if by magic, players gathered round as soon as he walked in, cards were brought out, and the game would begin. For us it was like a high mass, full of unchanging and incomprehensible ritual. Like a priest, or a king, Joseph sat shuffling and dealing,

4

shuffling and dealing. Sitting on the bench, we were lulled to sleep by the calls, the discussions, the arguments, the laughter and the brawls. We got to know intimately every corner and lump of those hard banquettes, trying to find ways to curl up comfortably; we'd always end up asleep somehow or other, thumbs in mouths. When the game was over, Joseph would wake us up and take us back on the delivery bike, dazed and yawning. The Pagnol film *Marius* came out around that time, with the famous belote game sequence. But we didn't know about that, Joseph never went to the cinema anyway, and only ever played poker.

As we got older, Maurice and I began to inconvenience our bachelor father rather a lot, and one fine day we found ourselves at a Jewish boarding establishment in Brunoy, one of the south-eastern suburbs of Paris. The place was well-kept, and made quite a pleasant change from the delivery bike, the sacks of flour, and the battered café banquettes. The only problem was that after one or two visits, Joseph seemed to decide that since we were fine he needn't come again. He didn't send them any money either ... The weeks went by and we started having problems with our linen ... and with other things: Jewish children not being visited by their parents! it was unheard of. Everyone knows that Jewish mothers and fathers are supposed to be crazy about the flesh of their flesh. But this sixteen-stone Jewish father had broken all the rules. I remember those Sunday afternoons waiting for The Visit. We would be sitting leaning against a big tree, with Maurice whining: 'Where's Joseph?'. Had he gone away, was he ill, or had he just forgotten us? Had he ever really existed? Or had I just made him up, complete with tall stories, appalling blind rages and sudden bursts of affection? If not, I thought, there's nothing else for it, he must be dead.

After three months of this, we weren't the only ones who dearly wanted to see him. The directeur and directrice were getting rather worried too: if this father — unworthy of the name — had gone for good, then what on earth were they to do with us? Especially since I'd started to show unmistakable signs of becoming thoroughly bad-tempered: I was unbearable, except to Maurice, of course, whom I protected as fiercely as a mother would have done. We were all-but orphans, living in a world of our own, cut off from everything and eveyone, Maurice the helpless one, and me like a spitting cat, with my claws out.

We'd just finished eating the sort of frugal meal we'd come to expect with three months' fees unpaid, when who should arrive but

Joseph, very nattily dressed, with a beautiful woman on his arm: 'Meet your new mother.'

Preambles never were his strong point. We swallowed hard. Our 'new mother' was called Thérèse, dark-haired, Polish to the tip of her tongue, and she didn't speak a word of French. She had great big gentle eyes, a lovely smile, and wonderful hands. She'd got the lot — and it was much too much of a good thing. Step-mothers just shouldn't be that pretty. So Maurice and I loathed her at first sight: she didn't have a chance.

Joseph paid the bills, plus a bit extra, and drove us away in the back of his spanking new Citroën coupé, while the usurper lorded it in the front seat. The directeur was as delighted to see us go as he was to be paid. And we were glad to see the back of the place too, all clean and tidy but very dull, where we'd learnt nothing much except that we now had a step-mother, and that was no thanks to the directeur!

Back in Paris we found Joseph still 'living above his means', but this time it was above a jam factory which he'd bought with the help of assorted loans arranged after a circuitous trip round all the financial houses from Lévy to Dreyfus, via Rosencrantz and Rosenblum ... he loved that sort of thing, and borrowed from loan sharks all his life. He was too casual ever to make his fortune, but too shrewd to have problems either. We were sent to school in the rue de la Folie-Méricourt. Thérèse couldn't have been sweeter to us, but we were real little beasts to her. Me especially: boarding-school had turned me into a right pest, and I blamed Thérèse entirely for those lonely miserable months at Brunoy. Her cooking was out of this world, and she tried to win us round with sweets and cakes. Maurice was tempted. I was furious with him: eating her food was treason! I wouldn't let him get away with eating a single mouthful without glowering at him, so he had to chew with his head down and swallow on the sly. Or else I'd kick him on the shins under the table. He gave up in the end, and pushed the plate away like I did. I'd won the mealtime battle, and got even thinner than I'd been at boarding-school.

When Thérèse started crying with exasperation, I told her exactly what I thought of her — in French of course, so she wouldn't understand. Which of course she did — and cried even more. Sometimes I was more calculating: I'd say something horrible to her, but in the sweetest tones. Her hopes would rise, and then as soon as she started to smile again I'd pull a hideous face at her.

6

More tears ... When Joseph caught me at it he kicked me up the backside several times and told me not to be so nasty: in Yiddish so that poor Thérèse would understand. He really did seem genuinely upset: it was his way of saying if he liked her, then so should we.

Things came to a crisis point one evening. Thérèse had just come in proudly showing off a new hairstyle — she'd had it cut short and dyed blonde! About turn. The children loved it, but when Joseph got over the initial shock, which left him speechless for a good ten seconds, he started yelling like a madman. He must have said it thirty times, in Yiddish, in French: 'Tart! You're nothing but a tart!' He was in a blind rage, and for the first time started to hit her. Maurice and I took one look at each other and knew: the two little monsters suddenly found they had soft hearts for their step-mother. We both dived in to protect her. We got our fair share of the blows, and I discovered that that's what love is, taking the blows for someone else. (In general, though, it's never stopped them coming!)

Thérèse let her black hair grow back after that. And she found that she'd gained a family at the expense of her filmstar looks. Joseph calmed down and was rather remorseful, and gave us both a bit of pocket money by way of an apology. It worked out quite well: we spent the money, and we forgot all about the fight.

Spring 1936, I remember hearing Léon Blum's name for the first time. And I heard the word 'Jew' in the street for the first time too. They raised the minimum wage, they lengthened holidays, but the papers still had it in for the Jews. I heard demonstrators singing 'The Internationale'. Music means a lot to me, and I loved that song; I learnt all the words, it was my favourite tune. So I was a musical follower of the Popular Front — hardly guessing I'd live through another Popular Front forty-five years later to the alternate strains of the 'Marseillaise' and the 'Internationale'. Anyhow, it made a change from Maurice Chevalier and Fréhel, whom I also tried to imitate — with a certain verve, and not much restraint. I wanted to be the greatest, and like so many children do, I dreamt I was destined to be a star or a queen.

The revolution that was brewing at home affected me a bit more personally than M. Blum's did. Joseph announced that we were going back to boarding school because Thérèse was pregnant. Pregnant? I didn't understand: explain please. They did, and one explanation was quite sufficient. Just when you start getting on with your step-mother, she produces a kid! The hatred welled up

7

all over again, but it didn't get much public exposure because we were whisked away to the new boarding-school, this time in Aulnay-sous-Bois. Joseph had it all worked out: but so had I. By the time he came to fetch us home again when the seven months were up, I'd made Maurice swear on oath to dislike whatever it was we'd find when we got back. Standing by the crib as if it was a coffin we saw a fat wrinkled ball stir. Their new daughter.

'Don't you think she's sweet?' said Joseph.

'Yuk. She's really ugly.'

Maurice didn't go into ecstasies either: 'She's all red ... she's dribbling ... that hair ...'

Maurice had learnt his lesson well, but he needed supervising; he didn't have my vicious streak, and his curiosity soon got the better of him. He would peer into the crib at the squealing infant without even being asked to. I had to get him under control, realizing that the more often he looked at the thing in the crib, the more likely he was to end up liking it. Because 'Eva', as the little intruder was called, should never have been there in the first place, I felt it was dangerous even to look at her. Much later, when I was cross with people, I just used to treat them as if they weren't there. That's how I tried to treat Eva ... but it wasn't easy.

As I feared, it wasn't long before Maurice went back on his oath — and in a most perverse way. He was a compulsive eater whose hunger was never quite satisfied, and my tactics were to prevent him eating his fill. Then one day I caught him drinking a glass of milk ... but it was left over breast-milk! Eva obviously hadn't been able to manage all her feed, and Thérèse had left a bit in the glass. I was absolutely furious with poor Maurice, and beat him up. I never have liked milk.

At school I kept to myself, and got the reputation of being a bit on the wild side. One day when I got back, I told Joseph how people had got me into trouble, and that I'd been beaten up. He'd given me a franc by way of consolation and told me sententiously: 'Don't turn the other cheek, always give as good as you get'. I'm not especially obedient by nature, but I decided I'd take Joseph's theory on board. The theory still holds good, and I was to make plenty of sparks fly: a party for a party, a knock for a knock.

The teacher was taking the register a few months later: 'Regine Zylberberg!' I didn't budge — my name was Rodstein. She called the name again, pointing at me.

8

That's how I learnt that my father had recognized all three of us together, Eva, Maurice and me. He'd just forgotten to tell us. All thanks to Thérèse, who liked things just so, and thought it went without saying that one recognized one's children. She had nagged him, and gone on about his moral obligations until she persuaded him to let a solicitor sort it all out once and for all. And so, thanks to my stepmother I became, if not a daddy's girl, then at least my father's daughter. The new state of affairs made me very happy; it was immensely reassuring to know I had the same name as my father. The battles at home stopped; everyone breathed a sigh of relief and Eva really did become our little sister.

I had a school friend who just couldn't manage the 'berberg' part of my name, and I remember telling her: 'Just call me Régine'. That's what I've been telling people ever since ...

The jam business, *Confitures Villiers*, was doing well, and we were quite comfortably off. But neither financial security nor official fatherhood seemed to make Joseph any more willing to talk about his own family. He didn't talk about very much anyway — apart from straight flushes and full houses, and was even less forthcoming about his parents or any possible brothers or sisters. At school, all our little friends had grandfathers, grandmothers, aunts and uncles ... but our family didn't materialize at all until after Joseph's death, as I've said ...

We got given presents and new clothes sporadically through-out the year, at times which bore no relation whatever to the dictates of the Jewish or the Christian calendar, nor to our birthdays either. They just came out of the blue, much as thick ears did! We accepted the mish-mash we spoke at home now just as unques-tioningly: it was a mixture of French, Polish and Yiddish. Even Thérèse had now started to speak a bit of French — if you could call it that. We were all in the same boat, adrift without much in the way of navigational aids or sense of time. Castaways who didn't question the captain of the ship, and who took the weather as it came, fair or foul. I'd banish rainclouds by singing something like Chevalier's 'Ma pomme'. It cheered Joseph up no end, and he'd give me five sous, or ten if he was with friends in a party mood.

But Thérèse had other plans for us, greater things than singing 'Ma pomme' for an audience of card players. If she could look impeccably clean and spotless, she decided we could look impeccably clean and spotless too. Easier said than done. It wasn't that we didn't want to, but things just didn't work out that way. There was

9

always some gremlin — no doubt from the ghetto of ages past — which returned to jinx her valiant attempts at turning us into model children. Lice for example ... She could scrub us as hard as she liked, and dress us like nice little children, but the lice always came back. So Thérèse would constantly be chasing the obstinate little beasts the length and breadth of our scalps with her long, graceful fingers and carefully filed nails. No messing about with the powder or the special lotions! We never did anything by halves, and Maurice and I caught impetigo as well. We were covered in purulent spots — it was really disgusting. Thérèse was undeterred and dragged us off to the Saint-Louis hospital where they first smeared us with horrible sulphurous stuff, and then shut us in a cubicle for an hour while it took effect.

Thérèse's activities didn't stop at being mother and stepmother by day. At night she slogged away in the little jam factory. She scalded almonds by the kilo, and then deftly removed the skins, one at a time, with those fingers that should really have been stringing pearls. Despite working hard at the jam business, Joseph still managed to fit in long rest-breaks on café benches ...

Maurice, who got everything that was going round, caught mumps and passed it on to me. While we were in quarantine we 'helped' Thérèse, stuffing ourselves with coconut and all sorts of other sweet things which were lying around. But I never touched the great vats of jam: red jam, yellow jam ... if there's one thing I can't stand, it's jam!

The delivery bike of the good old days had been replaced by a van, which we'd occasionally help to load. It was the family emissary, proudly driving round Paris with the magic words *Confitures Villiers* emblazoned on the coachwork. Joseph loved impressing people, and the van certainly did just that. People were always in and out of the factory, and now we had a maid as well. Funnily enough, she was a Polish Catholic, and a more fervent believer in God and Poland than any rabbi in Jehovah and Jerusalem. Talk about setting a fox to keep the geese, she'd taken us to church from time to time, all unbeknown. But one day, some neighbours must have told Joseph, because he was there waiting for us when we came out. We got such a hiding! We were strictly forbidden to enter the church of the gentiles ever again, although we didn't really understand why. We thought it was a lovely place. The church smelt so good; it was full of flowers and candles and pretty gilded statues. It wasn't as if we could compare it with the synagogue, since we'd never set foot inside one — Joseph not being the spiritual type. Anyhow, despite the hiding we got, we carried on going to church on the quiet, to get our own back on Joseph. It was our big secret with the maid. But while she was only too pleased to feel she was saving even a tiny fragment of our souls, for me it made a good bargaining point. Any time she tried to punish us for something, I'd threaten to tell Joseph all about the church — it seemed a fair deal.

Summer 1939. Joseph took us all on holiday to a house he'd rented in Brunoy. It was as if he wanted to gather his brood around him for the last days of summer, the last days of freedom, for the last few good times. We had huge slices of fresh buttered bread and onions. The wireless churned out an endless stream of songs, names and news bulletins: 'Bei mir bist Du schön' Chamberlain with his umbrella, Hitler's rantings (much worse than Joseph's), Edith Piaf, Maurice Chevalier, Trenet, Tino Rossi, Saint-Granier's 'disque des auditeurs' ... There was one word we kept hearing over and over again: war. Joseph would ask me to waltz with him, giving me five sous so I couldn't refuse.

War broke out — because people kept on saying it would, or so it seemed. We all went back to Paris. In the heat of the moment Joseph decided to sign up. He went down to the *Amis de la République française* in Belleville, where they were recruiting foreign Jews. By offering to fight, he was sure he'd finally get a bona fide French identity card. But no such luck: the French army didn't want an outsize diabetic like Joseph, a colossus with feet of clay. (The French Republic didn't want him either, as it turned out: his diabetes was the reason they refused to naturalize him at every subsequent attempt.)

Maurice and I were evacuated along with the other children from our school. There were grand farewells on the platform at Gare d'Austerlitz. Madame Joseph was in tears; Joseph was swearing he'd go and fight all the same. In the meantime, the train pulled out ... and I just watched them both standing there on the platform, getting smaller and smaller, still going through the motions. I didn't fully realize what was happening. War: a long journey, a holiday? What really tormented me was that I had been separated from Maurice. What would he do without me, his awesomely effective guardian angel? And there was I, all alone in the world, like a general with no troops. And not yet ten years old.

11

2

Château de la Patate

Eventually we arrived at the Château de Coulon, south of Moulins. The journey seemed very long, and we had tried to sing to keep our spirits up a bit. The grounds were large with magnificent trees, the rooms inside dilapidated and perishingly cold. The huge size of the rooms and the enormous number of windows, doors and corridors defeated the best efforts of the squat cast-iron stoves. There were draughts enough without the broken window panes. Winter's icy blast blew, and we could see we'd have to dance as well as sing if we weren't to die of cold.

My first morning there, three boys impressed me enormously by leap-frogging one of the stoves, which was full on. Needless to say, I thought I'd like to create an impression too and had a go myself. But I ended up in the sanatorium, with a serious burn on the knee and badly wounded pride to go with it. You can still see the scar. And I'm still in the habit, figuratively speaking, of leaping over hot stoves. (Not without getting burnt sometimes, either, and when that happens I stop and think, then put it out of my mind and start all over. Life's never been lacking in suitably hot stoves.) No sooner had they let me out than, stubborn as ever, and at the risk of smashing myself up completely, I had another go. Success, I'm happy to say, because I don't think I'd have tried a third time. As I'd hoped, my exploits had not passed unnoticed and I became 'the new girl who leaps over stoves'. Baron Münchhausen and the seven league boots had nothing on me.

There were lots of children from Paris there, boys and girls, from the eleventh and twelfth arrondissements; and I really couldn't make out why Maurice and I had been split up. I'm sure none of these kids had ever lived in a château before, and certainly not under those conditions, and they were having problems getting used to it. Some of them just drifted about like ghosts, trailing snot instead of chains, wandering listlessly and dwarfed by the enormous rooms. Groups formed, of course, including mine. The hard core consisted of a few girls from my dormitory, but there were some boys too, who got a kick out of being with the amazons and their leader with the burnt knee. I didn't just choose the strongest girls − physically or morally − but I picked those whom I felt were able to stand up for themselves, even though they might have appeared weak or shy. It was easier to impress them in the first place, and it meant I could protect them and foster that 'esprit de corps' which, later on, I was always able to create around me. A mixture of altruism and egoism, a need to protect and to rule. Some of these girls and boys, seeing me on television or in magazines years later, wrote telling me what good memories they had of those eventful months when I formed my first real gang.

I set up 'home' under a huge pine tree whose lowest branches were just the right height for a roof. On the ground I marked out bedrooms, living room, dining room, and very soon the other gangs copied us; so we all had different home corners. Having lost their real ones, they made the most of these − playing mummies and daddies, cops and robbers, kings under siege, exiled princes . . . Many of the children missed their parents badly. I missed them much less, never having had a family life really, and the whole situation seemed relatively normal. For me, my château 'family' was the only real one, and if any of them were unfairly treated by the powers that be I didn't stop to ask questions, I threw stones at the directrice's window instead. The situation was aggravated (for her) by the fact that her son was the leader of one of the rival gangs . . . Of course the two of us were at daggers drawn. It's a good thing I didn't suffer overmuch from being all alone in the world: that little creep being constantly spoiled and fussed over by his mother really got on my nerves.

About five or six months later I overheard a conversation between the directrice and one of our teachers. All the children were going back to Paris soon − the armistice had just been signed − except those whose parents hadn't 'come forward'. These children were to be sent on to another château while the office made further enquiries. I realized that with a stepmother who spoke no French and a father who couldn't write, it was unlikely that my parents would 'come forward'. If I wanted to get back to Paris then I'd have to find another way.

There were French troops stationed near the château. Horses, tanks and war-weary soldiers, the whole muddied lot witness to and proof of the recent débâcle. We didn't see the pathos of it; for us it was a fantastic diversion. The boys were fascinated by the guns, the tanks and all the equipment just lying there, some almost unused. It was a pitiful spectacle, and they didn't miss a bit of it. The French army was as good to watch as a circus show. We girls wandered about amongst the soldiers, very taken with these men who had gone to fight and were now returning to hearth and home. They were nearly all handsome men, with their shabby uniforms and tired eyes. One of them attracted me particularly, and gave me an idea — rather a strange one, but quite good. He was a fine young n.c.o. whose name I can't remember now. I came up to him fluttering my eyelashes just so, without simpering too much, and turned on the charm like I'd seen fast girls do. I was convinced I was irresistible — at least, that was the idea — and asked him if I could be his war-time pen-friend! Smiling, and without even trying to explain that the armistice had just been signed, he accepted my offer. He sat me on his knee and asked what he could do for me in return. He obviously realized that roles were a bit reversed and that, as far as pen-friends went, I needed him more than he needed me! I said: 'Since you're being sent back to Paris, would you do me a favour and write me a letter as if it came from my parents, saying something like "my darling daughter, mummy and I can't wait to have you back and hope we'll see you soon …"'

He looked puzzled, so I put my cards on the table and told him the whole story: about Joseph, who couldn't write, Thérèse being Polish, etc. He listened very carefully and promised he'd write me the letter. Anyway, a few days after they'd left camp a letter arrived at the château for Régine Zylberberg: 'my darling daughter, etc.' Success: three cheers for the lieutenant! (I learnt later that he had actually been to see my parents — I'd given him the address — and wrote the letter with their approval.) However it happened, there I was on the Paris train with the others, only too glad to be leaving that crumbling château. We were all singing and laughing, and I could already see myself back at home in rue Pasteur. The war's over, I thought; there was nothing to it, really, everything's back to normal.

But the new order wasn't quite the same as the old order, and very quickly I came smack up against it like a fly against a window pane. At Moulins, the train stopped to cross the demarcation line. I'd never heard that phrase before, and it sounded funny. Red Cross lorries were parked alongside the track. Men in uniform were all around — not in French uniform either. The teacher who was looking after us murmured: 'Germans'.

There had been much talk of Germans at the château, but we'd never seen any. We did this time all right. A big fat-bellied one plus two others with machine-guns got into the carriage and started calling the roll, compartment by compartment, ticking names off on a piece of paper. Total silence. As soon as he got to our compartment I had a premonition that something awful was going to happen to me. He bellowed out the names of the seven other children with me. Terrified, they answered one after the other, 'present'. One of them, obeying the schoolboy's reflex action, stood up, answered, but stayed standing as if nailed to the spot. The German dismissively motioned him to sit down again. Then it was my turn: 'Zylberberg!'

'Present.'

He looked at me, and without ticking my name off like he had the others, he showed me the door saying: 'Raus!'

I went out into the corridor where the teacher kissed me, with tears in her eyes, and said: 'I'm afraid you must get out, my love.'

I picked up my bag, walked along the corridor past the other compartments and got off the train. Everyone was watching me. Among them some friendly faces: the boys and girls from my gang. Goodbye 'home' under the tree, goodbye cops and robbers; hello Nazis.

A soldier led me to the station waiting room, where the Red Cross were based. I was given a drink, and a girl dried my tears: 'Don't worry, we'll take you somewhere.'

Well, there I was in another train, with other children, not so different from those I'd just said goodbye to. In fact some of them were from the Château de Coulon like me, and we all got in the same compartment. On the opposite platform a train was just leaving for Paris. Some kids called out: 'Where have you come from?'

'The Château de Coulon.'

'Where are you going?'

'We don't know.'

15

'Hope you're not going to the Château de la Patate.'

'Patate' or no, we'd soon see. I wondered why they didn't let me go to Paris too. 'They' must have found out that the letter wasn't from my parents after all ... I didn't make the connection between my name, Zylberberg, the Jews and the Germans. I didn't know that in occupied France they didn't want Jews, and that they'd put me with the children who hadn't heard from their parents. I just thought my well-laid plan had failed.

After a short trip, we reached the Château de la Patate, so called because they gave pride of place on the menu to the humble potato. Its real name was Château de la Brosse.

The children there were of all ages, classes and religions. Some had lost contact with their parents, others had been separated deliberately ...

'So, you're new are you?'

'Well, I'm not the lady of the manor am I?' I answered good-humouredly.

'Is it true you're Jewish?'

'So what's it to you then?'

Their questions stopped after this show of aggression.

My stomach was crying out for food by midday, when we sat down at big refectory tables in what had once been the stables. While I was eating I suddenly noticed a big hairy oaf of a boy walking along behind us pinching what he fancied off our plates.

'What on earth's he doing?' I asked out loud.

'He won the fight this week.'

'What?'

'He won the fight.'

That's how I learnt that at la Patate each table organized a fight on Sundays, and that the victor won the right to pick what he wanted from the others' plates for the next week. What delicious children!

For the guy doing the picking life must have been fun. I was mulling all this over on my third day there, while they were calling the kids to collect their post.

'Maurice Zylberberg! A parcel for you.'

'Is this some kind of joke?'

I was getting up to tell them I was called Régine and that (incredible though it seemed) the parcel must be for me when a kid at the next table shouted out: 'It's for me!'

I could hardly believe my ears, and looking round I saw a fat little boy rush up to collect his package. It couldn't possibly be the same Maurice I'd last seen eight months ago, thin as a rake, because, poor boy, I wouldn't let him eat the food Thérèse made us ...

But he wasn't unlike Maurice either; I went up to him while he was opening his parcel.

'Hey, have you got a sister?'

'Yes,' he said, not bothering to look up.

'Have you got two sisters?'

'Yes I have actually.'

'What are they called?'

'Régine and Eva.'

'I'm Régine. Your big sister.'

Finally he did lift his head up and looked at me with blank despondency.

No reaction. Someone must have completely brutalized this kid! What on earth had they done to him? I spoke again, and shook him. That seemed to jog his memory: 'Oh yes! Régine ...'

I plied him with questions and he told me how he'd been sent to Château de la Patate right from the start and that as he hadn't heard from our parents he had to stay while nearly all the others were sent back to Paris.

What with parental neglect and solicitous Germans, Maurice and I hadn't had much luck really!

Finding Maurice completely changed my life at the château. When he told me there was a 'victor' on his table too who took all the best bits of food, I decided I'd put into action an idea I'd had in the back of my mind. First I asked permission for him to eat at my table. Granted. Now I just had to fix it that no one took our pudding or portion of meat. We didn't mind about the spuds!

The next fight was the following day, and that evening I grabbed the victor by the arm while he was on his way round the table.

'Hey you, I'll fight you tomorrow!'

He treated me to a smug macho smile: 'You must be out of your mind! Challenged by a girl! Had a good look at yourself lately? Look at your puny little arms!' etc.

'Okay, if you've quite finished, what about weapons?'

Because like a duel you could choose your weapons. Not pistols or blades of course, but you could opt for kicks or punches, and allow or disallow blows below the belt, hair-pulling, slapping, scratching, or use of rulers ... I chose the most direct method: a fight with our bare hands, kicking permitted. No holds barred, hobnailed boots on.

The following evening, Sunday, six o'clock in the playground. A big circle gathered round us. From the window of their first floor flat — it came with the job — the directeur and directrice would be watching the fight too. They didn't have to worry: jumped-up little creeps, they were stupid and indifferent enough just to let us get on with it. The victor seemed more of a brute than ever, and sauntered up to me with: 'Let the little Yid show us what she's made of.'

What a clever boy: calling me a Yid made me boil with rage, and there's nothing like anger to make you lose your inhibitions. It was like Popeye with his spinach. I flexed my muscles and feeling my hatred entirely justified I lunged with my hobnailed boot and fetched him a hell of a kick in the balls. The effect was devastating, and not least to his masculine pride. He fell to his knees more in pain than admiration. I went on thumping him, scratching him, slapping him, pulling his hair. He clutched the site of the initial injury, as if reassuring himself that he still had them. I had indeed won.

Next day it was my turn with the plates. The fight had been hard, the foe hateful; there was no reason to give quarter, and from starters to pudding everything came my way. Maurice had a surfeit of cakes: my own, not Thérèse's. Every weekend thereafter I'd ask: 'Anyone care to fight me?'

But the image of the deposed champ writhing on the ground had been etched in their minds and no one stepped forward.

Another problem: chilblains. Maurice hadn't been looked after properly, or fed properly (until I came), and he had terrible chilblains on his hands and feet. Some days he couldn't even walk. Some nights he couldn't bear to put weight on his feet and wet his bed ... I was in a different dormitory and couldn't help him, and when he'd get teased by the other boys the next morning I got furious and would have given anything to get my hands on those creeps who wouldn't help my little brother.

In the day sometimes they hurt so badly I'd have to carry him to the refectory — the only warm spot in the whole damned place. I'd ask someone to help — Maurice was quite heavy — but often had to duff them up a bit before they would give me a hand. What's more his shoes were too tight and with the chilblains as well they were horribly painful. Since the directeur refused to give him new ones he often had to go barefoot, or just with old socks on, full of holes.

The directeur made me sick. Everyone knew he stockpiled loads of Red Cross parcels full of, among other things, all the mufflers, shoes and socks that we badly needed. With the help of the Red Cross he was able to go in for black marketeering, lining his own pocket at the expense of Maurice and others ...

I went to see him one day in his office, on the spur of the moment. Opening the door, I found him with his wife on his knee in a clinch. It didn't bother me too much, and I was so outraged at Maurice's condition that I announced, with bare-faced cheek: 'You've *got* to give my brother some new shoes. I'm writing to my father, he knows lots of important people, and telling him that you're stealing things and keeping them for yourself − I'll tell him everything!'

Being caught in mid-embrace like that, they took a moment or two to get a grip on the situation. While his wife was getting to her feet the directeur demanded: 'How *dare* you talk to me like that, Zylberberg?'

'If you don't give me some shoes I'll go and get them myself. I know exactly where they are.'

He thought better of getting riled, and changed his tune. In a tone which approximated to kindness he said: 'But what's your brother's problem? You should have told us about it!'

He took me to the store-room and told me to choose. I took what I needed for Maurice, and for myself, thanked him politely, and dashed off to present the little brother with his new shoes.

Banging your fist on the table is asking for trouble, but it also makes for a rosy future. I learnt very quickly that you don't get something for nothing.

When I got into fights at the château, it was mostly with good reason, but sometimes I did go over the top a bit and I realized there were some girls (rather than boys) who either hated me or were afraid of me. In the dormitory toilets one night I overheard two whispering: 'Tonight okay. Don't forget: you all shut up, and I'll get out of bed and pretend to be sleepwalking, and go over and thump her.'

It was crystal clear whom they were going to play the sleepwalking trick on. So I went to bed and waited.

My bed was the only one standing on its own. The others had pushed theirs together, to keep warm so they said, in fact so they could chat, and fiddle with each other. Lights out. Time passed and I could hardly stay awake. Suddenly a girl got up out of her bed and started to come towards me with her ams out in front. I pretended to be fast asleep. She began by tapping me on the legs,

19

gently at first, then harder and harder. But I didn't react; I didn't feel ready for a fight cold like that, in the dormitory, with hardly any clothes on, and no weapons ... Not to mention the terrible trouble we'd be in if we got caught! Noise at night was one of the unforgivable crimes. One of them came up to me the next morning, very sly: 'Didn't you see Marie last night? She got out of bed — she was sleepwalking.'

I acted dumb: 'No, I didn't notice anything. I sleep like a log, you know ...'

And then she started explaining that with sleepwalkers you have to be very careful never to wake them or else they might die, and so on. So that's what it was all about, the little cows! The whole pantomime just so they could get me when they felt like it without me being able to retaliate, for fear of killing the stupid girl! Some of them were so delighted with this brain-wave that they sniggered at me openly. Whatever the risk, it had to be worth it rather than let myself get pushed around like that: strong action was called for.

That night I slept armed, with my hobnailed boots! I waited ... nothing. Same thing the following night ... Eight, ten days went by ... still nothing.

I used to sleep badly even then: I always got the feeling (I still get it) that I was missing something important, that exciting things were happening somewhere else. But one night during this unbelievable episode I was really tortured with desire for revenge, and was having even more difficulty than usual in dropping off to sleep ... I was trying hard to think about something else, anything else, when the same girl got up, 'sleepwalking', and came over to my bed, tapping me once or twice. Encouraged by my lack of response, she got a bit closer. I uncoiled like a spring, and got her smack in the mouth! Shock, horror, turmoil in the dorm. The sleepwalker got taken away to the sanatorium with her mouth a bloody mess.

The next day I was summoned to the directeur's office and sent to Coventry. I had my hair shorn (particularly cruel punishment for the female of the species, although very fashionable after the Liberation). And for once I didn't have lice either, just my luck. The somnambulist, in considerable pain, had taken to sleeping horizontally again, and I could rest easy in my bed. They couldn't put me in a separate room because there wasn't one. So I had to sleep in the dormitory, although no one was allowed to speak to me, and I was forbidden to speak to them.

It was the same in class. Only the teacher was permitted to

address me: but I decided not to answer. Dumb. He was rather thrown by this. Some of my friends took the risk of passing me messages, either in whispers or on bits of paper, but I ignored them. So they send Zylberberg to Coventry do they? Well, Zylberberg sends the rest of the world to Coventry too! Coventry or no, it didn't stop me laying down the law, and whenever my brother came and told me someone or other had been nasty to him I'd go and sort out the family business there and then.

A bit later I heard via the directeur that Thérèse was coming to fetch me. He did nothing to conceal his pleasure — I was a 'trouble-maker' at the château, as he put it. I was delighted too, so we were both happy.

Thérèse turned up a week later. She was all dressed up, like the time Joseph was mad at her for looking like a tart. She was magnificent; platinum blonde hair, high heels, camel coat, properly made up and drenched in perfume. She came with a man from the Préfecture de Police who was a friend of Joseph's, enabling her to cross the demarcation line without difficulty. But why had she come and not Joseph? 'Too busy,' she said.

The directeur thought it only fair to tell her he'd had one or two little problems with me, but added that fortunately I was a nice child, in spite of it all!

So off we went, the inspector following in Thérèse's perfumed wake with 'Master Maurice' on his shoulders, while 'Miss Régine' brought up the rear in her hobnailed boots. A few francs for the guards on duty at the bridge marking the demarcation line saw to it that they turned a blind eye. This was the end of 1940, so the checks weren't all that strict, and Joseph wasn't being miserly.

Night fell. It was all very exciting except when the exhausted inspector passed Maurice over to me. Having to carry my brother brought me and the romance of our adventure back to earth. We stopped the night with a peasant family and ate fresh bread and butter and ham. It was wonderful and made such a change from all the spuds! Finally we caught a train and reached the rue Pasteur, Paris.

Confitures Villiers was still there, and business was booming. They hadn't started confiscating Jewish property yet. Joseph was making a fortune with his apple and grape jam (the grapes replacing white sugar, which was unobtainable), and was dashing all over the place — not forgetting, though, to line a few well-placed pockets just in case.

21

It was a wise precaution! Without any warning, they suddenly did start confiscating Jewish concerns and handing them over to so-called 'managers'. Despite hare-brained appearances to the contrary, Joseph had unusual flair and a considerable instinct for self-preservation (which I've inherited, I'm glad to say). Alerted by his 'friends' at the Préfecture, and with barely time to grab a toothbrush, we were sent off to an old couple in Aulnay-sous-Bois. Joseph packed his bags and went south, to Aix-en-Provence.

We didn't stay long at Aulnay-sous-Bois. The old couple we lodged with were very sweet, especially the old man. He used to come up to the attic, where I'd be browsing through old copies of *L'Illustration*, to keep me company.

'Your knickers are all dirty — show me!' he'd say.

He'd come closer to have a look — for me it was no different than someone saying: 'Show me if your hands are clean.' I could see no harm in it — he was such a dear ... He went into ecstasies over my little pants, then he asked me to show him my little bottom as well! I had no idea why, but I did, and he seemed delighted. After that, he'd give me five sous, and it meant Maurice and I could go to the local cinema.

There was such a surfeit of films; all the best ones of their day (*Premier Rendez-Vous, Regain,* films with Odette Joyeux and Danièle Darrieux). In the foyer I'd be in raptures over all the photos of my idols taken by Harcourt — one day, I told myself, I'll have mine done by Harcourt too.

On Sundays I'd drag Maurice around all the little cafés on the banks of the Marne. I loved music and dancing, and people were always surprised to see a kid of eleven dancing so well. I used to sing all the popular tunes too.

One morning out of the blue, the man from the Préfecture who'd got us over the demarcation line came to fetch us. He was to take us to Aix-en-Provence. Yet again we got our things together and boarded a train. In Aix Joseph was waiting for us. But he was alone. He and Thérèse had separated. Such is life ... such is love.

3

At the Convent

On arrival in Aix-en-Provence, Monsieur Zylberberg had ceased to
exist; he became plain Monsieur Joseph, new to the town. He had
taken to sporting a beret and had a pipe stuck in his mouth. He
seemed to have given up working. The first thing we asked was
where was Thérèse. In very dignified tones he replied: 'Madame
Joseph is a cow; she's gone.'

He might look different, but underneath it was the same old
Joseph! We were dumbstruck: Thérèse, gone? She had met a man
who was small, not very handsome, but very kind and who never
hit her. Quite different from Joseph, who remarked of him, in
Yiddish: 'I've seen him. His breath stinks.' Adding, with his own
particular brand of humour: 'What do you expect? He's a dwarf —
his mouth's not far from his arsehole.'

In his fury, he had taken back everything he'd given to Thérèse
(her fox-fur stole, her jewels ...) and told her: 'You'll be going to
your dwarf without so much as a pair of knickers to your name!'

He was unstoppable, and had us in stitches with an inexhaustible
string of insults, all in Yiddish. But deep down we were very sad to
have lost Thérèse. We really did love her and never forgot that it
was Thérèse who'd got Joseph to recognize us, and Thérèse who'd
come to take us away from la Patate. And then there were all
those times she'd kissed us better, and all those lice, too ...

He told us their story all over again. She'd come to Aix with him,
then announced that she was going to marry a chap called Albert.
And Joseph told us how he'd smashed this poor Albert's face in,
done him over; more or less left him for dead in fact. We could see

23

it now, this unfortunate dwarf, completely disfigured, the ex-Madame Joseph bandaging his head. The truth, of course, was considerably less tragic! When he finally met the (supposed) dwarf and (actual) husband-to-be, he treated them both to a big booze-up, tears in his eyes, overcome with emotion, wished them both every happiness.

That's how Thérèse told the story after the war. She always had a soft spot for her 'ex', and said laughingly: 'All Joseph's "corpses" are quite alive and kicking, believe you me.'

Joseph didn't appear to be working, but then he didn't seem short of money either. We childishly imagined he'd brought a suitcase-full of bank notes with him from Paris, or something. For a week we were looked after by a lovely couple, the Mariottis, who also had charge of Eva, our little sister. Joseph had insisted on having custody of her since Thérèse could do nothing but harm, to his way of looking! Monsieur Mariotti made matches for a living, and Madame Mariotti, good Provençal housewife that she was, fattened us up like geese.

As for schooling, Maurice went to the convent for boys, and I to the convent for girls, situated in a cul-de-sac off rue de l'Opéra. It was reputed to be the safest sort of place to be in the event of a German invasion of unoccupied France. Joseph took us out on Sundays. He was always well dressed and charming, and never came without a little something for us, and for the nuns too: perhaps some shoes or sweets ... in the eyes of the reverend mothers, Joseph, this loafer, this inveterate gambler, philanderer and inattentive father to boot, was a model of good behaviour. What a hypocrite! (It was true, however, that for once he did pay the fees regularly.) He used to drag us off to the casino on Sundays, vanish into the gaming room and not reappear until the evening. Maurice and I would eat by ourselves at one of the best tables in the restaurant; Joseph was a big gambler and got special treatment on account of his generous tips.

The odd times he forgot to fetch me from the convent, I'd manage to get out like this. Posted at the gate I used to reach through the bars, pull twice on the bell-rope, calling 'cooee'. The nun on duty, crippled with rheumatism, would open the gates from her lodge, thinking it was a nun coming back in. Before she had a chance to do anything about it I'd already run to the end of the street and disappeared into the crowds in rue de l'Opéra. I always knew where to find Joseph: in the casino.

After our Sunday lunch, Maurice and I would go into the auditorium and watch both matinées and sometimes the evening show
as well. That's where I saw all the big music-hall stars on tour:
Maurice Chevalier, Charles Trenet singing 'La chanson du maçon'
and 'Ça sent si bon la France' the Étienne sisters and Edith Piaf . . .
Of course I learnt their songs and was dying to be a star myself, to
sing and dance up on stage. And one Sunday I got the chance. The
casino had organized a children's singing contest. I went in for it,
singing 'J'ai ma main dans ta main', Charles Trenet's song. I
tripped up and down, smiling at everyone, miming love and passion.
I was in seventh heaven. But some parents of children at the
convent were in the audience, with their offspring. The children's
gasps of admiration when they recognized me were not echoed by
their parents, however. They were horrified and went to report it to
the Mother Superior first thing next morning. She called me in
afterwards and held forth with the conventional spiel about the
'school's good name', my 'immodest behaviour' and 'the need for
discretion', and so on. But I knew she was fond of me and I got the
impression that she was only telling me off in order to satisfy the
local hypocrites who were anxious about their pure little daughters
mixing with the likes of a showgirl such as me.

One Sunday Joseph turned up at the gates, minus his pipe and
beret. There was a calèche waiting for us outside. It was a much-
used mode of transport at the time − if rather expensive. Maurice,
Eva and another woman were sitting inside. I noticed straight away
that she was wearing the fox stole and jewels that used to belong to
Thérèse, Joseph said simply: 'Régine − meet your new mother!'

I'd heard that phrase before. He presented the Countess
'Kratoshkaïa' − or something like that − a flame-haired Hungarian
temptress with a distinctly scornful expression.

She edged away perceptibly when I sat down next to her, pulling
at her skirt with an air of disgust. I was all of eleven years old, but
my first thought was that she might well be a genuine Hungarian,
but she was certainly no countess. I couldn't stand her. She was
reasonably beautiful, but very different from Thérèse: just to be
polite I'd call her the 'adventuress' type. What's more, she was
wearing Thérèse's stole and jewels, and that shocked me. (It has
always shocked me, that habit of passing on valuables.) I held my
tongue, but not for long, and on the cours Mirabeau I burst out
with: 'Madame, I forbid you to wear Madame Joseph's things.'

And I snatched the fox stole from round her shoulders! Instantly

I received a masterful slap from my father, and delivered him a heavy kick in return. Yet another slap, yet another kick: Joseph was getting a taste of his own medicine. The exchange continued and the atmosphere in the calèche became quite crazy. The phoney countess looked as though she might faint, but was still tugging hard at the fox; Maurice and Eva yelled in unison so as not to be left out; Joseph and I were fighting more and more fiercely, he with his left hand, me with my right foot (the left foot was lashing out at the Hungarian . . .). Reaching the casino signalled the end of the round, fortunately, and after our minute's madness was up we each tried to regain our composure, or at least some semblance of dignity. Joseph and his Hungarian, both purple with rage, marched through the revolving door. Eva, Maurice and I made straight for the restaurant. Clutched under my arm was the fox-fur stole, my trophy!

Aix, like everywhere else in the south of France, had wine, oil and soap in plenty, but wheat, sugar, potatoes and coal were sadly lacking. As the months went by the bread got blacker-looking, and cakes were all made with buckwheat or chestnut flour. Buying a nice brioche to eat when I was out with my schoolfriends on one of our infrequent walks was right out of the question. Luxuries only came courtesy of Joseph, who was obviously doing a bit of black marketeering.

The old part of Aix, round the archbishop's palace and the convent, was a rabbit warren rather like the 'Pletzl' in Paris, but considerably cleaner. Here too were the old paved streets, and severe façades of grey dressed stone: but there were no tailors hunched over their work, no stale smells of Jewish cooking, and no kosher butchers. Emerging from the maze of narrow streets into the broad cours Mirabeau was like walking into a large garden, with its immense trees, people thronging the café terraces and beautiful women out for their promenade.

The convent was full of beribboned little rich girls with long names. I was much impressed to hear them call their parents *vous* when they came to visit on Sundays. I couldn't imagine addressing Joseph formally like that! But I was utterly flabbergasted when I heard one of the girls called *vous* by her own parents!

Going to the fountain at the bottom of the cours Mirabeau was my favourite walk. It was the best place in town. I wanted to cycle round and round it singing at the top of my voice all the latest hits I'd heard at the casino, which was only a stone's throw from the fountain. I'd fantasize about the calèches following me round the fountain, their drivers and passengers joining in the refrains ...

The classroom at the convent was long and white, and smelt of apples and chalk. The forty pupils, aged between twelve and fifteen, sat at six rows of desks. We didn't learn much — except how to stand up straight and not to make too many spelling mistakes. On the wall at the front of the class, next to the blackboard, was the familiar map of France with its départements, préfectures and sous-préfectures. I never did learn a single one. Behind us hung a big black cross and an engraving showing Saint François de Sales and Jeanne de Chantal founding the Order of the Visitation. The only patches of colour were provided by two golden-brown haloes, beneath which were the two saints looking bored stiff. I used to sit right near the picture, and thought it no wonder they looked bored if the Order had been created just in order to 'visit' the poor. The prints on the side wall were much more fun: there was Saint George slaying the dragon, and Joan of Arc burning at the stake with, flying off to the right, the dove of the Holy Ghost. Another devotional picture hung in the corridor leading to Mother Superior's office on the first floor: the photograph of Marshal Pétain looking just like a kindly old grandfather.

I went to mass every morning just like the others, but being Jewish was excused from confession. That meant I never had to tell anyone all the stupid things I got up to. In fact, I soon realized that no one told quite the whole truth. Some of them used to snigger as they came out of the confessional and boasted that they'd just said any old thing: I didn't like that. If God exists, then why bother to lie? And if He doesn't, then why bother to say anything at all?

The nuns didn't try to convert me; they were waiting for the impetus to come from me. At six o'clock every evening after school one of them gave me religious instruction. I had a lot to catch up on ... She told me about the mystery of Christ's birth, 'begotten not created', but I didn't understand. I wasn't in much of a hurry to understand it either; playing dumb, and playing the heathen for whom mysteries remained impenetrably mysterious, put me in a rather special position. I made the most of it — being a goat in the Christian sheep-fold, a bit of an ugly duckling, under the at once despairing and affectionate eyes of the nuns. Singing the convent song, 'Maréchal, nous voilà', was my saving grace.

I was forgiven for certain outbursts which wouldn't have been tolerated in other pupils. For example, at Easter a priest (he was a canon or friar of some sort) came to stay at the convent for a few days. In the chapel every afternoon he would explain and comment on passages from the Bible. One afternoon he read the passage where Christ says: 'Whosoever shall smite thee on thy right cheek, turn to him the other also.' It was the first time I'd heard that, and I burst out laughing, I couldn't stop. Everyone looked round, completely baffled. So was the priest who asked what was the matter with me. I managed to splutter out: 'I'm sorry, but my father always told me the exact opposite. He used to say: "Don't turn the other cheek, give as good as you get!"'

General laughter all round, quickly brought under control by the priest, who simply smiled and went on with his sermon. For a brief moment Joseph's good words took the place of Christ's. I must confess that I've carried on giving more credence to the first than to the second: that's my heathen nature.

One of my teachers, Mademoiselle B., was particularly interested in the progress of my studies. She found me a lively pupil, funny sometimes, with my own brand of intelligence but lacking in application. I liked her a lot, but we fell out at one point. One day she suggested taking me out for a walk the following Sunday because Joseph couldn't come. Sunday came, but for one reason or another not Mademoiselle B. I waited the whole afternoon. She didn't mention it the following day and when she ticked me off, very mildly, about something in class, I burst out with: 'That's as maybe, but a litre of oil won't buy me — which is more than I can say for some people I know!'

Now and again parents used to give teachers litres of oil as a favour during these hard times. I sat down, pleased as punch with such a mean and silly remark. Mademoiselle B. blushed scarlet and sent me out, trembling.

'Régine! Leave the room immediately and go and tell the Mother Superior what you just said to me!'

My pleasure was rather short-lived: suddenly I didn't feel at all proud of what I'd done and realized that I'd been horribly unfair to her. That was the first time I'd had words with one of the teachers at the convent too. It was ten to four. I left the classroom and went to Mother Superior's office. I hesitated outside her door because I could hear lots of voices. I decided to knock.

'Come in!'

I pushed the door gently ... and saw the most astonishing sight: a magnificent table (gigantic in my memory, though doubtless of modest proportions) complete with crisp white table cloth, laden with cakes, gingerbread, shortcake, *Calissons d'Aix*, fruit and hot chocolate. This Ali-Baba's cave with the forty cakes took my breath away. It was like the feeding of the five thousand. Surrounded by other nuns Mother Superior asked: 'Régine, dear, what has happened? Come here, come and sit down.'

'Um, well ... I've come to tell you ... that ...'

I shifted from one foot to the other, lost for words.

'Come in, come in! Come and sit by me and share our tea.'

As, miraculously, she didn't really insist on knowing to what she owed the pleasure of my visit, I closed the door and took my place next to her. Sweeping aside without a second thought the few good manners they'd succeeded in drumming into me, I let temptation get the better of me and shamelessly stuffed myself with cakes and hot chocolate. What a heavenly punishment!

Having discovered that these tea-parties happened every other Monday, I tried it on again several times with Mademoiselle B., who conveniently ordered me out of the room again to 'repeat that to Mother Superior'. I went, they sat me down, I ate some cakes, drank some chocolate, and, punishment over, went to join the others for my second tea in the hall ... I had become a quasi habituée of the most exclusive circle at the convent: it gave me my taste for 'clubs', and I've not lost my gift for opening (and closing) doors at just the right moment.

At this time, right in the middle of the war, Joseph, complete with beret and pipe, was out title-hunting: count, viscount or marquis! His Hungarian lady-friend was mad on titles, real or fake, and had told him she wouldn't think of marrying him unless he had one! He was thus naïvely searching the whole area for a minor aristocrat in reduced circumstances with whom he might come to some sort of financial agreement.

Alas (or fortunately), his noble impulses were cut off in their prime when the phoney countess severed relations, diplomatic and otherwise, with the aspirant squire. She'd just met a chinless wonder with a coronet, and dumped Monsieur Joseph and the rue Pasteur without further ado. It took him a good week to get over it, which was a long time for Joseph. And we were only too glad to see an end to that gloomy Carpathian interlude.

Joseph rapidly found another girlfriend, a dressmaker this time, who met with our complete approval: she didn't have a title, wasn't looking for one, and wasn't a Slav either. She was utterly normal,

Provençale, and sweet. She made me a pleated skirt and a sailor suit for my brother. So far so good. And for the first time Joseph introduced one of his mistresses without the 'Here's your new mother' bit. We hoped he'd leave it out for good from now on, but it must have just slipped his mind this time, because it was back to the old formula with the subsequent ones.

I was still just as thin as ever, despite my chocolate-coated punishments, and the school doctor decided that a spell in the fresh air would do me a lot of good. By chance, the Mariottis — who still looked after Eva — had some cousins who lived in the country at La Brillanne near Cucuron in the Basses-Alpes. Why not stay with them? So off I went to Cucuron a few days before the start of the summer holidays in 1942. The people I stayed with were a kind childless couple, who lived serenely in a little house with a small-holding. I got my strength back quickly, as well as a stomach-ache from too many cherries, and another (much worse) from too many peaches.

There was a low stone wall in the village square just near the house where the whole population (about sixty people) gathered in the evenings ... It was good to meet there, after dinner, to listen to people talking about this and that, in the semi-darkness. A month later, at the beginning of August, a young man of sixteen arrived in the village to stay with some relatives. He was called Georges, he came from Nice where his father was a baker ... yes, really! He had the dark complexion and regular features of the Mediterranean type, and I thought he was very handsome. As I was the only (even slightly) well-developed girl in the village, he was smitten with 'great love' for me. And me for him. He contrived to sit next to me on the wall in the evenings. I was only a skinny kid, not very pretty, with no hips, no breasts, nothing ... but I did my utmost to make myself seem more grown-up: I put my hair up for a start, it was all the rage and made me look at least three years older.

Apart from (very discreet) conversations in the evenings, we agreed to put each other little notes under a particular stone in the wall. We'd write these few lines when we woke up, to greet the new day. It took real redskin cunning to slip the note in and remove the other one. In the evenings we used the crossed-arms trick, which meant that we could touch and hold hands tightly, without anyone seeing. It gave me hot flushes and Georges got palpitations. The good folk I lived with thought it quite natural to leave me in his charge, given our respective ages (I was twelve), and their trust wasn't misplaced: contact between us was always very solemn and chaste. Sometimes we went on long bicycle rides with his brother, who was the same age as me.

One evening we walked over to Cucuron, about three kilometres away, and discovered that the film *Mayerling* was showing; it moved us terribly. As we left we decided to adopt the same motto as Archduke Rudolf of Austria and Maria Vetsera: 'United in life as in death'. On the way home we felt so happy it was like walking on air. I was in love for the first time.

One morning I felt very peculiar when I woke up. I felt sick and had a headache. I got up and saw, to my horror, that there was blood on the sheet. Scared stiff, I dived back into bed, pulled the covers right up, and thought hard. The important thing was not what was wrong with me, but keeping it well hidden. It had to be something to do with Georges. What had he done to me, what had we done, that could have produced such an effect? I thought I must be expecting a baby at the very least! But poor Georges had hardly done anything apart from hold my hand and kiss me on the eyelids ... I had no one to confide in, so furtively I washed the sheet, and said a little prayer for normality to return. I tried to avoid Georges and I stopped writing notes and collecting his. Two days later, the bleeding stopped. So that must have been it! Georges was very unhappy: he couldn't explain the sudden cooling off.

It was the end of August shortly after, and Georges came over one morning to say goodbye to us all: he was returning to Nice to start at art school (he drew very well and had decided to make it his career). He took advantage of the occasion to ask, in front of everyone, for the convent address: I could hardly not give it him! We shook hands respectfully, and I felt him pressing a note into my hand ... I read it as soon as I was alone. It was full of reproaches, tender phrases and promises, with the little motto 'United in life as in death'. Very grand! The note contained something else too, his instructions for 'properly' reading the letters he was going to write me at the convent.

The holidays were soon over and I went back to Aix. Georges did write ... at least twice a week. And very ordinary letters they appeared to be, written on very thin paper, saying things like 'My dear Régine, I hope you are well, that you're working hard and eating well ...; I'm well and working hard', etc. I'd told him that the nuns read all our mail and he'd devised a brilliant way round it which, even now, I find difficult to explain: he would stick two sheets of paper together, and you just had to pull on a hair which stuck out from one of the bottom corners for the two leaves to separate and reveal the 'real' letter. This one was full of 'my darling', 'my love', 'I think of you', 'don't forget me'. So the harmless-looking letter was just a cover for a passionate love letter. The nuns were completely fooled ... so I thought.

To get to our places in the refectory we had to go past the high table where Mother Superior and other nuns sat. As we went by we bobbed our heads. As I was bobbing one day, I got the feeling something was wrong. The nuns were looking at me strangely, with an unmistakable stiffness quite unlike the usual relaxed atmosphere of mealtimes. We had hardly sat down after grace when Mother Superior said in a loud voice, still standing: 'Girls, the devil is among you!'

Before she'd even mentioned my name I guessed that I must be the devil in question. Taking a sheet of paper from the table, she looked at me and said: 'Zylberberg, stand up!'

I got up, my cheeks burning.

'Girls, you see before you the living example of perversity and misplaced trust.'

Deathly silence.

'The apparently harmless letters received by Régine Zylberberg from a holiday friend bear witness, in fact, to the most perverse machiavellism.'

Ecclesiastical language was still beautiful in those days and full of devilishly suggestive images. Mother Superior's voice, trembling with emotion, accomplished the rest: we could feel the devil's thunderbolts poised overhead and the gaping mouth of hell opened at my feet ... And then I heard Mother Superior force herself to recite with some disgust all Georges's tender declarations of love! She got as far as our little motto, from *Mayerling*, which Georges followed with Madame Rosemonde Gérard's equally famous line, 'Today more than yesterday and much less than tomorrow'.

'The rest I shall spare you,' concluded Mother Superior.

All eyes were on me. It was a real triumph for a little girl dreaming of stardom! Before she sat down, Mother said: 'You will remain standing throughout the meal.'

Given the rationing, meals didn't last very long, but this one seemed never-ending ... When the bell finally rang, I wondered anxiously what other punishment I had in store for me. As I walked past Mother Superior she called me out of line and kept me behind, all alone in the refectory, with the nuns standing over me.

'Where are the other letters?'

I'd had time to regain my composure and said:

'I tore them all up.'

Which was true. After reading them, my one desire had been to get rid of them.

'Were all the letters you received of the same sort as the one just read out, which came yesterday morning?'

'No, Mother, absolutely not, I've never received letters like that before.'

'Are you prepared to swear that you didn't know what was in these letters?'

Without faltering I said, 'I swear it.'

At that stage in my life, it was a little phrase of no great significance. Joseph was always swearing on his daughter's life, or his son's life, that he had or hadn't done something or said something. His gambling partners, his mistresses, associates and employees would think twice before contradicting him. In fact they were flagrant lies ... He knew that we knew too, and would offer us bribes so we wouldn't choke on them, and so that he felt better about taking our lives in vain. I must confess I was not beyond indulging in a little blackmail in these situations ...

You only had to lie and perjure yourself ... so to spice things up a bit I said to the Mother Superior: 'I can write to him in front of you if you like.'

And I started scratching a letter right away, breaking things off with Georges in such an exaggerated style that he couldn't possibly fail to understand that I was writing under duress. I begged him not only to cease writing to me, but to forget me altogether, even my name! Did all this seem utterly hypocritical to Mother Superior? Probably, because that evening at dinner she announced that I was to be sent to Coventry from that moment on. It was the first time since I'd been at the convent that such a punishment had been inflicted on a pupil. It made me horribly sad: for the first time I was happy somewhere too ... and to make matters worse I had to have my head shaved again! The lice had returned in force to their traditional hunting grounds.

In the midst of all this shame, a message got through to me from the ever astute Georges via a friend, to say that he was in Aix and would be waiting for me at the top of rue de l'Opéra next Sunday. As Joseph wasn't in Aix at the moment, I was going to have to find some other excuse for getting out. The bell trick had become rather overplayed, so I opted for an outright lie. A big one: they're often the least suspicious. I pretended that as my father was away, Mademoiselle B. had invited me to her house (where I had been several times already). I just had to hope no one would ask her anything about it on Monday morning ...

I met up with Georges all right, and hand in hand we set off for the countryside, over towards Le Tholonet, to minimize the risk of unwelcome encounters. As far as encounters were concerned we certainly had one ... and a very unwelcome one too! Who should we see coming through the lavender but Mademoiselle B. She was out sampling the joys of the countryside too, but all alone! She was outraged, snatched me away from Georges, and took me straight back to the convent. She marched me along by the arm. From time to time I'd turn sadly back to see Georges who was following some way behind, hiding when Mademoiselle B. looked round and re-appearing when I did ... He followed us as far as the gates of the convent and blew me one final despairing kiss ... That was the last time I saw him. At least, the last time until thirty years later during a concert in Nice, when a man came to my dressing room and said:'I'm Georges.' Georges? And then the memories came flooding back, of young love, the vows we made, the little stone wall, *Mayerling*, the double letters ...

Needless to say I was given a hard time, and sent to Coventry too, after the romantic escapade in the lavender. But some extra-ordinary news alleviated the harshness of the punishment: one Sunday, Joseph came and told me proudly: 'Régine, in a fortnight we're going to America!'

America! I didn't know then that for a hundred years America had been the dream of all unhappy, hungry and persecuted Euro-peans: but I did know that it was my dream, especially since I gathered that the Zylberbergs were finished in Paris ... Joseph's wonderful news set me reeling. I thought about it by day and dreamt about it by night. America, the ship, the whole adventure! Joseph would be smoking like a chimney, Maurice became the lookout boy, I'd be flirting with the captain in the lounge, all dressed up in my white shirt and houndstooth check skirt, white socks and patent shoes. And Joseph, spying the Statue of Liberty looming out of the mist, would say, 'Children, meet your new mother!'

While I got ready for the great day, Joseph had to fetch some papers in Lyon. Three weeks went by with no news. Then one day the nuns started looking at me strangely again, but for once this

34

time I knew I hadn't done anything wrong. In fact, they were being unusually kind to me: the spell in Coventry came to an end just then and they seemed especially affectionate. What was going on? I found out very shortly. I was called to Mother Superior's office before long, she sat me down and said: 'Régine, I have something serious to tell you.'

She addressed me informally, which was unusual. Looking me straight in the eyes, she went on: 'You are going to have to accept what I tell you without asking for too many explanations. What I'm doing is for your own good ... You will no longer be called by the name of Régine Zylberberg.'

Of course, it took me a while before I understood that she wasn't trying to tell me that I was being expelled from the convent. It all seemed to fit together: Joseph hadn't come back (goodbye America), he hadn't paid my fees, I'd be out on the streets. I started to cry and threw myself at her feet promising I'd be sensible, wouldn't do any more stupid things, wouldn't go out without permission ... She picked me up, stroking my head gently, and said: 'You are even more at home here than ever, Régine, we will never abandon you.'

But why then, if everything was all right, didn't they want to call me by my proper name? I had almost forgotten about the German officer coldly reading out my name on the train ... but it suddenly all came back to me.

She had heard that Joseph had been arrested in Lyon, but didn't dare tell me, and explained what I would have to do from now on.

'You know the Germans have just invaded the south of the country ... Well, if they should come here asking for Régine Zylberberg – don't move under any circumstances. You're not her; she left here two months ago. We will say that someone came to fetch her. Don't worry, you're in no danger. It's just that from now on you are called X ... and that is the name you will answer to when we call the register.'

The peculiar thing is that, to this day, I can't remember what my other name was. It must have been a very easy name for someone who was so used to the long, complicated names from Eastern Europe ...

From the very next day, that's the name I answered to, to the bewilderment of my friends, who didn't understand a thing and thought that it must be some new sort of punishment!

Things came to a head about ten days later. Mother Superior

came to see me again: 'Régine, my dear, you'll have to pack your case, you have to leave us. Don't worry, it has nothing to do with the Germans. You just have to go with a very nice lady and gentleman and do whatever they say.'

She took me to the parlour, where a man and a woman were indeed waiting for me. They explained, with a great deal of tact, that Joseph had been arrested in Lyon carrying some papers giving the Germans permission to come to Aix and fetch me and my brother Maurice. Convents were no longer safe places after all, and so it would be better for me to go with them. They said they were members of the Union Générale des Israélites de France. It was the first time I had heard of such an organization. The prospect of leaving the nuns filled me with anxiety, and for the first time in my life I felt really frightened.

I discovered years later when I met the gentleman again that the nuns had been against sending me away, and that it had taken the intervention of a police commissioner from Aix, who was in contact with the Resistance, to persuade them of the danger I was in, and that they should let me go.

So I packed my belongings and they warned me that if we were stopped on the way and questioned, I should say I was their daughter! I wasn't quite ready for a change of name, place and parents ... As I gradually got used to these new 'parents' though, my one concern was for my brother. He'd been in a clinic for several months now, with calcium deficiency. What was going to become of him? They told me not to worry, that he was being looked after. As for Eva, she had recently been reclaimed by her mother ... I was not to see either of them again until the Liberation, both safe and sound ...

And so the journey to the end of my childhood continued.

4

Claude

The journey from Aix to Lyon was uneventful and no one asked us any questions. The couple I was travelling with were obviously used to being quiet and discreet, and spoke little. This marked the start of a new phase in my life, the underground phase. Seventy-seven rue de la Villette (a sad little street close to the railway lines) was a house which had been converted into an old people's home. The home was run by the sister of a Lyon clergyman and her husband, the Heymanns. It was under the joint control of the Union des Israélites de France and ... the Gestapo.

The Union Générale des Israélites de France had been created in November 1941 with the agreement of the Germans, who saw it as a means to administer the future French ghetto while making monkeys of the Swiss Red Cross on their occasional visits. Occupied Europe was full of homes like this one: whenever the Red Cross came they were able to exhibit these reasonably well cared-for old folks for all to see. It was one way to try and silence all the rumours about concentration camps and gas ovens. Some officials did indeed depart with the clear conviction that nobody was doing any harm to anyone — they'd seen as much with their own eyes. As for those who were more doubtful, or more curious, they were instantly invited not to concern themselves, and not to believe everything allied propaganda told them. But the UGIF did have a more positive rôle too. Although it might seem to be playing the Germans' game, and to be confining itself to offering 'assistance' of a purely passive sort, it was also in close contact with an important resistance group organized by a remarkable man called Maître Geissman.

With the brief of creating an acceptable image for the German occupation, the association did in fact improve the fate of numerous Jews, and even saved many from extermination.

Deposited with my new family at seventy-seven rue de la Villette, I sat down politely on the edge of the sofa not really knowing what I was doing there at all. I looked round at the very simply furnished room. Everything was sad and dismal, and I felt quite out of place. A rather rancid smell floated on the air. So far from Aix, from the convent, and from the casino, I thought it all ugly and felt terribly alone.

Madame Heymann, who was forty-four and from Alsace, took me upstairs to show me my room. There were seven beds, with an eighth squeezed in by the door for me.

'This is where you'll sleep,' she said. 'Obviously, if there's a visit we'll hide you somewhere. There should only be old people here. Therefore you don't exist ... do you understand?'

Yes, I did understand; it wasn't the first time I'd been told that.

It was the women's dormitory. The men's was opposite, on the same floor. The toilets were at the bottom of the staircase.

That evening at dinner, I ate with the Heymanns. I was rather glad, because the thought of eating with my 'room-mates' terrified me. The youngest was well into her seventies ... They ate together in the dining room at a separate table from the men. The men were much 'younger': the most sprightly must have been in his sixties ... all from Alsace. They introduced me: 'Well, so you're the little girl, are you?'

They had such a funny accent! They squabbled about the jam, about the chairs, about a napkin one of them couldn't find ... They had spittoons by their plates, which they used noisily and regularly. One of them was blind. He touched my face with his finger-tips and told me I had dark hair.

It wasn't much fun ...

The Heymanns had a son called Claude, a bean-pole of sixteen who talked schoolwork and mathematics. There were swift introductions: this is Régine, this is Claude; hello, hello. Claude got back from school at seven every evening, and slept in a tiny room leading off the dining room on the ground floor. His window opened onto the hall and staircase! A key position, so to speak. Monsieur Heymann's brother and his wife ate their meals at the home too, though they lived in town under an assumed name. He worked for a brewery and wore a beret like Joseph did to look like a real Frenchman. His wife helped round the house and in the kitchen.

The first few nights were a real nightmare. I was used to girlish giggles and whispers, and now had to contend with the assorted noises these ancient ladies made. They hawked, they spat, they kept getting up in the night to use the chamber-pots which were dotted all round the room on bedside chairs or at the foot of the beds ... The smells were not of the freshest, and neither were the complexions. In the morning, it was soiled sheets and false teeth clinking in glasses.

I hung about all day, bored and fed up, trying not to think about anything, and especially not about what was happening all around me. Madame Heymann (who had absolutely no news of my father yet) was waiting for me to get used to my new life. But it was all so strange for me ... as though I'd landed on a different planet. Friday evenings were the start of the sacred Sabbath, when we weren't allowed to touch a single electrical switch or anything you might call 'modern'. The one thing I did like was the synagogue ... I walked there with Claude and Monsieur Heymann. It was less exacting than the daily mass at the convent. My 'holy' war: first the soutane, now the skull cap.

Gradually, though, I got used to the decrepitude and never-ending quarrels. The permanent state of war between Madame Lévy and Monsieur Kahn even made me laugh in the end. They were both ninety-five and the big problem was sorting out which should enjoy the title of doyen: 'Madame Lévy,' said Monsieur Kahn, 'you are ill-mannered, too ill-mannered to be our doyenne!'

'Monsieur Kahn,' replied Madame Lévy, 'what you say is untrue, it is only my good breeding which is stopping me from telling you what I think of you!'

I pretended to be interested in the leadership question, and I wound them up a bit reporting back what each had said about the other ... but it wasn't a very absorbing occupation, and I'd continue my wanderings from room to room staring into the middle distance. One day I was sitting watching Madame Heymann down on her knees washing the kitchen floor. She straightened up, her hands dripping wet, and said: 'Tell me, you, you don't think you're going to just sit there all day long, do you? Give me a hand!'

I looked her straight in the eye, got up, and then kicked the bucket over: 'Never!'

It was a sublime moment for me; but Madame Heymann didn't

quite appreciate it. She grabbed me, thrust the cloth into my hands and made me mop it all up. It served me right, and from that day on I helped her with the housework and the cooking. It was all a question of knowing how to deal with me.

She took me shopping sometimes, to try and find an alternative to jam and fortified biscuits. But we often came back empty-handed. Lyon was one of the most disadvantaged cities for provisions. We saw crows for sale in the market at ten francs each, and in a town famed for its good eating everyone was having to make their mayonnaise without eggs, cakes without sugar and coffee without coffee. In terror I heard people talking about nettle soup and guinea-pig stew. At the house we ate lots of swedes and salsify. But we all had a feast the day the monthly rations came for the home. We'd have tastes of everything, and Madame Heymann used to make a prune 'kouglof', a special Alsace cake. I didn't eat much except when there was goat's cheese, which I adored.

We had the same problem with clothes: although fashionable tailors advised reversing jackets and transforming men's suits into women's suits, it wasn't much good if you had nothing left to make anything out of ...

Little by little, after a long period of frostiness, Claude gradually started talking to me and taking an interest in me. He asked me what I wanted to be when I grew up, what I liked doing, what I'd read, and so on. I replied quietly that I'd never read anything and that I hadn't quite decided yet whether to be a princess or a star. Then he started calling me a brainless idiot and I ran off and shut myself in the dormitory to cry.

I knew perfectly well he was better educated than me and it was maddening. His glasses and straight dark hair gave him an even more serious air, and he intimidated and irritated me by turns. He had done brilliantly in the first part of his baccalauréat and was now specializing in maths, with the inevitable self-satisfaction which came of being sixteen and brighter than anybody else around. His parents worshipped him. Because I was jealous I thought him pretentious. Clever, but pretentious ...

One day, Maître Geissman, a family friend, asked me: 'What do you want to do? You're a big girl now. You must either get some training or go back to school.'

'Some training.'

Apart from becoming a princess or a star I wouldn't have minded being a lawyer. For a liar and gossip like me it wasn't such an absurd idea. But he pointed out gently that I didn't even have my school certificate and that it wouldn't be easy. Coming down a rung I suggested: 'Perhaps I could at least be a legal secretary.'

I was enrolled, under an assumed name, on a shorthand typists' course on the avenue Berthelot. I could specialize in legal work later on. There was already enough to be getting along with, too much perhaps: I was to find other things to specialize in later, and never did manage that particular one.

I was entrusted to Claude for the journey to avenue Berthelot every morning. Just as he'd become nicer when he saw me helping his mother, he became nicer still when I started 'studying'. He behaved like a big brother, holding my hand along the road. He took care of me. He left me at the college door in the morning and picked me up there in the evening. As the weeks went by he got closer to me, in both senses: he used to put his arm round me in the crowded tram to protect me from all the shoving and pushing . . . and I gradually felt the pressure increasing as this protective gesture became more tender and less mechanical . . . His teasing, shy manner was already affecting me, and now that he was becoming warm towards me as well as mocking, he unsettled me even more.

He started to introduce me to writers who were too advanced for me, like Pascal! Although I was only thirteen, I was enthusiastic, less about Pascal perhaps than about my tutor. He also started me on Stendhal, not so dry, and better suited to the literary and sentimental education he was trying to give me . . . I read Zola too, and found some pages fascinating, no doubt because I felt close to the life-force he portrays, with the blend of cobblestones and gold, grandiose dreams and appalling misery. Claude seemed to understand that I'd never be a real intellectual, but that I did have a kind of instinctive animal intelligence which was worth developing: 'When you get angry, you're like a steam engine puffing fit to burst,' he said one day. A 'bête humaine' indeed! Of course, he was still as unenthusiastic as ever when I told him about my dreams and my ambitions: he thought my instincts too possessive, my imagination too wild and my plans for the future out of all proportion. The dreams of stardom and princesses, which I clung to for dear life, just made him laugh. But then sometimes he'd also shrug his shoulders, with an air of displeasure.

On Friday nights, at the synagogue, we'd always leave a bit early so we could have some time together on the way home. It was a hell of a walk, but love gives you wings to fly, as everyone knows. He

41

used words I'd never heard before, and I got the feeling that there was another whole world out there I knew nothing about. He sometimes asked me whether I understood what I was reading. I didn't dare tell him that I didn't understand everything, but tried to explain what effects certain things had on me ... One day, when I was making the beds in the dormitory, he offered to help me. Surprised, I asked him why, all of a sudden, he should want to do that. He told me softly that he loved me. I said I loved him too. So we declared ourselves, between two sheets. Too bad they weren't our own sheets.

He asked me to tell him I loved him again the next day. I did. After a long silence he said: 'Yes, but you don't really know what it means. And anyway, you've been so spoilt ...'

First, I just didn't see the connection. But the word 'spoilt' sent a shiver up my spine. Me, spoilt, who by? By what? At the convent a little, maybe. But otherwise? It gave me a shock because I realized for the first time that what others (even if you love them) think of you can be so far from the truth ...

After two months of flirting with each other he said: 'I won't believe you really love me unless you prove it to me.'

'How?'

'By doing something very simple.'

But what? What did he want me to do? He tried explaining, without really explaining at all: 'If you don't understand, it's because you're too young.'

It all made me very cross; him too. We argued constantly, and called each other all sorts of names. He deliberately went out with a fat blonde girl; I didn't hesitate to tell him how ghastly I thought she was.

'What can you possibly see in her? She's horrible.'

'She's charming, intelligent, and she knows what to do.'

'Ah, I see, so I have no charm, I'm not intelligent?'

I tried very hard to find defects in my character, but couldn't ...

One day he said: 'I want to talk to you, come to my room early one morning.'

'All right, I'll come. When?'

'When I tell you to. I'll arrange it.'

A little while later, when we were discussing my studies with the Heymanns, Claude told them I was very behind, for my age, which was true, and that if I wanted to get up earlier he'd work with me for an hour before we went off to school. Everyone thought it was an excellent idea, and saw nothing wrong with it. As he wished me goodnight he said: 'Come at seven o'clock tomorrow morning.'

I went next morning and we tried to work. He held my hands and gave me a grammar lesson which must have left him feeling a bit dissatisfied. Two days later he said, getting straight to the point: 'Come at five o'clock tomorrow. You'll prove to me that you love me.'

I kept pinching myself that night to stay awake. He'd lent me his watch, and at five o'clock I slipped out of bed to join him and give him this famous proof of my love. In my spotted flannelette nightie, barefoot, I opened the dormitory door and peeped out to check it was all clear. Horrors! There in front of me on the landing was the old blind man, like an apparition. The one who'd touched my hair that first day, and told me it was brown. There he stood with his eyes wide open, and his white stick. I was petrified and couldn't move. Claude's watch ticking in my hand sounded deafening.

'Régine?'

He'd sensed my presence. I hesitated, then answered,

'Yes, it's me.'

'Ah, good. I can't ever sleep, you know.'

I was on the point of tears, my throat all dry: I couldn't say another word, and went on past him down the stairs and locked myself in the toilet. I didn't dare come out again, so that's where I stayed with the frightful tick-tick of the watch. I was suffocating, and half dead with fear: 'What on earth am I doing here?' In spite of all this, I decided not to do things by half (the worst was over), and to join Claude in his room. I opened his door and whispered, still terrified: 'Monsieur Netter's on the stairs.'

'Shh. Come in!'

I entered his room and flung myself onto a chair. He started kissing me straight away — and on the mouth, for the first time. I wasn't really with it at all and thought to myself: 'So this is the proof?'

Tears of fear and relief ran down my cheeks. He told me to let myself go, breathe and part my lips. I was trembling and everything was spinning round ... I opened my mouth wide and closed my eyes. Then I heard him saying very gently: 'You can open your eyes now, Régine, we'll do some work. We'll talk tomorrow.'

I couldn't go down the next day, nor for three or four days afterwards. Claude went into a sulk and wouldn't talk to me. And I couldn't stop crying. Then one morning I thought I would go down, and got up at half past four. I walked past the blind man without speaking to him (he was still there listening to what was going on in the women's room) and went into the dining room, where Claude had decided to work from now on: it was just as quiet as his own room and there was much more space for his books. Strangely, he was standing there waiting for me, or so it seemed. He held me very tightly in his arms and said:

'Don't worry, I won't hurt you, you'll see. Lie down there.'

He pointed to the dining room table. I obeyed. He came over and gently started stroking my breasts, what little there was of them, talking to me all the time. Then he put the light out. In the darkness, I wondered if Monsieur Netter, the blind man, wasn't behind the door watching everything. Very gently, Claude explained what I had to do. I did it; so did he. It hurt. It wasn't what I was expecting ... and the whole experience left me with a bitter after-taste. And what if we'd been discovered?

Straight away afterwards, Claude told me I'd be his wife, when the war was over. He knew all about my 'story so far', the thirteen confusing, unhappy years, and he said: 'Up till now it's been as if you didn't have a family. Now you've got a father and a mother and me. We're your family now.' Say no more ... On that dining room table, Joseph's daughter started out all over again.

Over the days which followed, I continued to work with him. I never dared tell him but after the initial surprises and enthusiasm, I found the work itself very boring. What I did like was listening to him talk, telling me all sorts of new things: for all my mistakes, spelling didn't interest me either ... Sometimes I'd fall asleep again before going down and Claude would be waiting in vain ... then he'd sulk endlessly, and wouldn't even let me try to explain. He even slapped me one day! So much for criticizing my father!

Then Madame Lévy, the nonagenarian, got ill. She kept on calling for me one night.

'Régine ... Régine ...'

'Here I am, Madame Lévy. What can I do for you?'

'Ah, there you are, Régine, there you are ...'

I went back to bed, only to have her call me again ten minutes later. I jumped out of bed and went to her bedside.

'Here I am, Madame Lévy.'

'You're there ... Good, good. Stay with me ...'

In the morning she had her eyes wide open so I thought she was awake, and leant gently over her: 'Good morning: you really had a bad night, didn't you?'

She didn't answer. Her eyes were staring. I shook her, crying: 'Madame Lévy! Madame Lévy! Aunt Flora! Madame Lévy won't answer, I don't know what's the matter with her!'

Madame Heymann came rushing up in her nightdress. She looked at her, and then held a mirror to her lips. Ten seconds later she said: 'She's dead'. It was the first time I'd seen a dead body. 'Is she dead, really?' I said. Aunt Flora (that's what I now called Madame Heymann; her husband was Uncle Benoît) closed her eyes and looked at me saying: 'Come on, we'll get her washed'. In fact, I didn't do anything, I just watched her prepare the poor scrawny body. I was very upset, but watched without crying. Then suddenly, I couldn't help it, I started laughing hysterically. I rushed out of the room spluttering; I was so ashamed, I ran and hid on the stairs ... I was to get that nervous laughter several times during my life, at moments of intense emotion.

Aunt Flora called me back: 'Régine, Madame Lévy was very fond of you. She would have wished you to put the white socks on for her. Go and get a pair of yours.'

So I learnt that according to one tradition a body mustn't be buried with bare feet, and that whoever provides the socks and puts them on remains happy for the rest of their days. The dead person, shod for all eternity, would watch over them. As I was putting her into the socks I said to myself, 'I'm going to have good luck and happiness all my life.' I did have good luck and happiness, it's true, but not without effort and hard work: help yourself, and socks will help you too!

With Madame Lévy gone, there was one inconsolable old man with no one to dispute seniority with ...

The grief I'd felt was quick to pass. The house and its ghosts became oppressive, the noises from inside and from outside seemed muffled. Madame Lévy was dead? Well ... Whole families from Lyon had been arrested and taken away in their nightclothes? We lived with horror and in anxiety but life had to go on. I was much more frightened that one day Claude and I would be caught in the act or, worse still, that one day he would no longer be by my side ... By now, we made love anywhere we could, and not without risk; in the nearby woods, behind gates, in the cellar ... I liked it in the cellar because Aunt Flora put all the provisions down there three times a week after market: so I could indulge my passion for goat's cheese. Of course Claude told me not to touch anything, but he let me anyway because I was hungry and because

45

the rations upstairs in the dining room had become even more restricted.

Naïvely, I thought the Heymanns hadn't noticed our relationship. But years later, Madame Heymann told me they suspected as much, but could hardly throw me out. But then, Claude was their only son, and he must have told his parents, as he'd told me, that he'd marry me later on. And then sometimes when I was peeling potatoes with the old folks they'd ask with knowing smiles how I was getting on with my fiancé, and whether he was kind to me. I'd shrug my shoulders. Shut up, don't be ridiculous! I couldn't bear to think they knew! They'd laugh, like deaf people do, and shout, 'Go on, Régine, tell us what it's like with your fiancé!' They wouldn't stop, so I'd get up and leave the room.

The stories about the Lyon Militia and the deportations were gradually becoming more detailed and terrifying, and the atmosphere in the house became unbearable.

Later I learnt that this corresponded exactly with the arrival in Lyon of S.S. Obersturmführer Klaus Barbie, in November 1942. He was very efficient. One of his best catches was the arrest, on 9 February 1943, of eighty-six Jews and members of the Resistance at the Lyon branch of the UGIF in rue Sainte-Catherine, our own self-help group. That day, the UGIF had arranged a meeting of nearly all the local members, some of whom were linked with the Resistance. The Gestapo were there before anyone else arrived, and took each one prisoner as they came in. They were lined up against a wall in front of Barbie who ordered them all to be deported. Not one came back. Only Michel Thomas miraculously escaped the concentration camp, and is now an American citizen, one of the principal witnesses for the prosecution in the Barbie trial. He was a very experienced Resistance worker, specializing in false papers, and told Barbie that he'd walked into the UGIF building to sell paintings and didn't really belong there at all ... This round-up had a terrible effect on our little refuge. We felt we'd all been given a stay of execution.

Four months later, Jean Moulin was arrested, and a year later forty-one children were seized in the Jewish colony at Izieu near Lyon. All were deported.

The alarms were on the increase in Paris too, and they were rounding people up in the Jewish quarters where I'd lived as a child. The canteens for Jews between the République and the quartier Saint-Paul — rue Vieille-du-Temple, rue Elzévir, and rue

Béranger — were offering their 'customers' a last bowl of soup, thus making it easier for the police to take everyone away. There were 'ghettos' elsewhere too, such as the last carriage on the metro, the only one Jews were entitled to ride in.

All of us at the home lived in terror of what might happen, to us or to others. Against this rising tide of fear nobody had time or inclination for futile romance, but Claude and I lived out our dead-end yet intoxicating passion. Sometimes I had the awful feeling we were taking advantage of the situation ...

Then Claude had an excellent idea. Very early each morning Monsieur Heymann's brother-in-law arrived at the home with his wife, hung his jacket in the cupboard, put on his blue overalls and left at seven on the dot for the brewery where he worked, leaving his wife at the home. He left the key to their flat in his jacket pocket. Their flat! Claude decided that we'd skip classes after prep and go there to make love. He borrowed the key in the morning and put it back again before a quarter to six when his uncle came back to change. We'd meet there at four o'clock, and had an hour and a half of love-making in front of us. With four walls around us and a locked door we were much more comfortable, mentally and physically, than in the cellar, or various doorways, or with the rattling breath of Monsieur Netter spying on us behind the door ... It didn't stop me being ashamed, but I was less scared.

One day on my way to the flat I decided to buy some mimosa for Madame Heymann: the classic guilty gesture.

'What on earth have you got?' said Claude when he saw me coming.

'I've bought some mimosa.'

'You must be mad, it smells ghastly. Don't bring it into the flat. Leave it on the landing.'

'All right.'

I left the mimosa on the doorstep and we went in. Claude went first, with his eyes peeled, because there was always a 'trap' in the flat. So that he'd know if someone from the Gestapo or the Militia had been there, Claude's uncle always set a trap before he left — always the same sort, fortunately: a hair stuck across the crack of the door with saliva, a little bit of paper in the groove, some flour on the carpet for footprints, etc. When we left, we had to put everything back as it was, which often took quite some time and sometimes made us late ...

We were so late the day I bought the mimosa that we had to run for the tram. We just made it when I remembered: 'Claude, the mimosa! I've forgotten the mimosa!'

'Never mind, they won't know who left it there, it doesn't matter.'

The thought of the bouquet left lying on the doorstep tormented me all the way home.

Claude only just managed to put the keys back in time, jostling in the cupboard against his uncle who'd got home at the same time. His uncle wasn't surprised because Claude had made a point of keeping some of his books in the same cupboard so he'd always have a good excuse for rummaging about there.

The next night when we got in we heard his uncle in the dining room saying: 'We're going to have to move out. Someone in the block knows we're Jewish ... It must have been a warning, we'll have to go.'

'What are you talking about,' asked Claude, 'what's happened?'

'We found a little bunch of mimosa on the doorstep last night when we got home. Someone must have left this small yellow sign to show their sympathy and warn us of some danger.'

Catastrophe! Everyone was devastated, for different reasons. I didn't even dare look at Claude. I could have died with shame. The others were all discussing it and talking about going to pack their cases straight away.

'Don't be ridiculous,' said Claude, 'maybe someone just left it behind by mistake ...'

'No, no ... we'll have to move out.'

That same evening they moved into the home, lock, stock and barrel, and we were all just a bit more cramped. Claude was worried: 'You and your stupid ideas! Who was the mimosa for anyway?'

'For your mother.'

'Why for my mother?'

'Because I'm ashamed of myself.'

'It's stupid to feel ashamed, because I'm going to marry you.'

Fortunately, the aunt and uncle quickly found another flat, not far from the home. They carried on as before with the keys, but we couldn't bring ourselves to start that business all over again. So on Sundays we started going out into the woods by bike. We told them we were meeting friends. We made love in the undergrowth, under the pine trees ... It might sound poetic in books, but in reality pine needles are very slippery, prickly and sharp, and it became a real bore. And once we'd got there, there were endless good excuses to put it off: I was tired out, my back hurt, shh didn't I hear footsteps, etc. Claude hated me for it and started saying I just didn't love him any more. 'But I do, I do love you, but I'd prefer it if we could just talk.' It was the same old story whenever the inconvenience of loving outweighed the advantages.

Soon after this, very suddenly, Claude got very ill: with pleurisy. We didn't make love then for several weeks, and I started to realize how much I missed it, and that I really needed him physically. But it was out of the question: he was much too weak. Now it was my turn not to understand and to accuse him of not loving me. To annoy him I went out with one of his friends ... He didn't have the strength to make love to me, but mustered just enough to sulk at me for days on end.

I became obstinate about everything. For example, I'd refuse to go down to the shelter when there was an air-raid, or a warning. But since I was scared stiff that the house would collapse on me, I'd rush out into the streets like a mad thing as soon as the sirens went off.

On Friday evenings I still went to the synagogue, with Monsieur Heymann but without Claude. It was the one time that I wondered whether perhaps they'd invented the whole story about concentration camps! Because we went there openly, came out again without fear, and could walk home again without rushing. The synagogue was only three hundred metres away from the Gestapo headquarters and was protected by an agreement between the Germans and the chief rabbi of Lyon: it was understood that no Jew would ever be arrested during a service.

When I got back, I told Claude how some extremely handsome boys had been giving me the eye in the street ... but that he must certainly not get jealous because it would only make his temperature go up even more.

At last I got some news about my brother. He'd been very ill and was safe in a medical centre in the country. UGIF agents had dressed up as German police motorcyclists to get him there by ambulance! As for Thérèse, she was living with Eva and Albert the 'dwarf' ... Still no one knew what had become of my father.

From time to time, the UGIF would hide Jews on the wanted list in the home for a couple of days. One such was a very religious ten-year-old boy who stayed longer than most and who refused to have his curls cut off and on the Sabbath refused to touch light switches, even during an air-raid alert.

The Germans came from time to time, sometimes with the Red Cross, to check there were none but old folks in the home. Then Claude and I would hide in the cellar. And once we hid in a hole dug in the garden . . .

By March 1944, after three months' illness, Claude was well again, and working harder than ever. He was about to take his second baccalauréat, and was completely obsessed. Since I judged him to be paying his mathematics far more attention than he was paying me, I nagged him: 'Claude, are you sure you love me?'

'I've told you. I'm going to marry you, aren't I?'

It was all crystal clear to him and he didn't understand why I kept asking him . . . My periods had never been very regular, so we were always counting the days, re-counting, getting it wrong, hoping for the best, despairing again . . . I lived with the threat of pregnancy hanging over me, which didn't make our love-making any easier . . . If I was even a day late Claude would be in a state of panic and would rush off to get me lemonade-flavoured purgatives from the chemist. I don't know where he'd read about them, but he assured me they worked and made me take four at a time. The lemonade (clearly quite ineffective) made me sick as a dog: and with four times the recommended dose inside me I was never far from the toilet.

On his birthday at the beginning of June, Claude decided to go and have lunch with his Uncle Dreyfus, whom he loved and respected enormously. I asked if I could go too.

'No, stay here. In any case, I want to talk to him about us, and I don't want you to be there. But I'll see you back here at three-thirty.'

I felt sad and let down, but I didn't insist. I knew how difficult he found it 'living a lie' with me. It was quite understandable that he should want to talk to his uncle about it. I waited impatiently for him to come back. Half past three, and no Claude. He was always so punctual (it was absolutely essential for all of us in any case, because even being slightly late might mean the worst), so I was worried. Four o'clock, half past four, still no Claude. I was terrified. Monsieur Heymann came in: 'Where's Claude? Not here?'

'He's not back yet.'

'When did he say he'd be back?'

'Half past three.'

He went pale, and rushed madly out again; I went too. He ran down to the brewery to see his brother; I jumped in a tram going to the quai de Tilsit. I got to the synagogue door, and was reaching for the bell-pull when a man touched me and whispered: 'Get out of here quick. The Gestapo have been.'

I ran off and got the tram back to the home. I couldn't speak and collapsed on a chair in the dining room. Just then, I heard Monsieur Heymann's voice in the hall: 'They've been arrested!'

Everyone started crying, and I fainted. When I came to, I couldn't speak at all. And I remained voiceless for three days.

What had happened? Uncle Benoît had gone to the synagogue just after me, with his brother. He'd rung, but the concierge didn't answer. So he called out, and Benjamin Dreyfus's wife opened a window on the first floor where their flat was. He asked her where her husband and Claude were. She had no idea. She too was surprised they weren't back, and that the concierge wasn't there. She was desperately worried by what Monsieur Heymann told her and barricaded herself in the flat and started praying. Uncle Benoît carried on the search and finally found someone who could tell him something: the Militia had received an anonymous letter accusing the concierge of black marketeering. They came to arrest him just as Claude and his uncle were about to ring the bell. The Militia took them all away, without going up to the flat.

The next day, Uncle Benoît heard that they'd been sent to the fort at Montluc. The Germans had offered to release the uncle, but he refused to leave without his nephew. From what people said, Montluc didn't have a good reputation: they said prisoners were particularly ill treated, and malnourished, and that it was a transit camp for Drancy and eventual deportation.

Three or four days passed before I surfaced from the lethargy I'd sunk into, and one morning, at five o'clock, I suddenly decided to take a parcel to Claude. Stealthily, I packed some chocolates and fortified biscuits that we were given for the old folks. I slipped out and went up to the fort, completely oblivious of the danger. It was six o'clock in the morning. People were still asleep.

There were some big double doors, which opened and closed at all hours of the day and night, letting lorry-loads of men, women and children in and out. To one side was a small armoured door. Between the two, the guardroom where they operated the doors from. I rang on the little door. A very young German looked out through the guardroom window, and two seconds later the door slid aside and disappeared behind the wall. I went in, the door slid to behind me, and I found myself in a corridor closed off at the other end with another armoured door. On the right, behind a grill, two German soldiers. They can't have been more than forty years old between them.

'I want to give this parcel to a friend who's been arrested.'

He looked at the name I'd written on it in big letters — Claude Heymann.

'Jewish?'

I hesitated ... 'I don't know ... He's a friend.'

They looked at each other and then suddenly said:

'Get out, quick! Raus! Germany kapput! Schnell! Raus!'

One of them opened the door signalling me to go straight away. But the other one had looked out of the guardroom window and shut the door again before I'd even moved. I started weeping, crying 'I want to get out, I want to go!' They put their fingers to their lips saying shh, looking anxiously out of the window. I squeezed between them to have a look.

Two light fifteens had just pulled up outside the fort, followed by two coaches. It was pouring with rain. The unfortunate people who'd been piled in the coaches were ordered out by men from the Militia and the Gestapo, among them some officers. Some of the people were in their nightclothes, or half-dressed. Quite clearly, they'd been arrested in their homes at dawn. I could even see a family I knew, with the children barefoot. The man giving the orders might have been Klaus Barbie.... I'd seen round-ups starting and the checking of identity papers before, but I'd never seen the full horror of it at close range. I was actually witnessing one of the tragic, banal events like the dozens we'd only heard about over the last three years.

The two young Germans gestured to me to crouch down, but because I did not obey fast enough they pushed me to the floor. Outside, a German came up to the window and asked them: 'OK?'

'Ja!'

I was scared to death. Five or ten minutes went by. I could hear them ordering different groups of people here or there: some went into the fort, some went back in the coach. Then they bolted the big doors again, the coaches and cars started up and then silence returned. The two young Germans stood me up and opened the door. 'Raus!' I picked up my parcel and ran. Thunder rumbled in the early morning sky. My eyes were blind with rain and tears.

When I got back to the home I told Aunt Flora that I'd been up to Montluc fort, but that I hadn't been able to see Claude. I told her what had happened: 'But don't you realize what you've done! You must be mad! What made you do it?'

She raged at me, crying and gasping, all the while clasping me tightly to her breast. Before long, all the old folks gathered round too, gesticulating, weeping and berating me. Aunt Flora, through a sob, managed to say: 'Dear little Régine, you mustn't.... Claude ... do you understand ... You are our daughter now ...'

It was as though she were saying he would never come back.

After the initial shock, everyone began hoping once more. We knew that the landing had been on 6 June, Claude's birthday, and that Liberation was very near. Aunt Flora had a change of heart and kept saying: 'They will come back, they will. Because of the landings, they can't have been taken far.' Alas though ...

A few weeks later, after the Germans had started pulling out of Lyon by road, I wandered over to the railway carriages which had been sitting there, right near the old folks home, for at least two months ... I ventured across the rails and saw that one of the Red Cross trucks was partially open. I got in. There were thousands of pairs of shoes, rucksacks, packets of cigarettes and tins of corned beef, just waiting for someone to help themselves. I spread the word among the neighbourhood kids and it was like the gold rush. They cleared them out in no time. Others followed suit and forced the doors of the remaining waggons, making off with the contents.

The Heymanns had closed their shutters while the Germans were on the run, but with our eyes to the slits we watched the tanks, cars and lorries rolling past the house. A few days later, shutters flung wide, Lyon welcomed the first *Forces Françaises de l'Intérieur* and allied troops with open arms. Notices were posted up on walls asking for the return of all the merchandise stolen from the trains, so it could be fairly distributed ... I don't think the FFI got much back. I kept a rucksack, telling myself that after wearing the same three or four garments for two whole years I deserved a little treat from the Red Cross.

It was holiday time in Lyon, like everywhere else, then time for recriminations. Going from place to place, I saw women having their heads shaved in public, and others already shaven going around under escort. They didn't seem to know what was going on:

neither did I. I was carrying the unloaded revolver which I'd found somewhere or other; it seemed quite natural to be carrying one, everybody did. The streets were full of 'last minute' Resistance fighters ready to tell you about the Jews they'd saved. (Even now, forty years on, I never quite believe it if someone tells me his best friend's a Jew.)

One thing seemed very strange to me. The Germans may well have gone, but you still had to walk miles to fetch milk. The enemy had fled, but the bridges were still down and the only way to get across was to hitch a ride from the Americans and cross further upstream. Mile after mile with my rucksack on my back, full of potatoes, was enough to put me off walking, potatoes and rucksacks for the rest of my life.

One evening, our American benefactors were throwing chocolate down from their trucks to the poor starving French, and I'd wormed my way in among the seething mass of people to catch some, too. With my eyes heavenward following the trajectory of the chocolate I managed to fall into the entrance to a shelter. I was pulled out and taken to the home, and thence straight to the hospital. I was in there for ten days with both ankles badly sprained.

Back at the home, we expected Claude and his uncle back any day. One day, Aunt Flora went to see a fortune-teller she'd been recommended. I waited for her, full of hope. But when she came in she dissolved into tears and murmured: 'We've got to forget all about them: Claude won't ever be coming back, it's all over. You're my daughter now, you'll stay with us.'

Not only could I not give up hope that Claude would come back, but I was dreadfully perturbed by my new status as 'daughter' — now almost official. I was convinced that she thought of me as Claude's younger sister, and that she would start to hate me if she realized what the true nature of our relationship had been. Hence the remorse I felt when I thought about what we'd done. In fact the Heymanns knew perfectly well that, despite my age, I was more of a daughter-in-law than a younger sister, and it was modesty which prevented them talking about it ...

My hope was fed by a prediction the fortune-teller had made about Aunt Flora having another baby, at 47! If she was wrong about that, then she might well be wrong about Claude ... But she was right about the baby and, alas, right about Claude too. Claude and his uncle were in one of the last trainloads of deportees before the Liberation, or perhaps even the very last, on 11 August 1944.

Whichever train it was, it would have rolled out on the line we could see from our window. We never knew where they'd been taken to, but they never came back. Claude would never again mock me for my dreams of stardom, nor correct my spelling mistakes. His uncle had gone to the abyss rather than abandon him.

All I know is that to this day he still protects me.

Life looked up again, and by the end of 1944 I'd started venturing out to the famous American dance-halls, where they did the swing and the jitterbug, the dance that Boris Vian had just made fashionable in the Paris nightclubs of St-Germain-des-Prés. I did my best to look elegant, on very slender means, and often in cast-offs from the help agencies. A kid in women's clothes wasn't much to look at, but who cared! I turned up all the hems myself, and not very well, so they were frequently gathered, very uneven, and prone to coming undone ...

I watched the Lyon *zazous* in amazement with their thigh-length jackets and narrow trousers, big shoes, knitted ties and hair slicked back with salad oil. Their dropped shoulder-line was quite different from the female of the species, who wore square shoulders. The girls had polo-neck sweaters, pleated skirts, thick stockings and heavy flat shoes, but rarely wooden-soled ones. They all looked a bit like Popeye's girlfriend Olive. The *zazous* had plenty of money: either they'd always had money, or their fathers had made a mint on the black market. Thus *zazou* links were made between good families and the black marketeers (called BOFs after *beurre-oeufs-fromages* − butter, eggs, cheese − dealing in which had made them rich). I watched and took it all in. All this little crowd sang and danced 'Je suis swing', the Johnny Hess *tube* (a record was called a *saucisson* − sausage − until Boris Vian invented the word *tube*), and looked down on the poor behind-the-times creatures who preferred 'Je suis seule ce soir' by Léo Marjane or those with nostalgia for Paris who were cheerfully humming 'Si tu vas à Paris, dis bonjour aux amis' ... It was also the beginnings of the Compagnons de la Chanson.

Since Claude's disappearance, and despite my hopefully alluring finery, I hadn't yet met anyone who appealed to me, and no one, needless to say, who I had the slightest desire to make love to. But then one day ...

I was coming back from the Red Cross with my fortified biscuits when it started pouring with rain. I stuck out my thumb (everyone hitch-hiked, even in town) and a jeep pulled up, driven by a young American who can't have been more than twenty-five, and who spoke pretty good French. He looked like Claude: the glasses, high forehead, serious expression, straight hair ... He looked so much like him that when he suggested we make love I agreed. We didn't know where else to go, so we did it in the jeep, and about as uncomfortably as in the dining room at the home.

I told him immediately afterwards that that was the first and last time I'd make love with him. He didn't seem to believe me and insisted on seeing me again. He even came to find me at the home, and very politely asked the Heymanns' permission to take me out. One evening he told me he wanted to marry me. Then I told him my story, and that the only thing that had attracted me to him was his likeness to Claude. I started to cry. He didn't seem at all put out:

'It doesn't matter, we'll get married and I'll take you to America.'

'No, it's no good, because I'm not in love with you and I'm only fourteen and a half.'

That did it. Not the fact that I didn't love him, but that he'd never imagined I might be that young. But instead of giving up the idea, he seemed to panic at the thought of having 'compromised' a child, and started proposing marriage all over again! Since I still refused, he said, as sure of himself as a Roosevelt: 'I'll wait, and my parents will come and fetch you.'

He wrote to me for a long time after he left. To begin with I answered his letters, but then ... And now I can't even remember his name. One thing's for certain though, he was the first of the men in my life who were like Claude (though he was the most similar to look at): after Claude I always had a distinct preference for tall, quiet, cultivated men with glasses.

In the middle of all this came another proposal of marriage, by letter. This time from Georges, my little baker friend from La Brillanne. He had managed to find my address and wrote: 'I have heard that your father has disappeared: there is room for you with us and when you are old enough I will marry you, if you are willing. I haven't forgotten you and I still feel the same: I hope you do too ...' No words of love from *Mayerling* though. I wrote back that I was very touched, but that so much had happened since we last met ... And then, I still wasn't fifteen yet ...

My brother was still in hospital and sending me such sad little letters that I tried to boost his morale by writing long funny letters back … It wasn't always easy to find amusing things to tell him and one day when I was chewing my pencil, trying hard to think of something, someone knocked at the door and came in. I turned around; it was Joseph! Dumbfounded, I heard him cry: 'My daughter! My daughter! Here I am, I've come to fetch you!' And he recounted his epic story.

Just as he was getting everything ready for our departure to the States, he had been denounced, arrested and put in the fort at Montluc, a year and a half before Claude and fortunately just before Barbie arrived in Lyon. Then, with two French officers, he tried to escape. They had found out the times of the freight trains which stopped near the fort, they stunned a guard and then ran hell for leather while the gates were open for a convoy to pass through!

Joseph's second sense had warned him what was in store at Auschwitz or elsewhere: he'd rather be shot in the back. The Germans set their dogs on them, and Joseph's calf muscles were half torn off before he managed to jump into a truck. Safe! He got to Grenoble, then to Toulouse where Albert and Thérèse lived. They sheltered him and that was the start of a true friendship between the 'dwarf' and the 'giant'. Just before Toulouse was liberated he was captured again during a round-up and thrown into prison. The Militia tried to make him confess he was Jewish, but he stuck to the story his false papers gave, making him out to be a Pole of purest Aryan stock. He managed not to let slip a single word of French. To make him crack, they tortured him, working on his ankles with a mallet and putting cupping-glasses on his back and smashing them with mallet blows. Just after that the town was liberated and Joseph managed to get his hands on one of his torturers and killed him with an iron bar. Well, that's what he said, anyway; but I wouldn't like to count on it. One thing was for certain, though, he'd developed a limp and had to walk with a stick …

Having duly recounted his tale, doubtless with embellishments (though the worst bits always seemed the most probable), he left, promising to be back soon:

'I'm going to Paris. I'll be back in a week and we'll get the whole family back together.'

And off he went again. Although the Heymanns were delighted for me that I'd found Joseph again, they were a little sad too:

'We're ashamed to tell you, we shouldn't really think it, but we'd have preferred him not to find you, you're the only thing we've got left ...'

Alone, without a family, I was their daughter. But with Joseph's reappearance I became no more than their beloved son's last girlfriend.

And so life, no respecter of tragedy, went on ...

5

La Lumière de
Belleville

Three weeks later, of course, there was still no Monsieur Joseph. I
decided to look for work. I saw some advertisements for typing and
secretarial assistant jobs, and went along straight away. A man
ushered me in and asked my age.

'Fourteen and a half, Monsieur.'

'People don't start work at fourteen!'

'But I must, Monsieur, I really must work.'

I told him my story, I told him everything, except about Claude.
He seemed moved.

'I see, well, I think there just might be a job for you. Go back
home now and I'll come and see Monsieur and Madame Heymann
this evening. Your job, if you agree, will be looking after my three
young daughters, and it will mean coming to live with us. That's
why I really must come and talk to them.'

He came round. Aunt Flora and her husband were very surprised
at this new development, and asked me if I was sure I wanted to
go. But my mind was made up and I answered tearfully: 'Yes, I
want to go, because my father's still alive and it's not right that you
should be looking after me. I want to go to work, and then I can
pay you.'

I had become obsessed with the need to have some money of my
own, and to help them ...

My determination scared them, and Aunt Flora ended up saying:
'Perhaps it's the best thing after all ...'

So I did go and live with Monsieur S. where my main duties were to look after his three little girls: I took them to school, fetched them home again, corrected their homework, heard them reading.

My room contained a grand piano, a bed, and me. We went to the country at weekends ... nothing too exciting. I took the Heymanns little presents when I went to see them, and bought myself some fishnet stockings to wear when I went out. I had several little flirtations at the dance-hall, and danced like crazy, like one possessed, danced till I almost dropped with exhaustion.

I hadn't forgotten Claude, but gradually the pain lessened. I'd been a child, and that was all over now. Memories became less sharp, and my whole body yearned for the future. I was hungry for life.

Monsieur S. called me into his office one morning and said: 'I'm going to Paris tomorrow. While I'm there I'll try and find your father. I think it's a bit odd that he hasn't been in touch at all. I've been making a few enquiries and I think I know where I might find him. Somewhere round Belleville.'

He came back a few days later and proudly announced: 'Régine, I've found your father. He's coming to collect you next week. Aren't you pleased?'

No, I was not pleased. Next week: what did that mean in Joseph's book? Next week, next year ...

For once, though, he kept his word, and appeared wearing a blue pin-striped suit, sporting a diamond ring, a felt hat, very much the gentleman, very much at ease, and so charming that my rancour just melted away. I decided to go with him.

Farewells and kisses all round for the S. family, and then we were off to the old people's home to tell the Heymanns we were leaving for Paris. Everything had happened so quickly ... I felt stunned, happy and rather anxious all at once. The Heymanns couldn't believe that this time I was going for good. And Joseph, while thanking them, wanted to recompense them as well, clearly taking the home for just another boarding school. He was blithely oblivious to the love, affection and lack of self-interest shown by these people who had been my real family for two whole years. I would never ever forget them.

As we walked away I couldn't help turning round again and again, and at the bottom of the road I was seized by a desperate desire to run back. I confessed as much to Joseph, who promptly pulled out all the stops and sent rumblings of deep family feeling resonating through me: what about my brother, my sister ... what about him? The Heymanns' understated little melody couldn't compete and I gave in. Especially when he told me I'd have my own room in a beautiful flat in Paris, and new dresses and new shoes. He believed what he was saying; so did I. I shouldn't have done. The bubble was to burst very quickly.

During the journey he told me the least surprising news: there was a new Madame Joseph, whom of course he swore he was going to marry soon.

'You'll see, I'm sure you'll like her very much. She's very intelligent. She's not very beautiful, but she's more intelligent than the others.'

I listened without flinching, merely looking at this man who had reappeared in my life only to tell me that there was going to be yet another Madame Joseph. My pleasure at his return gave way to unease, and I started asking myself whether, all things considered, I would really have minded very much if he'd never come back at all. But then, going to Paris was an exciting prospect, and Joseph kept on saying: 'You'll see, you'll have piles of dresses, you'll have dozens!'

'And what about Maurice? We'll have to fetch Maurice and Eva.'

'Yes, yes. Later . . . later.'

We arrived at the Gare de Lyon in Paris. But no taxi for us. We took the metro to Porte Dorée, in the twelfth arrondissement. Joseph led me to rue Marcel-Dubois. That's where he and the lady lived. We went upstairs. He rang the doorbell on the first floor and, horrors! A frightful woman in a pink spotted dressing gown opened the door; her hair was frizzy, she had a scar on her cheek, blood-red lips and a cigarette stuck in her mouth. Opening her arms in welcome, with a gruesome smile, she cried:

'Oh Joseph! Oh my little girl!'

Panic-stricken, I dropped my suitcase, ran back down the stairs and out into the street. With my back pressed against the wall, I cried uncontrollably. I'd heard Joseph shouting my name as he ran down after me, and there we both were on the pavement, he bewildered and me in a heap.

'I don't want to stay here, she frightens me.'

'Stop Régine! Ettie's going to love you very much, and you'll grow to love her too.'

We talked, we bargained: a new dress? . . . all right, then, two? . . . and a real lady's handbag . . . Are you coming then? So back I went, trying hard to smile. But the damage was done. My new stepmother, still in the dressing gown, but smiling rather less, had taken a dislike to me. And she knew what I thought of her.

Since she'd decided to treat me like a skivvy, and I had pretensions to stardom, we were incompatible from the start.

Next morning, we had a repeat of the scene we'd had with Madame Heymann: Ettie asked me if I'd like to help her clean the dining-room floor; I declined, kicking the bucket over and telling her she could damn well do it herself. And after sticking my tongue out at her, I went off for a walk, slamming the door behind me, and leaving her cloth in hand. I came back that evening — I had to, I was starving hungry — to find Joseph playing the lion-tamer, belt at the ready. Before I realized that I was the wild beast in question, he set about me in front of Ettie. When it was all over, I looked him straight in the eye without a word, thinking: 'You'll never make it to heaven, mate!'

As the days went by I gradually realized that this woman only had room in her heart for one, and that was Joseph. The rest of the world could go hang. That was Joseph's problem, not mine.

With the atmosphere at home as it was, I was hardly ever there, and I found myself thinking more and more about Maurice. I started waging a war of attrition on Joseph, nagging him constantly with the same question: 'When are you going to fetch Maurice?' So much so that, for a bit of peace, he though he'd kill two birds with one stone: he sent me down to fetch Maurice, who was with the Mariottis near Aix, convalescing after his illness.

I stayed down there for several days, delighted to be with Maurice again, and thrilled to be near 'my' casino again too. But the atmosphere was all different. The discreet charm of the war years had gone; everything was Americanized . . . and much more fun. There was a huge ball there one evening. I took my brother along, and danced the boogie-woogie outside all night long like a mad thing in front of fifty musicians. The next day, still trembling from the excesses of the night before, I went to see the nuns at my old convent, who welcomed me like the prodigal child. We took the train to Paris that evening: it was completely packed so we had to spend the night standing in the corridor.

Two shady-looking characters propositioned me, but I told them to bugger off . . .

We arrived at the Porte Dorée. I hadn't told Maurice much about the new stepmother . . . he'd see for himself soon enough. And the face he pulled when she started coming over all maternal with him was a real treat. He didn't exactly make for the door, but it was clear that he'd rather be elsewhere.

Shortly afterwards, we got Eva back as well. Thérèse and Albert had come back to live in Paris, and though she adored her daughter, she gave her up to Joseph, who had insisted on having her. Eva had just one failing in our eyes: she was too young to detest Ettie the Romanian. (Yet another East European: Joseph seemed to be working his way through the lot.)

Monsieur Joseph was a dealer. Foreign currency? Cloth? Whatever it was, he dealt in it. He made quite a bit of money, and not for the first time played cards down at one of the cafés on the place de la République. And he drank. Before the war he didn't touch alcohol because of his diabetes. He didn't seem to give a damn now, and practically ran on booze. It didn't take much to make him drunk, and when he was he started taking it out on the stepmother. We thought it very funny but she didn't trust him and kept a close eye on him so as to keep the damage to a minimum. When she thought he was about to let rip, she'd gently remind him that it was time to go home. But she was often too late and he'd come out with something like: 'Shut up you old crock!'

He called her 'The Antique' as well, although she was actually six months younger than he was.

'My women have always been beautiful! But you, you're an Antique, a Titanic.'

His friends guffawed with laughter every time he said it.

One day I'll never forget I'd gone to the café with Maurice and Eva. We had come to get Joseph, who'd promised to buy us some new clothes for the holidays. But he must have decided to celebrate some other way, and was completely sozzled. Bye bye new clothes! He insulted Ettie and, with a drunken wave of the arm in her direction, addressed the room in general: 'Just look at her! My daughter, she doesn't love my daughter! I'll have to choose between them! . . . and I'll choose my daughter, because I'm a father you know! And I've always done everything I could for my children! . . .'

And so he went on, trying to persuade the customers that his wife was no good, that she was trying to separate him from his children, etc. All in a mixture of French and Yiddish, which was funny for everyone except us. We were so ashamed of him we didn't know where to hide. We begged him to come home with us.

Finally he agreed, and there we were, me, Joseph, Maurice and Eva, on our way to the Porte Dorée. The stepmother had sensibly made herself scarce.

With difficulty, we got as far as the entrance to the metro at République, just by a shop called 'La Toile d'Avion'. I was admiring myself in the shop window: I'd got my hair swept up like two great shells, with ribbons in it, and was wearing a red, white and blue crêpe dress, red platform shoes, and carrying a large handbag given to me by my stepmother (I had been sorely tempted to refuse the gift, but the bag really was too nice to turn down). I was fifteen years old, with smocking under the bust to make me look bigger, and a dead-drunk father to return to the fold.

Right in front of the shop, Joseph came to a halt declaring that he was not going down into the metro, and started haranguing the passers-by. People began gathering round, while Joseph launched into: 'The Titanic wants to part me from my children! But I'm a father, I've always done my best for my children! It's all over with the Antique! I'm keeping my children with me!'

Wanting to show the assembled company the fruit of his loins, he suddenly realized we weren't there any more. We were so embarrassed that we'd hidden behind the crowd that had gathered round him. Now he started yelling: 'My daughter! Régine! . . . where is my daughter?'

I tried to squirm away but he saw me.

'Régine, come here!'

I came up to him, the two huge loops of hair on top of my head, the platform soles, the dress, the big bag, and said: 'Papa, it's time to go. Come on, everyone's looking at you.'

With Maurice and Eva (both in tears by now), I took his hand and pulled him, and he finally followed us into the metro. It was the middle of July, and it was stultifying in the train. Joseph slumped onto one of the folding seats. I was standing next to him, staring straight ahead, pretending not to be there. Suddenly, still in tears, Eva tugged my hand: 'Look at Papa . . . look what he's doing . . .'

I glanced round, as if he was nothing to do with me. And what did I see? Monsieur Joseph was drying himself off on the skirt of my dress. He'd taken a whole section of it to wipe his sweat and blow his nose on. Crêpe is nice stuff, but being acetate, its disadvantage is that it shrinks on contact with water. The singer René Paul had had a big hit three years before with a song taking the mickey

64

out of synthetic materials which turned trousers magically into shorts with the first shower. 'It's slightly inconvenient,' he said, 'but when you know what to expect, at the first drop of rain you simply remove the trousers, tuck them under your arm and off you go shouting "women and children first!"'

I couldn't exactly tuck the dress under my arm, and just watched while the section so generously watered by Joseph instantly shrank to half way up my thigh!

I didn't say a word, and just stood there steadfast against adversity. There were eleven stations between République and Porte Dorée. So there I stood for eleven stations, staring into the middle distance. People were laughing, I could hear them, but I didn't look round. We got there at last, and had to get out. We pushed Joseph out onto the platform. If anyone had told me my troubles were only just beginning, I don't think I'd have believed them; but it was true! Once he was out of the carriage, Joseph slumped onto a bench and promptly threw up. I thought I'd die when the man on the metro popped his head out and yelled, 'Just you get that cleared up, right away!' So I had to dash off in search of a mop and bucket from somewhere … And clear up Joseph's revolting mess, with my dress like a rag, my bag in a safe corner, my brother and sister flopped on the bench next to Joseph, who was still spewing. Train-load after train-load of people went past, all laughing, I was sure.

Once we were back home, I didn't speak to Joseph for several days. The next day he said he wanted to buy me 'seventeen dresses'. Why not twenty? I couldn't even bear to listen to him.

'I'll buy you lots of dresses, Régine. Whatever you want!'

I didn't give an inch. He followed me around, promising me the moon, but I was so angry with him that nothing, nothing could ever make up for the humiliation he'd made me suffer.

The whole episode got blown up out of all proportion: for three months after that I wouldn't go near the station in case the ticket-collector recognized me, and used to walk right down to Daumesnil, the next station along.

The more I dreamt, as I did often now, of my prince charming, the less he looked anything like Joseph. And the nearer I got to the dream, the further I drifted, irresistibly, from Joseph. The trouble was that Joseph was precisely thinking of marrying me off, and to no prince charming either.

In the rue Notre-Dame-de-Nazareth was a café-restaurant where he often went because they did such good Polish-Jewish food. He got on so well with the boss that they began making plans to marry me off to Marcel, the boss's son. The stepmother, whose one wish was to see the back of me, was right behind them. To soften me up and make me accept the contract, she quite suddenly became remarkably congenial and offered me a white gold engagement ring set with some sort of red stones and minuscule diamonds. This ring, which must have been about as genuine as my stepmother was, fascinated me, and I started saying to myself, 'Well, after all, why not? What have I got to lose?' And the fiancé was a nice boy too, called Marcel: not David or Solomon, but Marcel. It made a change from Joseph's other friends, who treated our house like their favourite ghetto. A bit of fresh air wouldn't be a bad thing.

We go to know each other a bit better and went to the cinema together, and decided without further ado on a date for the engagement. Thérèse, my ex-stepmother, who now ran a little dressmaking workshop, made me a beautiful long blue crêpe dress for the big occasion; it had lots of tiny buttons down the front and the inevitable smocking under the bust.

The morning of the party, I made myself up to the nines, with the two shells of hair swept up higher than ever, and put the ring on over my glove so that people could see it better. It was a big party, with a proper lunch, and people taking photos. I felt radiant. But at about five or six o'clock that evening, when we got back home, my heart sank — the ring had gone! I couldn't remember whether or not I'd taken the glove off at some point, or whether perhaps someone, regretting that I was now spoken for, had shaken my hand and slipped the ring off as a kind of consolation prize. In tears, I started to hunt high and low for it, but in vain. It all seemed like a very bad omen, and my feelings for Marcel, lukewarm at the best of times, turned even cooler. I begged him to leave me be. Since he demanded an explanation I explained once and for all:

'Look, I've been thinking it over. Let's break it off. I'm too young, and I just don't want to get engaged after all!'

It was a shock for him, because he was in love with me.

I plucked up courage one evening, and told Joseph: 'I've broken off the engagement.'

'What do you mean, you've broken off the engagement?'

'I've broken it off! I've told Marcel it's all over! That's all.'

First I lose the ring, then I lose the fiancé! It was all too much for Joseph, who started trying, unsuccessfully, to take swipes at me. My stepmother, the while, droned away in the background with: 'There you are, I told you so, she's no good. She's just a "bitter-schtik" [Yiddish for a bad lot]! You'll never make anything of her, Joseph, believe you me! I never want to set eyes on her again!'

I couldn't quite see the connection myself: I wasn't getting disengaged to spite them, it was because I just didn't want to be engaged after all. I felt they'd had a bit of a nerve to hitch me up at fifteen, with a ring that had a mind of its own, to someone I was only half keen on. But Joseph was beyond reasoning and yelled at me:

'Okay, if that's the way you want it — back to boarding school with you!'

He was playing his trump card, so he thought; he'd always been convinced that I hated boarding school because I missed him. He couldn't have been more mistaken — I liked it. It was better than stepmothers, anyhow. First I'd kick up a bit of a fuss, then I'd find my niche and then I'd feel fine. Back home with Joseph, there was never a niche to find, just a bear-pit full of stepmothers.

Pension des Lilas, The Lilacs boarding school. I started in the middle of August. There were barely a dozen other girls there. They were there, I suppose, either because their parents hadn't wanted to take them on holiday or else because they weren't going away anywhere.

The dormitories were all shut up and so we slept in the sanatorium. There were high windows which gave onto the road. I'd taken my own gramophone, my records and the photos of my engagement — for the dress. All my chums were duly impressed: think of that, she's already been engaged to be married, at fifteen! I taught them how to dance to my records and the directrice, a friendly, attractive woman, who'd started life as the school wardrobe-keeper and then married the directeur's son, used to come and join in.

When the other girls came back at the beginning of term, I'd already got quite a reputation. It must be said: I'd been working at it.

Joseph had bought himself a café: La Lumière de Belleville. He came to fetch me on one of our free days and took me by metro from Porte des Lilas to Belleville. Appalling memories of that other metro incident at Porte Dorée flashed through my mind ...

We arrived at the café. Animated groups of men and women sat around laughing and drinking, speaking Polish, Romanian, Russian, Hungarian, and Yiddish when they couldn't understand one another. The atmosphere was folksy and quaintly exotic.

I had hoped that Joseph might have changed his mistress along with his job and house, but no such luck. The unsinkable Titanic was there too, moored to the till, cyclone-proof, tight-fisted as ever.

With barely a 'good evening', I asked her where the flat was.

'First floor, last door.'

As in Anderlecht and in rue Pasteur, Joseph was living 'above his means'. There were just two bedrooms − Joseph and the Titanic's, and another with two single beds, plus a toilet with washbasin and shower. No bathroom. It was pitiful compared to the old flat at Porte Dorée, and I told them so. But stepmother made out that we didn't need a kitchen or a dining room, since we had the use of the restaurant.

I hung about in the café to see what went on.

Joseph introduced me to his partner: another Joseph. To distinguish them, we called them Baker-Joseph and Ginger-Joseph. Joseph was no longer a baker, but the other was genuinely and permanently ginger-haired.

Everyone gathered at the café on Sunday mornings. It was a real tower of Babel, an Abraham's melting pot. Ginger-Joseph served at the bar, the stepmother rang up the till, and our Joseph mingled with the customers in the café. He was the master of ceremonies, the life and soul. The stepmother also supervised the cook who was busy making the meatballs, kasha and cheesecakes. As in the cafés around the Carreau du Temple and Place de la République, the talk was of dollars, real and forged, the war, houses, flats, women, missing children, unknown countries and cities far away. Everyone's eyes bore the traces of recent tragedy, but not of sadness. A sense of humour from elsewhere, cruel and funny at the same time, gave all their expressions, their words and their gestures a festive air. Some of them must have been to hell and back a hundred times over, others had fled from country to country, and they'd all felt the war open up the ground beneath their feet, yet each one donned his Sunday best and they flocked like so many butterflies to La Lumière de Belleville.

Many of them had recently arrived in Paris, and were looking for work: until they found a job, they got by somehow, happy just to be alive.

Eva joined me at the school a few weeks later; and it was thanks to her that my school career came to an end, even earlier than expected: just six years' education in all ...

What happened was that she got an ear infection almost as soon as she arrived. Her temperature soared. And I was told to take her back home post-haste. Very kindly, the directrice lent me a blanket to wrap her up in, and phoned the café to tell them I was on my way. It was a Saturday. When the stepmother saw me coming she shouted furiously at me: 'What am I supposed to do with her on my hands, and it's Sunday tomorrow, the best day of the week!'

I put Eva in the room she had shared with Maurice before coming to the school. And on Monday I went back to the Lilacs, with the blanket under my arm. I was a bit late. I heard people talking in the directrice's office, and because I didn't want to disturb them I left the blanket on the doormat and quickly went to the classroom. At two o'clock, after lunch, the directrice made a solemn entry into our classroom. She stood at the front of the class and spoke to me:

'Mademoiselle Zylberberg, I've just learnt to my cost that you can't make a silk purse out of a sow's ear.'

She upbraided me for the way my 'mother' had spoken to her on the telephone, and for the cavalier fashion with which I'd returned the blanket. I wasn't surprised to hear that Ettie had treated her scornfully — she was as stupid as she was pretentious. But what really maddened me was that she could have taken the Titanic for my mother! And as for the blanket, I had deliberately left it outside the door out of consideration for her privacy, and I was furious that she chose to reproach me for this excess of zeal — especially as such things were so rare.

She repeated her previous phrase, apparently delighted with the sound of it: 'No ... Sow's ears decidely don't make silk purses.'

'That's as maybe,' I retorted, 'but wardrobe-keepers don't make directrices either! And incidentally, I'm leaving: I'm not staying a moment longèr in your filthy little school!'

And slamming the door after me, I left the room, and the school too, without even bothering to take my things.

While I was on the metro, I worked out how best to describe the events to Joseph. When I got home I told him: 'Dad, I've left that school because she called you a pig!'

Joseph nearly choked with rage, and leapt up to go and give the good woman a piece of his mind. Restraining him by the coat-tails, I assured him that she'd already had her come-uppance. He trusted me in these matters, because we were both cast in the same mould, and he calmed down. I never did go back to that school, nor to any other, by the way. Joseph thought I'd learn more about life with a job.

Fortunately, I was allowed to choose for myself. I'd met a seventeen-year-old girl called Monique out dancing one evening, and her parents owned a dress-fabrics shop opposite the *France-Soir* offices on the corner of rue d'Aboukir and rue Réaumur. She asked me if I'd like to be a sales assistant in the shop. Some good news at last! I started work there, and Monique fast became my best friend, and her house my home. I stayed with her adorable family whenever I could. What's more she had a brother my age who was a darling, and whom I flirted gently with. He had lots of friends and they became my new crowd. And a much more fashionable crowd than I'd ever been part of up till now, too. Dress fabric was selling like hot cakes, my commission went up, and in the evenings it was the high life.

We used to go dancing at the Schubert in Montparnasse. I wore bobby socks, a pleated skirt and a corduroy jacket. I became better acquainted with jazz and bebop than was possible in Lyon. Monique often used to lend me stockings, platform shoes and hats to play at being grown-up. It was wonderful. Most of the time I slept at her parents' beautiful flat in rue Mouffetard: the trot from Montparnasse to Belleville was enough to discourage the most devoted gallant knight, but Montparnasse — rue Mouffetard was much more reasonable. And, more than anything, at the flat lived a happy, well-balanced family who offered me what I'd scarcely ever known: warmth, security, and an ordered life without shouting-matches and crises . . .

To start with Joseph could see no harm in my sleeping at my employer's house. But the venomous stepmother, little by little, sowed the seeds of doubt in his mind: 'She says she's spending the night at these people's house, but that doesn't prove anything, does it?'

Monique woke me up one morning with: 'Did you know, your father came here to check that you really were sleeping here. Promise me you won't make a scene about it because he made me swear I wouldn't tell you.'

I swore all she wanted me to so she wouldn't worry about it, and then that evening I broke my promise just as she'd done: lips

My Family Album

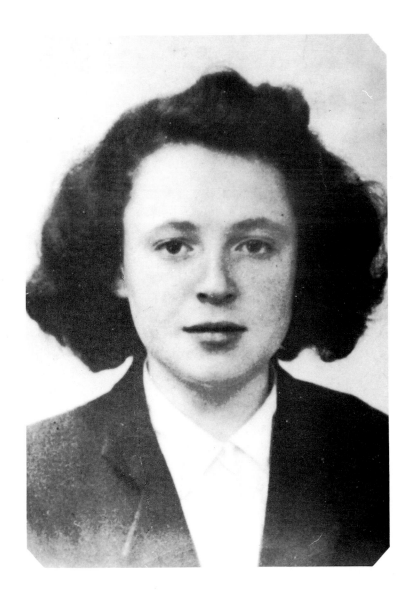

Joseph, my father.

Évelyne and me.

Lionel and his wife on their wedding day.

6 December 1969. I become Madame Choukroun, under the serious eyes of our witnesses, Françoise Sagan and Jean Poniatowski.

Roger is the man who taught me to swim.

pursed, thundering brow, footsteps ringing, I set off for Belleville.
I called Joseph every name under the sun, and I cried, and poured
a carefully chosen torrent of abuse on the Titanic: the gist of it all
was that you only accuse other people of things when you're guilty
of them yourself. Backpedalling, she started explaining that caring
parents have to take an interest in the company their precious
daughters keep. That really blew it and I shouted: 'So I'm a
precious daughter, am I? I've got caring parents, have I? And what
little education I've got I owe completely and utterly to other
people, not to you!'

More shouting, more tears ... Just another typical evening en
famille.

I didn't only discover the warmth of family life with Monique's
parents, but also with Thérèse and Albert, whom Maurice, Eva and
I visited regularly. As far as Maurice and I were concerned, Thérèse
was still the only, the real Madame Joseph. She was equally affectionate with us as we were with her, and Albert was wonderful to
us. When we got there, he gave us all sorts of treats because what
he'd heard about Joseph led him to think we must be dying of
hunger. He had a great deal of charm, told dreadful jokes, but had
a real talent for telling funny stories. He knew hundreds of them,
and once he got going, after the second or third, he just wouldn't
stop until Thérèse said, 'That's enough, Albert.'

At long last I was discovering that life could be very good when
you had the right to choose whom you spent your time with. My
short existence had hitherto led me to believe I was some sort of
monster, but I now came to realize that I too could be good,
faithful, heroic even, when friendship demanded it. For example, I
used to go to the turkish baths with Monique — who thought she
was too fat — every Saturday afternoon. I was as thin as ever
myself, but would keep her company in one of those appalling
boxes, and I'd come out practically melted. But it was worth it:
what we lost in weight we gained in friendship.

I didn't see my father now, except rarely. He'd got his rue
Pasteur jam factory back, and was in the middle of negotiating the
purchase of large new premises in rue Villiers-de-l'Isle-Adam, still
in Belleville, but on the twentieth arrondissement side. He took us
round. Very amusing. For the time being it was used to raise
chickens, and there were thousands of baby chicks cheeping in the
hen houses. What a noise; what a smell!

'This is going to be the new *Confitures Villiers*!'

It was a good name, and very distinguished-sounding for a factory bottling fruit, making jams and supplies for pâtisseries. The premises were magnificent, as overflowing with chickens as they were devoid of even a single piece of equipment for making jam. So Joseph was going to have to borrow a lot of money to get the place set up ... something which, like everything else he did, was going to have very direct consequences for my own life. But I didn't realize that yet.

I was making the most of the cinemas and 'dancings'; the Mikado, the Mimi Pinson, the Schubert, the Coupole, having a good time, and spending Sundays in the country with Monique and the gang. Till Joseph put an end to it all. His partner, Ginger-Joseph, had taken over another café at the Carreau du Temple, and Joseph, who was very busy setting up *Confitures Villiers*, took me aside one evening and started explaining that the time had come for me to take on some extra responsibilities: 'You've got to run the café.'

As shocks go, it was a pretty big one. I protested violently. There was absolutely no question of me running the café! Joseph kept his hair on for once and explained that I'd be the boss, I'd look after the till, that people would be under orders from me, and that I'd have half the profit. That's just the bit I should have had my doubts about. But instead, my resistance crumbled and I told myself that when it came down to it, it didn't make much difference whether it was selling cloth or cheesecake, and that at the café I'd be able to invite all my friends for drinks on the house!

'And,' he added, 'you'll have the flat to yourself.'

That persuaded me: I wouldn't have to put up with my stepmother any longer. Still, I asked Joseph if I could have a day to think about it. I'd let him know tomorrow. There was one condition: I'd have to start within forty-eight hours. Hardly time to catch my breath.

It was a difficult decision to have to make. I didn't want to be parted from my friends, especially since Monique and I had just started going to smart places at Saint-Germain-des-Prés and on the Champs-Elysées.

And then I started to think what it would be like starting work at five in the morning, putting out the chairs, setting up the coffee machines, taking the orders, cooking, washing up, and then all the tidying up at night, bringing the chairs back in from the terrace, and other exciting things. And as a finishing touch, having to wear a lovely blue rubber apron ... very trendy.

But all in all, the advantages outweighed the disadvantages, and so I made my official entrée into the café business.

I settled into my new job, scalding myself on the percolators every three minutes, and developed a fixed smile serving lemon teas morning, noon and night. And all for a pittance. Because I discovered that all Joseph's promises were precisely that . . . just promises. The stepmother came by every evening to collect the takings which I, poor idiot, just handed straight over to her. She counted it up in front of me. I hadn't to be a single sou short. If by mistake I'd forgotten to ring something up, she looked at me suspiciously and then started to go through all the orders one by one.

At the end of the month, my promised half of the profits didn't materialize, and I took Joseph to one side. That's when he informed me that my board and lodging had to come out of those profits as well, and that we'd sort out the sums later. What's more, he said, he was in debt up to his eyeballs . . . and didn't I realize that he was doing all this for us, his children, and that I should be ashamed of myself asking him for money! I stood there gaping. No way out . . . he'd got me again, like he always did.

And what's more, I was so worn out by the day's work that I had neither time nor energy to see my friends or go dancing. I felt as pale and faded as the Lumiére de Belleville itself, but I was trapped in the tedious daily round, with no possibility of basking under the hot lights of the 'dancings'. When the cook, or the washer-up, or the waiter was off duty, I had to fill in. And since the Lumiére de Belleville never closed, Mademoiselle Régine had her nose to the grindstone seven days a week.

My fingernails broke, my hands roughened, I must have smelt like a burnt chip pan; in short, my dreams of stardom withered as the days went by. As consolation, I stuffed myself with cakes. Four months later, having always been as thin as a rake, I'd put on over a stone. To cap it all, Joseph — whom I never set eyes on during the week — used to invite each of his creditors in turn for Sunday lunch at the café, en famille as he liked to call it!

Joseph still had it firmly in mind to cancel his debts by marrying me off to the son of his principal creditor. Maurice was on my side, and used to warn me whenever there was something fishy going on. 'Watch out, Dad's invited your future fiancé and his father to lunch.' I'd disappear for the day, and steel myself for a bollocking when I got back. Then he started trying to catch me out by not mentioning it to anyone, so Maurice was only able to alert me at the last minute when he saw how many the table was set for. I'd make a dash for it as soon as I realized. Joseph saw he'd get nowhere by underhand methods, and tried reasoning with me.

'Look, be nice, won't you? We owe this man a fortune, and his son's really very pleasant. At least talk to him, so it doesn't show me in too bad a light. Don't put me to shame, or he'll never lend us any more money; and we really need it for the business!'

My good nature got the better of me: 'All right, I'll have a go, if you really want me to.'

He introduced me to the little chap in question, a boy half my size at the very most. When I got Joseph on his own I said: 'Can you really see me married to that little squirt? You'd be ashamed to see us together!'

He readily conceded that he was on the small side, but kept pointing out other advantages.

'He's a very pleasant boy, you know; he's intelligent, and intelligence is worth a fortune. And what he's worth is more important than how big he is.'

'All right, I'll have another go, just to see.'

The fiancé in question had invited me to the theatre, and I decided to accept. Not great. I went out with him again; not much better than the first time.

He bored me to tears. He kept trying to get close to me, and hold my hands, but I sat on them and he didn't dare try and get at them down there: peace at last! What's more, he had terrible halitosis. In the end, by way of thanking him for all his kind invitations, I put my cards on the table: 'My father only wants us to get married because he owes your father a lot of money. I must warn you here and now that I am not prepared to sacrifice myself like that. And also, I'm much taller than you, and I've always wanted my husband to be taller than me, or I'd go off with someone else for sure ...'

He started to laugh, shrugged his shoulders, and then said: 'But I like you a lot. You're very sweet, and I'd really like to marry you.'

'Out of the question. I'm absolutely against it.'

We parted amicably though. He was intelligent, it's true − and rich: his father had a wholesale haberdashery business which was booming, and with the interest he was charging on his loans he was hardly going to go broke. But it was all over for me. Joseph wouldn't hear of it, and carried on organizing Sunday lunches. He started using his strong-arm tactics again to make me stay. But it couldn't go on much longer and one day I had a word in the fiancé's ear: 'Look, I've really had enough of this! Every time he invites you to lunch, I get a clout instead of an aperitif to help me make up my mind. It's not funny. Since you're a nice guy, let's come to some agreement: we'll eat and then pretend to go out together afterwards but go our own separate ways. It doesn't mean I won't go out with you once in a while, though.'

'All right, it's a deal. On one hand I don't want to force you into it, but on the other you will get to know me a bit better the times we do go out together ...'

We did go out together two or three times. Joseph was rubbing his hands together, with a big grin all over his face. On other occasions I went off to have a good time with Monique and our friends. But I didn't really enjoy doing it that way: it was complicated and wasn't getting us anywhere. So I told my 'fiancé': 'Really, we can't go on like this. You'll have to tell my father that you don't find me attractive.'

'But that's not true!'

'You can tell a lie, can't you? You'll have to tell him that, because anyway even if my father kills me I'm not going to go out with you any more. And you don't want my death on your conscience, do you?'

My earnest tone convinced him. He came to see Joseph and told him in front of me: 'Look, I've been out with your daughter, but we don't get on very well. We don't have the same tastes or the same ideas about things ...'

'Never you mind, never you mind, my boy! She'll change.'

It was like a bad dream and I shouted: 'No I won't! I'll never change!'

The fiancé could only nod in agreement and said: 'No, I don't think she ever will change.'

Joseph, who was already building himself castles on the proceeds of the haberdashery business, looked from one to the other and shouted: 'Just you wait and see how she changes!'

And whack! A slap in the face for the fiancée. The poor boy was devastated by this: 'But you shouldn't hit her like that!'

In a rage, I began smashing plates and kicking the furniture around. Joseph came after me again, arms flailing like a windmill. The suitor just stood there. He can't have been at all unhappy at the thought of how narrowly he had escaped the clutches of such a family of lunatics, and went off bewildered but probably much relieved. Joseph was very worried indeed: the son of his major creditor! I learnt later of the details of their deal: he was to part with his little Régine and receive a marriage portion equal in size to the debt he owed.

So he ended up with huge debts and a daughter still on his hands. I was delighted, though: better to be poor but free in Belleville than rich and locked up in a haberdashery. Especially when one has ambitions!

6

Paul

In Belleville, Monsieur Joseph's daughter was quite something. Sixteen years old, chic, hard-working, her outbursts of temper offset by having lots of laughs with her friends. In spite of Joseph's debts, I was one of the most sought-after young ladies in the district. I was a romantic too, especially while reading *Gone with the Wind*, which I kept on the counter: it wasn't bedtime reading because in the evenings I went out. When people ordered drinks, it was Scarlett who extricated herself from her adventures to serve them in person.

Whenever I had a couple of hours to spare, and a few sous, I'd be at the cinema. There were cinemas everywhere; two opposite the café, three more on the same street, and another four on rue de Belleville, a few steps away. It was the golden age of the cinema. So, leaving the cotton fields of the deep south behind me, I plunged with delight into the world of Humphrey Bogart, musical comedies, and horror films. The stuff of dreams. I didn't know that thirty years on, they'd be called classics. What interested me right then was working out which role I could play.

The shows at the *Folies-Belleville* were another, more fleshly, source of fascination. Whenever Yves Montand was on, I used to get really dressed up. As Ettie was living with Joseph at rue Villiers-de-l'Isle-Adam, but had left some of her things 'above our means', I used to borrow, without permission, all her most eye-catching clothes. I got all dolled up, and went there in the fond hope that my idol might just happen to look my way.

One day I met an old school friend from the Lilacs there. She told me some great news, which changed her life, and considerably improved mine: 'I'm getting married to the boss's son. You'll be able to get in free from now on.'

She kept her word, and so I got to see all the shows, just like I'd done in Aix. When Joseph did his star turn at the café on Sundays, I went to both the matinée and evening performances. I came back punch-drunk from the songs, the music and ... the dreaming. Burning to be in the spotlight. That's how I saw Piaf, Trenet, Francis Lemarque and even Fréhel, just before he died.

The cinemas and music-halls were a real godsend; I don't think I could have put up with the rigours of the café and the rubber apron without them. All day long, doing the dishes, I could play the heroine who'd fallen on hard times among people who didn't appreciate her beauty or her many talents. A real Cinderella. But, of course, fame and fortune were just around the corner, and would be all the more glorious ... Trouble was, the golden haze vanished the moment I found myself nose to nose with the impatient customers, who were neither producers nor impresarios. What's more, they would insist on ordering tea or booze rather than 'discovering' me. It was all a cruel joke.

In the spring of that year (1946), two young men, brothers, started coming to the café. They met for lunch every day. One of them was very handsome, and kept calling me over every five minutes: 'Mademoiselle! Mademoiselle!' He's not bad-looking, I thought to myself, but he gets on my nerves. He made Scarlett step off her cloud, put a glass on the crucial page (of which there were plenty), and come down to earth in Belleville. I'd go over with my pencil, my order book and my apron, and ask crossly: 'Yes, what do you want?'

'Would you mind getting us some salt?'

'But you've got some salt!'

'No ... no, I don't think we have ...'

'It's right there, behind your elbow!'

'Oh, I'm sorry, I couldn't see it. Sorry to bother you, Mademoiselle.'

There was always some good pretext. He told me later that it was his younger brother who put him up to it: 'I bet you don't dare call her!'. A withering look put an end to their little game, and I was back in the tempestuous world of Scarlett O'Hara. Once I'd finished the book though, I started to get really bored, and it was my turn to be all smiles to them. Summer came, and we began to chat. The handsome one was called Paul. He was nineteen. He invited me to go swimming with him. Not a good idea ... I didn't like the water. I turned my nose up, but he insisted: 'I play water polo; I've got a match tomorrow.'

I didn't really let on, but it sounded fantastic: a champion sportsman, very nearly a genuine hero! He explained that he'd just been picked for the junior team. With the prospect of the athlete in trunks, I let him persuade me. We arranged to meet at the Belleville metro at midday the next day.

The following morning, classic situation: Ettie knew something was up when she saw me titivating myself, and plagued me so much that I told her to get lost. Joseph stepped in, there was a scene, and I was forbidden to go out. So I had to ask Maurice to go instead of me, and explain to Paul what had happened. I tried to describe Paul, without getting too carried away, but it was hard not to: 'You'll see, he's tall, good-looking, well-built, with a nice smile. He's got a little moustache. He looks like Laurence Olivier. You can't miss him.'

So Maurice went off to Belleville metro, looking for the most beautiful guy in the world.

But Paul had been having problems too. The girl he was going out with had wanted to prevent him seeing me, and succeeded: so he'd sent his brother too! Obviously the two substitutes missed each other. Maurice came back and said laconically: 'There wasn't anyone there.'

I pretended not to give a damn, but inside I really let rip with the abuse. What a turd, standing me up like that! Who dares stand up Régine-Scarlett Zylberberg-O'Hara! So I told myself it was all up; next time he came in here, it was simple, I just wouldn't look at him, wouldn't speak to him, wouldn't serve him.

I waited a good ten days just to show him that I was going to ignore him when he came in. He had told me that he lived nearby, that he was a leather-worker. Was he going to come back, or not? At the end of August he did reappear at last, with his brother. He got the works; I looked him disdainfully up and down, and deliberately ignored him. They must have called me ten times, but I didn't once look their way: 'Mademoiselle! ... Mademoiselle!'

Finally though, when they were just about to give up and go, I went over to take their order, frosty-faced, an icy smile: 'What can I get you, gentlemen?'

'I must explain ... I couldn't come ...'

'Come where?'

'Please don't be angry! My mother was ill, and I had to send my brother instead. He must have missed you.'

As if it was of no consequence, I paused and then said: 'I'm not surprised he missed me. I sent my brother, because I couldn't come either.'

I turned on my heels and went. But it was no good; all the time I was trying not to look at him, he was all I could see. So I might just as well look at him properly. Finally we made it up, and he invited me over to his house for a drink.

It wasn't far to go: they lived in one of the more dilapidated houses in the old part of Belleville, not dissimilar to our own. It was a dark and dingy little street, in need of repair, made only marginally more cheerful by a few flowers in window-boxes. I felt a bit alarmed as we went up the uneven but well-scrubbed staircase. Once we got upstairs he told me that his father had died after deportation, that his mother had been ill for a long time and couldn't work, and that he'd had to give up his studies to work and look after her as well as his young brother. He worked in the leather business with his uncle. He showed me some photos of him in his FFI uniform. (He'd been a sergeant in the Alpine troops.) That did it. I immediately invented a glowing future for him, in recompense for all the sacrifices he'd made. He really was the hero I'd been dreaming of.

In the evening he took me to see *The Grapes of Wrath*. Though I didn't tell him so, my wrath had completely subsided, and I was sitting there waiting for him to hold my hand in the darkness like other boys did. But he didn't even try to, and sat stock still as if I was his little sister. I waited for the end of the film in the hope that he would take advantage of the half light from the screen, but he didn't, not even the slightest little touch. He'd played his cards right: it made a great impression on me. He walked me back to the café afterwards. On the way he told me he was a 'marxist'. Mar-what? I didn't know what he was talking about. He tried explaining ... Just to please him I said I'd go and sell *l'Humanité-Dimanche* on the streets with him. The Communist Party was in its heyday, and there were almost as many fellow-travellers as there were activists. So it was in the cause of love that I came to do my bit of hoof work for the cause of the proletariat, shouting half-heartedly: '*Huma*, buy *l'Huma-Dimanche*'. I didn't actually read any of the stuff I was selling, but I was struck by the similarity between the wooden-sounding words they used and the sound of the wooden-soled boots we'd worn during the Occupation.

We saw each other often. He held my hand now, but gently, very gently. One day he told me he wanted to be many things to me: not least a father, a brother, a friend, in short, the family I'd never had. I sensed how heartfelt his words were and burst into tears. I told him everything: about the convent, the old people's home, Claude ... He listened and then said: 'You know, I didn't have very much better luck than you did, and as for Claude, it's not important. It was war-time, you were all alone in the world, and too young.'

His gentleness made such a change for me, and I fell madly in love with him. There was great passion, and very soon a physical relationship, with all the problems that that entailed. The first time was on one of the café benches at one in the morning. We weren't in luck because for some reason or other, Joseph had started sleeping in the flat now, instead of in rue Villiers-de-l'Isle-Adam. One night when Paul and I were downstairs in the toilet together one of the pipes started making a terrible racket, I thought it was going to wake the whole neighbourhood. The noise stopped soon enough, but I heard the door open upstairs, and Joseph muttering something on the landing. Fortunately, he went straight back to bed ...

Just like it had done in Lyon, the fear of being discovered gave me a pain in the gut; a real pain. Paul got dressed again as fast as possible after we'd made love, and only because he cared for me so much did he not rush off straight away. He was still very much in awe of Joseph.

After several months of clandestine contortions, the inevitable happened. My period was late. I was terrified, and without saying a word to Paul, I made a dash for the famous purgatives I'd used in Lyon. I swallowed them four at a time. Still nothing. Days, then weeks went by. Finally I told Paul what was going on. He was very scared, and tried to find someone I could go to, with all the prudence that required. I didn't have a clue myself, and no one I could get advice from. I tried to find out what was going on inside me, and how everything worked. But there was only one thing I understood properly: I was very much afraid, and despite Paul, I was all on my own. I spoke to Monique about it, who looked at me in surprise, and assured me she knew nothing about things like that. I could believe it. At last, more than two months after the first sign that something was wrong, Paul managed to get the address of someone who could help. An old girlfriend who'd had the same problem had come up trumps. But it was going to cost twenty thousand francs. It was a lot of money for two kids who didn't have a bean. Paul started to save as much as he could from his wages and

I nicked money from the till. It was a long month of scrimping and saving, and being scared shitless. I felt sick all the time. I only had to smell food cooking to want to disappear into the toilet, and I got so nervous that I started eating all the cakes I could get my hands on. I was visibly growing fatter. Fortunately, my stepmother, who'd also come back to live in the flat, was so busy sorting out the paperwork for the jam factory that she didn't notice how much weight I was putting on. And Joseph would never notice something like that anyway.

It was a struggle, but we finally managed to get the twenty thousand francs together, and we headed for Pigalle, where the man we needed lived. We waited in a dingy little room. There were old prints on the walls. It was filthy. Paul held my hand, and I just looked at him. My mind was blank.

A little man opened the door and motioned me in. I went into a grey room and got undressed. I got up on the table and shut my eyes. He said: 'You'll feel the first pains in twenty-four hours. You're very far gone, and it will probably be very painful. Don't panic. When it's all over, the probe will come out of its own accord. Then you'll have to get a bowl of boiled water ready, and wash yourself very thoroughly, to make sure you don't get an infection. Use this to wash with.'

And he handed me some stuff which I thrust into my bag.

Then he added: 'If you need me, or if it hurts too much, call me using the password ...' (I can't remember what it was). 'You will have to come and see me, and I'll give you an injection.'

I went home. Luckily Paul's mother had gone to the country for a rest so the coast was clear. When the pains started I was to go round to their flat, which was just near the café.

Twenty-four hours went by, and nothing happened. I started getting terribly worried. 'If it doesn't work, and I have the baby, Joseph'll kill me.' Forty-eight hours, and still nothing. I scurried round to Pigalle. He had a listen, and said everything was all right: 'There's no problem, you haven't got a temperature. Just go back home and wait.'

Yet another day went by, and still nothing happened. I went back to Pigalle again the next morning. This time he looked a bit worried and said: 'If nothing's happened by tomorrow, come back and see me.'

I worked all day long in the café as usual: in fact I worked twice as hard as normal, trying to forget the fear which gripped me, and the constant nausea.

That night, at about four in the morning, I suddenly got the most dreadful pains. Joseph and the Titanic were asleep in the bedroom next door, and Maurice was in my room.

It hurt so much that for a moment I didn't think I'd be able to stop myself crying out. At five o'clock, practically unconscious with the pain, I got dressed and staggered out of the café. It was still dark outside, a sinister drizzle soaking my dishevelled hair. I looked like something out of a lunatic asylum. I was bent double with pain, my eyes wild and staring. I reached Paul's flat and managed somehow to get up the stairs and knock. Paul opened the door; it was all I could do to get to the bed and lie down, I couldn't speak for the pain. It scared Paul's brother to see me materialize out of the night in such a desperate state and he said: 'What's the matter with her, Paul? She's not going to die! What on earth's the matter with her?'

Paul turned pale, and sent his brother back to bed. He didn't look much better than I did, but he managed to carry me as far as the kitchen and stretched me out on the floor. He was in the middle of boiling the water, when all of a sudden I began crying out.

A few minutes later, and it was all over. I didn't look. It felt as if my insides had been ripped out. I let Paul do everything for me, and then he carried me, practically lifeless, into the bedroom. I fell asleep utterly exhausted.

When I woke a couple of hours later he was beside me. We lay there silent, not daring to speak, not knowing what to say. The same sadness and the same loneliness overwhelmed us both. I understood then that for some time now I had been finding very little to like in myself or Paul.

Paul said: 'I swear it won't happen again. I'm going to ask your father for your hand, and in the meantime we'll be very careful.'

In actual fact what we were most careful about in the following weeks was to make sure we had some privacy. We gave up the café benches, Paul's flat, and anywhere else a mother, brother, a Joseph or a stepmother might suddenly pop up. So we started going to the public baths on a Saturday afternoon or a Sunday morning. There, in a bathroom for two, we'd make love in the steam, under the shower, to the sound of gurgling water, almost forgetting the crisis we'd just been through. We were certainly not the only couple doing naughty things in the public baths, but we thought we were, and naïvely took everyone else for young married couples living in flats without a bathroom. And as for those who could by no stretch of the imagination be young married couples, we felt far too guilty ourselves to ask too many questions ... It was the same every time, we crept in on tiptoes, and left sidling along the wall. I thought to myself that, really, what with pine needles, cellars, dining-room tables, café benches and public baths, this love business was very complicated. When was I going to have my own bed; when were we going to have our own bed?

At Christmas, our first Christmas together, Paul asked me to choose: 'What would you like better? Going out for a meal, or spending a night in a hotel: I can afford either, but not both.'

I didn't have a sou to my name, being fed and lodged, but still not paid; I chose the hotel room on the principle that a sleep's as good as a meal. We ended up in the sort of hotel which was more of a brothel on boulevard Jean-Jaurès. It was about as cheerful as the waiting room in Pigalle. Some of the window panes were cracked, the floor squeaked and the bed was just about to give up the ghost. But none of that really mattered. We tried to forget the past and think about the future, which we hoped would be a glowing one. We had a bit of a windfall and were able to afford something a little more special for New Year's Eve. This time, the hotel was a good quarter of a star better than the previous one, and was situated over one of the huge cafés on the Boulevards. We heard the revellers playing out 1946, and at midnight we kissed. The year gone by had been both a hard and a good one, and together, sensually, we made our resolutions for the year to come. This time the room was a big one, and the bottle of sparkling wine we'd bought ourselves made it seem very special. So 1947 started off bubbling. I was just seventeen.

We carried on making bubbles, too many doubtless, in the public baths: in spite of our 'precautions', I got pregnant again. And so we had to go through those agonies all over again. Why not get married? Because Joseph was being very stubborn. I'd talked to him seriously about Paul several times already, but each time he'd declared that he wouldn't have Paul for a son-in-law. So, once more, Paul and I had to get out of the mess we'd got ourselves into. We went to a different chap this time, and everything went much quicker: it was all over by the following day. In the evening I was feeling fragile and had a sudden craving for oysters, and Paul very sweetly took me out to a restaurant on the Boulevards. After this second ordeal, he'd made up his mind: 'I'm going to see your father tomorrow, and if he says no, I shall tell him that it's too bad, we'll get married without his permission.'

The next day, Sunday, we took our courage in both hands and

went over to Belleville after closing time. But from a distance, as we came out of the metro, we could see that a crowd had gathered and there was a lot of shouting going on. We got closer: Joseph and the Titanic were really fighting it out in style this time. Joseph was drunk, and had obviously been hitting Ettie, because she was covered in bruises. We kept our distance, and Paul, who'd never witnessed a scene like it, blenched visibly. No asking permission today: so, hand in hand, we retraced our steps to Paul's flat. On the way back, speculating about what Ettie could possibly have done to deserve such a beating, I found myself in tears. I was so ashamed: 'We'll never manage it, you'll never dare ask him.'

'Régine, I swear I'll ask him tomorrow.'

He came into the café first thing next morning, while I was still upstairs. Joseph was downstairs behind the bar. Paul didn't beat about the bush: 'Monsieur Joseph, I'd like to talk to you.'

'Yes?'

'The thing is, Monsieur, I want to marry Régine.'

'What did you say? Never! Never! I want you out of here!'

Paul didn't budge, and said very calmly: 'Even if you don't approve, we're still going to get married.'

Then Joseph yelled at him: 'Never! You haven't a sou to your name, you wouldn't even be able to support her!'

'That's my problem, not yours.'

I could hear everything from upstairs, and feared the worst. Fortunately, Ettie was in her room, tending her wounds. Then I heard Joseph shouting: 'Régiiiine!'

Down I went.

'This boy here says he's going to marry you! What is all this? What have you two been cooking up together?'

'We're getting married, that's all. If you don't agree it makes no difference, we're still getting married.'

Then came the histrionics: 'Over my dead body!'

'I don't care what you say. We're engaged anyway, and Paul can come here as often as he likes. Otherwise, I'm going to leave.'

'No, he's not coming here, and you're not going to leave home either, do you understand?'

He was choking with rage (or pretending to be), but Paul didn't take any notice: 'I'm not setting foot in this place again, and Régine's coming to live with me; and there's nothing you can do about it!'

And he walked out.

When it was just the two of us, Joseph softened up and changed his tune completely, telling me that Paul should come back again tomorrow and they'd sort something out. Next day, he was all smiles and treated Paul like an old friend: 'Well, if that's how it is, you'd do better to come here, young man. You don't want to put Régine to shame, do you? Right, you've got to come here. What's your name?'

He explained to Paul that because the jam factory was nearly ready, he needed me more and more at the café. But that wasn't news to us. What was more surprising was that he started introducing Paul as his future son-in-law, just as if he'd planned it all himself. Suffering from delusions of grandeur again, he promised us a wonderful flat, as if he was worried this ideal son-in-law might change his mind! After seeking out all the rich boys in the neighbourhood for me, here he was patting Paul on the back, telling him: 'You're in luck, my boy, marrying a girl with a dowry.'

It was easy to see why such sincerity on his part would fail to convince me. He boasted to his friends about the new recruit to the Joseph circus: 'He's handsome, honest, well brought up, from a good family.' Exactly what Joseph meant by a 'good family' no one ever really found out.

He made one proposition I was supposed to find tempting: 'If he wants to marry you, the boy should come here and work with you.'

Paul wasn't exactly enthusiastic. He knew nothing about the job and didn't think it would be very exciting. But thanks to Joseph's special brand of persuasion, and to please me as well, my leather-worker rolled up his sleeves and got stuck in behind the bar. Now it was his turn to find out the hard way what life at the café was all about: five o'clock in the morning, the terrace, the percolators, the little cups of coffee, etc.

We were waiting for Joseph to fix the date of the wedding, but he seemed to have forgotten this minor detail. I said: 'Papa, we can't go on like this forever! We want to get married quickly!'

'Why's that? Why so fast? There's no rush, you're doing all right as you are. You're both a bit young yet. If he loves you, there'll be no problem. Waiting a bit like this, it's good experience.'

A few days later, nevertheless, he announced a marriage, but not ours: his, to Ettie! She'd made herself so indispensable at the till and in Joseph's life that she'd forced him into making a decision. I wonder just how many times I'd heard him say: 'I'll never marry the Titanic, never! I say I will just for a moment's peace, but I'll never marry her.' Marriage was the interest payable on Ettie's loan.

But the night before the big day, Ettie started hunting all round the neighbourhood: 'Where's Joseph? Where is Joseph?' No one had seen him. Joseph had disappeared. It was a ghastly night for Ettie. She spent it in the café, on the look-out for Joseph, receiving the neighbours' condolences. Maurice and I had great fun hoping he, Joseph, wouldn't be found in time for the ceremony. In the morning, there was still no Joseph. The town hall was booked for midday. At eleven, Ettie phoned round the local police stations. While she was on the line to the station down at Place de la République she suddenly whooped with joy: Joseph had been picked up in the small hours in one of the bars down there. Thoroughly plastered, he'd spent his stag night playing 'passe anglaise', which was an illegal game. In the cells, he took care not to show signs of life, probably hoping, in an alcoholic haze, to miss the ceremony! But he underestimated Ettie's determination. She was very attached to her Monsieur Joseph: she wanted to get married properly, in good bourgeois fashion, and she hadn't put up with all the knocks just to end up on the shelf. She went down to collect her betrothed from the cells all smiles, without a word of reproach. She knew that if she missed this morning's 'I do' it could well be a hundred years before Joseph thought about going anywhere near a registry office again. It all went ahead as planned and Ettie became the most official Madame Joseph Zylberberg in the world.

We were desperate to get married too, but Joseph, now in no position to be critical of matrimony, had a different argument up his sleeve: he'd waited five years before marrying the Titanic and we should do the same! It was no good rushing into things, etc . . . I'd given him all the papers to sign a month ago. There was nothing we could do.

One day, a miracle happened! He rushed into the café in a real state, shouting for us.

'The papers, quick, I must sign the papers. My brother, my brother's arriving in Paris, he's sent me a telegram, you've got to get married straight away.'

No one could quite see the connection, but that's how it was: it took the surprise visit of a brother he'd not seen for forty years to persuade Joseph to make up his mind! The brother lived in America, and we'd heard the wildest rumours about him and his varied life: he'd started out as a society dancer, half gigolo, half actor, and then since the war had embarked on a sparkling career with the *Voice of America*, where his way with people and his gift for languages had got him a directorship. We'd been put in touch with him through Maurice Prywes, the son of Joseph's older sister. (He was the only cousin we traced, and had spent the war in Russia as a surgeon, and then gone to Jerusalem. He was to become the head of the medical school there.) Joseph was so impressed with the American uncle, that he decided he would throw a big party for him, and follow it up on the Sunday with our wedding.

We'd only been asking him for a year for the wedding to be held as soon as possible, and now we were in luck. It was a real race against time. The banns were read in the twentieth arrondissement, where *Confitures Villiers* was based, and Joseph, with great difficulty, booked two rooms at the Hotel Lutétia. My stepmother suddenly dug up something approximating to motherly feelings (as she always did when I was about to be married off) and decided that she wanted to help me with my trousseau. My father gave me five thousand francs and Ettie gave me a thousand francs too, miraculously. At the fleamarket — where they sold new things cheap — I bought myself three pairs of sheets, two tablecloths, tea-towels, a dozen hand towels ... I didn't exactly go mad, but I had enough, providing I washed them as I went along.

Joseph told us: 'You'll be living in the flat over the café.'

But Paul, who knew what he wanted, said that not only would we not be living in that flat, but that we wouldn't be looking after the café any more either. After an initial and violent reaction, Joseph simmered down and even suggested that we take over the flat in rue Pasteur, which he'd just recovered along with the old jam-making premises from pre-war days. We accepted his offer this time, and moved into the empty flat a few days before the wedding. Thanks to presents from Joseph it wasn't to remain empty for long. He bought us a Louis XVI style bedroom suite which I'd fallen in love with in Faubourg Saint-Antoine. Everything was sugar-pink, with two pouffes to match. Another little extravagance was the brown satin 'salon' ... The flat consisted of a living room, a bedroom and a dining room which we planned to convert into a bedroom for the (numerous) children we were going to have. The toilet was off the kitchen and the bathroom was off nowhere; there wasn't one. So we said our fond farewells to the public baths in the nineteenth arrondissement, and took out a season ticket for the ones in the eleventh.

The banns had been read, the date (7 November 1947) fixed, and all I had to do was to choose which outfit I was going to wear to the registry office, and which for the religious ceremony. A dress-maker in Pigalle made them both, without undue expense, while I bought an orange-blossom circlet from *Trousselier*. It was a bit expensive, but the family thought they'd splash out just this once.

The decorations were complete . . . Let the party begin. Only the uncle from America was missing, and we were to fetch him from the Gare Saint-Lazare two days before the wedding. We were all dusted off, smartened up and well scrubbed. I was impatient for a glimpse of the miracle-uncle, this man to whom I owed my wedding. I imagined him stepping off the train, staggering under the weight of presents for all the family. The train pulled into the station. Butterflies. Joseph cleared his throat and patted his tie. Ettie smoothed her hair and started smiling bountifully. The train came to a halt and the passengers got out. The two brothers recognized each other immediately, even after forty years, and hugged one another tight. The uncle was very handsome, very Rudolf Valentino from the back, hair oiled and slicked down, and extremely elegant.

'My brother!'

'My brother!'

They kissed, they cried, they laughed, all in Polish. The uncle was whisked away to the Lumière de Belleville, where a big dinner-dance was organized. After dinner, Joseph, who loved making toasts, stood up and made a speech, with tearful interruptions and lyrical flights of fancy. To wind up, he explained with great emotion how the wedding should have been two months ago, but that he had postponed it in honour of his brother. Our mouths dropped with the cheek of it all, and even Ettie looked surprised — and for a long time now there hadn't been much that could have surprised Ettie.

At that moment, at the height of emotion, Joseph, sitting opposite me, pulled the big ring off his finger, the one he had promised me for my wedding day. My heart was racing, tears came to my eyes, and I was already offering him my hand when something completely insane happened: Joseph took his brother's hand and quite calmly put *my* ring on *his* finger! I nearly fainted and through a fog heard Joseph saying: 'My brother, I bought you this ring as a souvenir of this wonderful day.'

So, not only did the uncle arrive empty-handed, but now he was kissing Joseph, tears in his eyes, and thanking him for having given him my ring! I was flabbergasted and wild with rage at the same time, and tugged Joseph's arm telling him it was my ring. To placate me, he said (so his brother, who had noticed my reaction, could hear): 'No, no, you will have Ettie's ring. This one looks much too masculine.' Some choice: one quite pretty 'masculine' ring with a small but decent diamond, and a 'feminine' ring which was just some cheap stone full of flaws. The damage was done, and I had nothing to lose: I looked over at Joseph and hurled this remark at him: 'If that's the way you want it, you can keep your ring, your brother and everything else!' I stormed out of the room, Paul running after me to calm me down.

Back at home I told myself I mustn't let a bit of bad luck get me down, and as for diamonds I'd buy them myself one day. Flawless ones too. The registry office ceremony took place next day, and on the Sunday it was action stations at the Hoter Lutétia, where the survivors from French concentration camps had been welcomed back two and a half years earlier. The religious ceremony and the reception were to take place in the two rooms Joseph had booked, one upstairs and one downstairs. There were more than a hundred and twenty guests. Family and close friends accounted for fifty; the rest were various 'friends' Joseph hardly knew but had invited over the past couple of weeks as the mood took him. If I hadn't been wearing a long white dress and a coronet of orange-blossoms, most people wouldn't have known who the bride was. That was Joseph's style: bonhomie, conspicuous largesse, see-and-be-seen. All tightly organized.

The Titanic steered a course through the crowd with her flags fluttering: two green plumes atop a little brown hat. In the front row were Paul's mother and brother, and my family including the inevitable uncle from America with my ring on his finger. Joseph was strutting about in front of the rabbi telling him a joke — a Jewish one doubtless. Then Paul and I positioned ourselves under a canopy while the rabbi started off the marriage chant. Then came the solemn bit. My senses were sharpened, perhaps rather cruelly, as I registered everything that was going on inside me and around me. There was Paul, very serious, and very handsome in his navy blue suit; the men holding up the canopy (chosen by Joseph for this great privilege), who weren't quite the same height, thus causing the canopy to tilt annnoyingly; the whispered attempts of the assembled crowd to get them to straighten out the heavens above us; and last of all the spotless white dress, after two abortions ... The rabbi had spoken the words which joined us in marriage and Paul was searching feverishly in his pocket for the ring. My fingers had swollen in the hot overcrowded room, and Paul had difficulty slipping it on. Then, according to the custom, we drank wine from the same glass and then smashed it. The more bits of glass there were, the greater our happiness would be, and the more children we would have. I can't remember how many bits there were that day.

Then came the big moment when everyone shouts 'Mazel Tov'. I watched huge tears rolling down my stepmother's huge cheeks. Whether it was amazement at seeing her cry or the emotion of the day I don't know, but something made me start laughing uncontrollably. I was shaking with it; fortunately people took it for tears of joy. Paul squeezed my arm very tightly and Joseph hugged me to him, covering me with kisses and half suffocating me. Then came the kisses for the bride. It was hard to stop the giggles, and my thick layer of make-up transformed itself into a lava flow. At last, stifling and streaked, I left the room to make my way upstairs, where the banquet was about to begin. I stopped off in the powder room to re-do my make-up. But when I saw what I looked like, the giggles started all over again. With Monique's help, I tried to repair the damage.

In the upstairs room, everyone seemed to be enjoying themselves, and Joseph was revelling in it; people of all religions, all classes, all sizes and all countries . . . He was holding forth loudly and tearfully, doubtless forgetting it was his daughter's wedding day: it was party time, and you could tell he'd all but lost sight of the reason for the celebration. Two Russian-Jewish gypsy bands were playing folk tunes, and the waiters started bringing round various dishes which had mostly been prepared at the Lumière de Belleville: there was gefilte fisch (Jewish stuffed fish), pastrami, pikel-fleisch, bright pink tongue and assorted hors d'oeuvres: minced liver and hard-boiled egg with onion, aubergine caviar, cream cheese with paprika . . . I was at the head of the table with Joseph on my right and the uncle on my left. During the sweet course, Joseph got up on a little platform and, very relaxed, made his speech. He said how happy he was to see his darling daughter married to a boy from a good family, and he raised his glass to Paul's mother who had brought up her two boys on her own. We applauded the deserving widow and drank. Then he thanked his brother for coming over specially from America for the wedding, and added that, in honour of this happy day, he was giving a large sum of money to the charity 'Pour nos Enfants Malheureux' which my cousin Maurice Prywes worked for. Everyone shed a tear and applauded Joseph's generosity. He was quite the star of the show, king of the castle, and absolutely in his element.

The dancing began, and Joseph asked me for the first dance. I remembered that holiday in Brunoy, in 1939, the last before the war. I'd hardly danced with him since then, and it brought memories flooding back. Afterwards I sat down with Paul, who kissed me. The guests whirled happily around us. Thérèse and the Titanic were billing and cooing, Eva and Maurice spun round like tops, and Joseph was playing the bountiful host with compliments and quips for all and sundry. In the cold light of tomorrow's dawn, he'd be trying to work out how to pay for it all. The American uncle was only too pleased to find he had a millionaire for a brother. What mattered to Joseph was that the French side of the Zylberberg family looked a pretty smart bunch.

At proper weddings, it's all organized so that the newly-weds can slip away discreetly during the celebrations: but of course, in our case, no such thing, and we had to borrow some money before we could go off for the miniscule honeymoon we had in mind. I approached Joseph and asked him for my 'dowry'. But I'd interrupted a wonderful dream and he just stared at me. He fished about in his pockets, but obviously didn't find much. So he went over to someone, had a quiet word in his ear, and borrowed a few notes. He came back over to us, brandishing a miserable twenty thousand francs, saying loudly, 'Here, take this for your honeymoon', with a sweep of the hand as generous as the hand-out was meagre.

A few minutes later, totally exhausted, Paul and I were back at rue Pasteur, and we left for our honeymoon the next day. Not Venice or Capri for us, but a simple little hotel in the Chevreuse valley which we'd discovered some time before and wanted to go back to. It was called Les Trois Clochettes. We took the metro, then a coach from the Bastille, farewell Paris!

When we got there, it was a disaster. We thought we must have got the wrong place. There was nothing, or hardly anything, left of what had once been such a charming hotel. Half the building was derelict and the other half was being repaired. Workmen were sawing and hammering wherever we looked, and the smells of the forest had been replaced by the all-pervading odour of fresh paint. Paul had even spoken to the proprietor on the telephone, but he'd conveniently forgotten to mention the builders. The toilets in the rooms weren't quite in working order yet either, so we had to go down the garden — it was October, too!

After lunch (with only the whistling wind for company), bitterly disappointed but with absolutely no hope of going elsewhere, we decided to go and keep warm in bed. In the evening, just before dinner, I suddenly got dreadful stomach pains and unpleasant stinging sensations. I dashed to the toilet, once, twice, three times. Now I knew what I'd got: cystitis on my wedding night. This bad luck just wouldn't go away. First an engagement without a ring, then a marriage without a dowry, and now a honeymoon without the good bits.

Next morning, we rushed out to the chemist to get some methylene blue. He told us it would take a couple of days to work — and we only had two days' honeymoon left! We decided we'd just have to laugh it off, and despite the cold we went for long walks in the forest, with frequent fits of laughter and lots of kisses. We were so young ...

Back in Paris, and all kitted out in rue Pasteur, we came across major problem number one: no money. Apart from what was left of the glorious twenty thousand Joseph had given us, we had not a bean. So until something better turned up, Paul went back to his old job in the leather business. He wasn't a communist any more, and was thinking of setting up on his own. We wanted a different sort of life-style. That's why we'd given up the café and the accompanying parental pressures, the scalding percolators and cast-iron tables that weighed a ton ... At that moment we shared the same ambitions, the same desires, and we thought that's how it would always be.

Wherever we went, we walked: we couldn't even afford the metro. Because I had nothing better to do, I started copying the fashions from magazines, and tried dressing like Maria Félix or Jane Russell. In front of my reproduction Louis XVI dressing table I'd play at Du Barry, concocting at my leisure huge chignons, the inevitable ringlets, swept up shells and false plaits which made me look five years older. Once the hair-do was finished, I'd paint my nails blood-red. I thought I had nothing to worry about: Joseph had promised us a two-hundred-thousand franc dowry. He would give it to us one day, wouldn't he? While I was waiting, I listened constantly to records by Montand, whom really I loved. I used to be the 'Gamin de Paris' or on the 'Plaines du Far-West'. To say nothing of the papers that I read by the shovel-full.

The longer we waited for the dowry, the grander our projects became. We were certainly counting our chickens. One day, I woke up in my Louis XVI bedroom, and felt sick; the feeling was unmistakable. With immense joy I shouted: 'Paul, I'm pregnant!'

Pregnant, freely, and happily so. That's when I made up my mind.

'I'm going round to claim my dowry. If he won't give it to me, I'll give him a piece of my mind!'

I set off straight away for the factory in the rue Villiers-de-l'Isle-Adam, and arrived full of pluck. Pregnancy had given me wings and voice. Joseph wasn't there. I approached the Titanic, who was watching the till, as cold and majestic as ever. I'd hardly begun to speak when Joseph arrived back. So I turned to him: 'Papa, I'm expecting a baby!'

'That's wonderful, my darling!'

He came up to put his arms round me. I backed off a bit.

'Yes, it's wonderful. But it would be really wonderful if you'd give me what you promised me: my dowry.'

Frankly he looked put out.

'Yes, the dowry you promised me.'

'Which dowry? What did I promise you?'

It was exactly as I'd feared ... My anger erupted.

'Promises, promises, that's all it's ever been. It's about time you kept some of them. The trousseau, the bedroom suite, the rue Pasteur flat, they're all very nice, but it's still no real recompense for all the work I did at the café. You've got to give me the two hundred thousand you promised me. If you hadn't been so stupid and spent all that money on our wedding, we might have been able to start up on our own. But no, you just had to play to the gallery ...'

He chose to ignore that one, and went back to the two hundred thousand francs. He could at least deny all recollection of that: 'But I never promised you anything of the sort!'

He turned to Ettie: 'Ettie, did I ever promise her such a thing? You be the judge.'

The Titanic was listening avidly to the conversation, obviously, and was of the same opinion.

I spun round and turned my attention to her.

'Of course, you viper! He couldn't promise me something like that with you around, could he? He's very generous when you're not there! Imagine it, that's what he promised me in his state of euphoria when his brother arrived. And by the way, to make up for arriving here empty-handed my uncle promised me a transistor radio. Well, I'm still waiting for that too! And when I think,' turning back to Joseph, 'that you gave him my ring!'

I carried on insulting my stepmother right and left, addressing her in the polite (*vous*) form. I had told her quite categorically one day that I could only ever address familiarly (as *tu*) people I really liked. And she was not among them.

'And anyway, shut up if you don't mind, Ettie! I didn't ask you for your opinion. I'm talking to my father, not to you!'

That's when I started shouting any old thing that came into my head, and chucking things about in the office. The workers, who could see and hear everything that was going on through the glass door, had stopped working by now. Ettie began yelling at Joseph: 'And are you going to let her treat me like this?'

But I'd seen those crocodile tears of hers before, and I wasn't going to let them bother me. I grabbed whatever pots of jam came to hand and lobbed them at the glass-fronted cupboards. On the desk there was a lovely stack of tins, like they have in supermarkets, and in good Buster Keaton style I pulled a couple out from the bottom row. The structure collapsed and the whole room was soon awash with *Confitures Villiers*.

Joseph could see his ship about to sink beneath the jammy waves and decided to take action. He started chasing after me, threatening me, but I managed to stop him by shouting: 'Careful, I'm expecting a baby!'

He restrained himself, with much gnashing of teeth. Then he begged help from on high, his arms raised to heaven. Since I just carried on smashing things, all he could do was follow me round fuming and counting the broken windows. He took the occasional swipe at my face; so much the better, I needed a bit of fresh air. I accused him of enslaving everyone, even Maurice who was barely fourteen. Of course I was exaggerating somewhat, but he had to work every bit as hard as the others, and Joseph picked on him too. A snide remark to Ettie: 'Thank God Eva's with Thérèse! There's a whole world of difference between a mother and a stepmother.'

It was nearly time to call it a day (you couldn't move in the room for pots of jam and broken glass), and I gave Joseph a long hard look and told him:

'It's all over now, papa! You no longer exist for me, I will never see you again!'

I left, slamming the door so hard behind me that the glass broke in that too. By the end, Joseph was left speechless by the tornado, dumbfounded that anyone, even his own flesh and blood, could make more of a noise and a scene than he could. As for the Titanic, she sank without trace.

I got back to the rue Pasteur in tears, and told the whole story to Paul, who comforted me and suggested very gently that perhaps I shouldn't have gone to claim my dowry after all. He said he wasn't bothered about the money.

'Don't worry, darling, it doesn't matter at all. You'll see, everything will work out fine.'

But no, everything didn't work out fine, because once I'd given my word I stuck to it. And for all Paul's tenderness, my raid on the *Confitures Villiers* had well and truly failed. There's nothing wrong with failure, providing you can forget about it. But how could I forget it, when we hadn't got a sou? Fortunately, Monique's parents had agreed to Paul's idea that he should be an agent for their fabrics. It worked quite well, but didn't bring in much money. And not enough to have a Christmas party, to celebrate my eighteenth birthday. Just like previous birthdays this one wasn't spent in the bosom of the family either, not counting Paul of course. On Christmas Eve we walked over to his mother's, who'd made us dinner. After the boudin blanc, we had yet another choice to make. If we took the metro back, we wouldn't be able to go to the cinema . . . So we walked back to Belleville to see a Maria Félix and Pedro Armendariz film. I often see adolescents today queueing for the cinema hand in hand, above their heads a huge poster of a Maria Félix or someone similar, so close yet completely inaccessible. And every time I see them I feel full of regret, as if I was mourning a past which will never return, but which I wouldn't really wish to re-live anyway. And Maria Félix stepped out of her poster, and is now a good friend of mine.

After that wonderful evening out, we went back home to the rue Pasteur. I put on a pink rayon nightdress, put a bow in my hair, and stretched out on the bed to watch Paul getting our little nightcap ready. He didn't need any help because the feast only consisted of a cup of tea and some biscuits. And he'd hardly poured it out before I got an attack of nausea. I couldn't swallow a thing and stayed silent for several minutes. Then suddenly, I solemnly declared: 'Next year, for Christmas, I want a hundred roses, a fox-fur stole, and an American car.'

Fox-fur stoles (silver fox, of course) really fascinated me: for me they were the symbol of success. I'd seen the first few Madame Josephs wearing them, and all the filmstars. Of course, I didn't distinguish between presents from Joseph and presents from film producers. It was all fox to me. And the roses; they were to satisfy my need for romance (which up till now hadn't been exactly pandered to), and the car, that was to give Father Christmas just one more chance. Paul didn't hesitate to promise me them ... Promises cost nothing. We slept in each other's arms and, instead of sheep, I counted roses.

7

Divorce

Financially, Paul was beginning to pull through, and our circumstances were improving. He'd heard that Germany, ruined by the war, was buying in supplies from the Sarre region of France, and that the province had been transformed into a veritable emporium. Plenty of business opportunities there. We launched into this new venture and soon stopped having to think twice before buying metro tickets. I'd buy the fabric, put it in a big wicker basket, and Paul would go off for three or four days a week to sell it. When he got back, I put my heart into preparing him tempting little dishes which I myself had to refuse because I was putting on much more weight than the pregnancy alone could account for.

Joseph turned up three or four times at the flat, to try and see me. He'd knock at the door: 'Who is it?'

He'd answer, in his funny accent: 'It's myself.'

'Well, myself can just go away again!'

One day he came round and said, still from behind the door: 'Listen, Régine, I'm going to give you the hundred thousand francs.'

'You promised me two hundred.'

'You'll never get two hundred thousand out of me!'

And he went off again. This haggling like two rag dealers was extremely irritating, but I sensed he was about to capitulate: it was not the moment to give up. I knew, in fact, that when people asked him how things were going with us, now I was expecting a baby, he'd say everything was fine, just fine, and then change the subject rather shamefacedly. When people asked me, I didn't mince my words and told them how the one time he could do something to help, he wouldn't. This latest business severely dented his reputation for generosity, and he wasn't happy about it. More knocks at the door: 'Who is it?'

'Régine, it's myself. I've got the hundred thousand francs now, but you mustn't breathe a word to Ettie. You know what she's like. I'll give you the rest later.'

'When?'

'Next week.'

This time, however, we badly needed to invest in the business, and my confinement was going to cost a packet, so I moderated my terms. We came to an agreement over the hundred thousand, and he was allowed in to contemplate my bulge. It made him so happy he was moved to tears. You'd have thought he was the father.

'Listen, Régine,' said the grandfather-to-be, drying his tears, 'you can come and ask for the other hundred thousand from Ettie. It's to be your official dowry, and she agrees to it.'

Ettie definitely held the purse-strings. In fact she held them so very tightly that I never actually got the other hundred thousand.

I showed Paul the money when he got back. With a sum like that we'd be able to buy up and sell a great deal of material, and, miracles, afford taxis as well. We were on our way to making our fortune. It had all turned out for the best, but still disaster was just around the corner. While we'd had no money, something stopped me from being too demanding and high-handed. The thing about the car was just a dream really. But now the immediate problem was solved I felt my hands weren't quite so tied. I started convincing myself that I'd married Paul not just because I loved him, which of course I did, but also as a way of leaving home. I had got married for the opportunity of being a different person, and I now realized that I hadn't changed. I was suffocating; I wanted to do things, all sorts of things, but what?

We started having rows. One day, Paul, probably quite rightly, refused to buy me a particular dress. In a rage, I smashed the glass in the kitchen door and cut my hand quite badly. Another time I broke a block of ice (we had no fridge at the time), put it in a bowl, and stuck my feet in it: not a sign of blissful contentment for the expectant mother. Not surprisingly, Paul started wondering what was going on. We weren't really communicating and he became very distant. His spells away from home didn't help, and as soon as he got back I'd beg him to take me out dancing. It wasn't such a good idea for someone in my condition but he agreed and we went off to the banks of the Marne where there were lots of little bars and road-houses. Chips, mussels, glasses of white wine, mazurkas and tangos ... I just loved music and dancing. Seeing me bop around like that, people thought it must be a 'craving' I had because of the pregnancy. But it was just a woman's craving, full stop. Paul, who had, after all, promised he'd be a husband, father, mother and big brother rolled into one, didn't miss the opportunity to tell me:'It's very bad for you to dance like that. Don't forget you're pregnant!'

'I haven't forgotten, it's all I *can* think about!'

Quite honestly though, that wasn't true. My mind was actually a complete blank at that time. The one thing I did know was that I'd married someone far too 'bourgeois' for my liking. He'd been so sure that marriage would make a sensible woman of me, and help me forget the past. But the wounds of the past were deep, the scars unhealed, and it had been more than just a string of minor worries and more major disappointments. I was carrying it all around with me, and that's probably why 'sense' had nothing to do with it.

The more Paul earned, the more solid his principles became, and the number of rows increased. Everything became a problem. I felt suffocated with him near me, and suffocated when he was away too. With him or without him, I felt I was missing something, not living properly. Everywhere felt like a prison to me, except precisely those bars full of the hum and buzz of people living like there was no tomorrow. They were having fun and enjoying themselves, and I discovered, with wonder, the pleasures of living for the moment.

The baby was due in a month's time. A kid knocked at the door one morning and handed me a letter saying, 'It's from your brother.' Maurice had written: 'My dear sister (his usual solemn style), war has just broken out in Israel and I'm going to fight. Life here is impossible. I'm going to fight — I feel it's my duty. Love from Maurice.' He was fourteen years old.

This time, I thought I really was going mad. I rushed round to Joseph's and created yet another scene. I shoved everyone about, broke a few more things, and was rude to both of them. The second visitation by hurricane Régine chez Zylberberg. I told them that if Maurice got killed in the war it would be entirely their fault. On my way out I yelled at Joseph, then at Ettie: 'You, I forbid you to come to the flat, and as for you, I never want to speak to you again.'

I went back home, and put Paul in the picture as soon as he came back. 'We've got to get Maurice back, he's gone to Marseille.' Paul took the first train he could but got there too late; the boat had gone.

Shortly after, we learnt that the boat had been torpedoed in sight of the Israeli coast! Fortunately Maurice escaped, and when I finally found out where he was, I wrote telling him to return immediately, and that he was too young to fight. Not much of an argument against an idealist who'd chosen to reject mediocrity.

On Friday 13 August 1948, I gave birth to a baby boy, whom we called Lionel, in a clinic in the ninth arrondissement. It was a very difficult labour. I was in excruciating pain for twenty-four hours. The midwife, who seemed to find me quite hateful, kept telling Paul to go and have a walk outside, but with great stoicism he stayed by my side.

During the pregnancy, and bearing in mind my nerves, I'd been obsessed by the notion that there would be something wrong with the baby. But he was a big bouncing boy whom my stepmother absolutely insisted on calling Léon. It was her husband's name, and Hebrew custom dictates that a baby must be called after a deceased grandfather. This suggestion didn't arouse much enthusiasm, and we compromised with 'Lionel'. Paul and I loved the name and my stepmother put up with it, not without commenting that it was just another of my little 'originalities'.

For the first few months, Paul and I got on better, but it didn't last. Symbolically, I refused to feed Lionel myself, because I didn't want to ruin my breasts. I don't know where I'd read about it, but I would have done better to concentrate on my weight: I had put on three stone. It didn't stop me wanting to go out and be seen, quite the opposite. Paul was trying to put some money by, but my feeling was that with the kind of future I had before me, why worry about the present. What did all this hoarding of candle-ends have to do with the bright lights of the movies? Paul looked at me like I was a dog with two heads and said, worried: 'You're mad. We've got to do something. It's not right.'

However, next Christmas (I was nineteen), he gave me the famous fox-fur stole, and the one hundred roses, and announced that he'd just found a good second-hand blue Mercury with beige leather upholstery. As one last present, I asked Paul to take me to the Bœuf sur le toit for New Year's Eve.

'What's that?'

'The place everyone's talking about.'

I read all the gossip columns avidly and I knew that all the stars went to the Bœuf sur le toit. Paul agreed in the end, but the thought of going to a place like that terrified him. When you're only twenty, a bit shy and you've never had much money, it's only normal to feel like that. I was the one who was 'abnormal' ... He asked how we went about it, just turn up or book a table. I didn't know, but assumed that it wasn't like the Lumière de Belleville, and that you had to book. We phoned — or rather Paul phoned. I told him we had to sit downstairs, not upstairs. So he asked for a downstairs table, and replaced the receiver.

'All fixed?'

'Yes.'

'Have we got a downstairs table?'

'But why downstairs? They told me it was all full up, so they've put us upstairs.'

'But all the rich people, the famous people go downstairs.'

'Exactly, but we're not rich or famous.'

'But one day I'll be famous.'

'Famous for your mad ideas, you mean! Anyway I think it's pretty good that we're going there at all.'

To tell the truth, I was thrilled. So, New Year's Eve saw us at the Bœuf sur le toit. We were taken straight to what I later learnt was known familiarly as 'Siberia'. (You could watch everyone arriving, but there was absolutely no chance of being seen by them. But I'd have chosen the view over unseeing famous heads any day rather than dine tête-à-tête at home with Paul.) I couldn't keep my eyes off the best tables, and I spotted Henri Salvador, one of my idols. I'd seen him at the Alhambra with the Ray Ventura Orchestra. He'd really made me laugh. He was with a gorgeous brunette. I knew she was called Jacqueline; all the papers said they were about to get married. I told Paul all the details, but he just laughed, and I added: 'I am going to be down there with the stars one day.'

My one obsession.

As if he could read my mind and wanted to bring me back to earth, Paul started talking about the menu, about the décor, about the past or the future, *our* future. And since I didn't always answer him, he asked: 'What are you thinking about?'

'Nothing ... nothing ...'

For me, the place oozed wealth, pleasure, and luxury. My one goal: to be like these people some day, to talk like them, to move like them, to smile like them. I knew that some twenty-year-olds went off to tend lepers, and I knew that my own ambition was not of the highest order. But mine it was, and I clung to it like a life-raft. These were the beautiful people, and I didn't doubt for an instant that their lives were one long fairy tale. Laughter for them was easier than breathing for me, and I imagined the slightest of their murmurs having more effect than any amount of my fuss. Like the infatuated poet describing his beloved, I thought I saw pearls and blossoms fall from their lips. I wanted pearls to drop from my lips too, and for my conversation to be a matchless jewel. Any word of theirs I could catch reverberated deep within me. Each gesture was a diamond, each word a gem, and the laughter crystalline. For people like them, every moment was sublime. What pure pleasure to be able to believe the world was yours for a handful of jokes and a little sparkling wit. Obviously, for the moment, I was a long way from achieving that blissful state, and I looked more like a little girl lost and a bit the worse for drink than an inaccessible and radiant star. I threw streamers down in the hope that a famous face would look up and see me. Was it pathetic? Well, show me a newcomer to the political or literary scene who hasn't at some time begged help from an old hand!

Back home, in familiar surroundings, I felt out of place again. To forget my frustrations and doubtless to punish Paul for not being some sort of prince I helped myself to a huge slice of bread and butter with onions before I went to bed. The morning after, I realized it was just myself I'd punished; I had the most enormous hangover. Onions and champagne obviously don't mix. Fortunately though, I did remember how much I'd enjoyed the evening out and I said thank you to Paul, while still harping on the same old subject: 'You'll see, one day we'll be right there with them!'

Even though I'd sobered up, I was just rambling on as far as he was concerned.

Lionel was six months old now, and when Paul was away on business (from Monday to Thursday morning) I started going out discreetly, leaving the baby with a neighbour, a kindly old grand-mother. Out dancing I could dream, and forget. I wasn't looking for a lover. The abortions I'd had, and the difficult labour with Lionel, had put me off seeking physical pleasure and I was still attached to Paul anyway. The only thing that interested me, like it did when I was a kid (all of two years ago ...) was dancing. My lovers were the Royal lieu at Richlieu-Drouot, the Berlitz underneath the school, the Mimi Pinson and the Club des Champs-Elysées. The day I realized that the old lady next door wasn't really a perfect babysitter I arranged for a nanny to come, and carried on dancing in the afternoons. From Thursday to Sunday, when Paul was home, obviously I didn't go out, and tried to give an impression of calmness. As far as I could.

One day, when I'd been without news of Maurice for some time, I suddenly got a phone call from a woman who wanted to meet and talk to me. She had met him in Israel where she had been to help and to find the son of a friend of hers. We arranged to meet at our flat. The doorbell rang. A beautiful woman stood on the doorstep, immaculately dressed.

'I'm Madame Biedermann. I'm pleased to meet you.'

She came in and handed me a letter from Maurice. I was dying to hear everything she could tell me.

'He's very well; I saw him only last week. The war's over and he hopes to be back in six months when he's demobilized.'

I opened the letter, which also contained some stripes. My heart jumped, I read the following words: 'My dear sister, I am happy and proud to entrust you with my sergeant's stripes.'

Madame Biedermann said: 'Your brother told me all about the situation at home. Don't you agree that it would be better if he didn't have to go back to that factory?'

I certainly did agree. We spoke about it at length and then, seeing some fashion magazines on the table, she asked me whether I ever went to fashion shows. I said I didn't, and she asked me if I'd like to go to a fur show with her that same day. Would I like to? There's nothing I would like to do more, I replied, overcome with emotion.

So off we went in what they used to call a chauffeur-driven light fifteen. I can't remember where we went, somewhere near avenue Montaigne; to a beautiful apartment block with a lift twice the size of my flat. The room where the collection was shown was lined with wood, with gilded decorations. I learnt later that it was called panelling. The models emerged onto the catwalk one after the other, wearing the most fantastic fur coats I'd ever seen. I was absolutely desperate for a fur coat by the time we left the show. I thought about it for two days and told Paul of my latest whim as soon as he got back to Paris. 'I've seen a baby seal coat; I want a baby seal coat.' He sent me packing, saying we just couldn't afford

104

it. I knew we couldn't, but it didn't stop me flying into a terrible rage. He was terrified and went straight out and bought me one. It wasn't exactly the one I'd been dreaming of but at least it was a fur coat. I wore it when we went out together, and also when I went to other fashion shows with Madame Biedermann over the next few months. As she was leaving for Israel again, I gave her a letter for Maurice.

Maurice himself returned shortly afterwards, and gave us the gist of what had been going on at the factory prior to his departure. Mainly, Joseph kept accusing him of not working and of being a good-for-nothing. He decided never to go back there but to look for another job, and came to live with us. Joseph had heard he was back and came round three times to beg me to tell him where Maurice was. We didn't let him in, and he began threatening and supplicating from outside the door. He kept this up for a quarter of an hour, and then just went back to his card game as if nothing had happened. But then one day, after he'd found out that Maurice was actually staying with us, he lay in wait and cornered him at the bottom of the stairs. With his usual expertise in the art of persuasion, he talked Maurice round. True, Joseph didn't spare his promises.

'I'll make you the manager of the factory. And you'll have some capital.'

Yet once more, Maurice believed the miracles would happen. Joseph's machinations over the café hadn't really struck home for Maurice: he really thought he'd be if not the boss then at least the boss's son, with an important job to go with it.

So Maurice settled into his 'new' job, proud as a peacock. He played at manager in a suit and tie. But nine days on, the illusion crumbled and poor old Maurice was back in overalls again. Joseph had remained true to form. That evening, Maurice came home in despair. Nothing had changed at all, he said, it was all exactly the same as ever. I begged him not to go back and phoned Joseph myself. For at least the tenth time in my life I told him I never wanted to hear from him again. Then we called Madame Biedermann to see if she couldn't help find Maurice a job. I told her what had happened and she said straight away: 'He could come and work in our workshops with my husband. He's fond of Maurice and would be glad to help. But only on one condition: he mustn't let himself get taken in by his father again, nor must he talk about us to his father. I don't want Joseph coming round here to fetch him back in a week's time.'

I could see her point. She'd met Joseph just once; and once had been enough. Not that she didn't like him, just that the serious side of his character hadn't come over very strongly. That's how Maurice started his new life as a stores manager with the Biedermanns. He was fifteen and a half. He was treated like one of the family and slowly but surely he worked his way up through the ranks until he became managing director of a big international clothing firm. And it was all down to his own hard work, his own creativity, and his gift for leadership. Both of us ended up finding substitute families to take us in hand, the Heymanns and Monique's family in my case, and for Maurice the Mariottis and then the Biedermanns. We found families where we could, and then built up our careers afterwards. Joseph remained a shadow in all this — a shadow we kept changing our opinion of, but still a shadow. He wasn't mean, but his attempts at generosity constantly fell foul of his personal demons, blunders, and particular brand of folly. He hadn't had an easy life himself but what we most resented during those years was his apparent inability either to provide a real family life or to help us in any substantial way. And we held that against him.

Ettie only made matters worse — she was immediately jealous of Maurice's new life and furious that she didn't have him under her thumb to do her chores any more — and she set herself against Joseph, who cast himself as the victim.

I was kept up to date about Joseph by Mademoiselle Hubert, a very proper spinster who was employed as secretary but who played an important rôle in the Zylberberg clan. She was the sort of person only Joseph could have dug up.

She was the archetypal spinster, about fifty, an ex-teacher, with a very long nose, hair on her chin, a boyish haircut and pebble glasses. She was from a 'good family' (as Joseph would say), and the one love of her life was a long-haul sea captain who'd spent but a short time at her port of call. After that, no one. Her conversation was cultured and her accent impeccable, so Joseph took her on with instructions to 'teach me to write and speak proper'.

In fact she was everything from nurse (she gave Joseph his insulin injections) through secretary, to teacher, and was the perfect intermediary between Joseph and us. She was goodness personified, and we adored her, and Maurice would never have run away when he did if she'd held the position then that she subsequently held in the family. She spent most of her time trying to reconcile people; and that was practically a full-time job in itself. She explained to

Joseph that he didn't always behave how a father should (understatement) and to me that 'Monsieur Joseph' adored us really, but didn't know how to express it. We shouldn't turn against him, she said, because he's very unhappy; we should show him how much we cared . . .

In fact she did know what she was talking about, as she had a lot to contend with herself. If she corrected his French when he wasn't in the mood to play the model pupil he might shout, 'Shut up you old loony!', adding a few choice insults in Yiddish. Mademoiselle Hubert would stiffen up and say, 'Oh Monsieur Joseph! You have no manners! I might not understand what you're saying, but I can see by your expression that it's not very polite!'

In truth, she was a little in love, and was far from unhappy to play a rôle that Ettie never could have sustained. Where Ettie the Titanic foundered, Mademoiselle Hubert sailed through. Rue Villiers-de-l'Isle-Adam harboured a bizarre trio indeed. And twenty-four hours a day too, since Mademoiselle Hubert lived in the flat above her beloved employers.

At rue Pasteur love was retreating in confusion, though it didn't stop us moving house. We found a larger flat on the corner of rue Réaumur and rue Saint-Denis; fifth floor, balcony, no lift. The block was close to Les Halles, and to the 'ladies of the rue Saint-Denis': when I went down to the café to make phone calls, I chatted with one or two of them, and even used to leave Lionel in their charge for a few moments. No sooner had we arived than a fellow resident warned us that the flat brought bad luck. The two previous occupants had started having problems the very day they moved in. I just didn't believe in that kind of twaddle. But I should have done, because two months later we had the most enormous gas bill: thirty thousand francs worth. Pretty expensive baby feeds! The gas board came and couldn't make head or tail of it. The fittings were all completely up the spout and I half believed that the entire block must have had its pipework running through our meter. It was a bad omen for the future.

Paul's absences grew longer. Not three or four days, but seven or eight. And when he got back he was irritated by the places I took him to, 'fashionable' places, not members only exactly, but full of people I found elegant, funny, cool. He didn't understand how anyone could want to spend their life dancing, meeting people, hanging about in night-clubs. We went to Carol's one night, somewhere I went back to often with friends after Paul and I separated.

107

It was a very elegant little place run by Fred (a woman). Women danced together, but men were happy to go there for a drink. That's where I first heard Annabel (Bernard Buffet's future wife) sing, dressed in a dinner jacket: and Maria Lergos, the Mexican girl, sang there too in a very sexy sequinned dress split to the thigh. It all left Paul quite cold of course, but that didn't stop me taking to the floor all on my own.

I dressed in an increasingly eccentric fashion: shoes which laced up above the ankle, crazy dresses in dark green taffeta, impossible hairdos ... Although it wasn't essential for fashionable women to be skeletal in those days, and though I wasn't hampered by my extra stones, I did start dieting seriously. For the first but not the last time! Long before it became trendy to diet, I spent three days lying in a darkened room (while Paul was away) sipping cherry-stalk tea. I got up on day four, totally exhausted, in a filthy mood to greet Paul ... The next week, while the cat was away, the slimmed-down mouse went out dancing again, from five to seven, or often from four to eight, and then more and more from nine to midnight ... Paul was furious when he discovered that I went out at night and not just during the day. I tried telling him that dancing didn't harm anyone, least of all him, but he was quite convinced that I left the dance floor now and then to jump into bed with someone. The arguments were getting us nowhere, so he tried another tack and started writing me long letters telling me to calm down, and warning me that if I didn't he'd be leaving. Since he was away for longer and longer stretches I had plenty of time to reply and one day I wrote that I cried a lot when I was alone. He thought it amusing to send me an assortment of handkerchiefs by post. I can understand his reaction a bit better now. But at the time I could have throttled him.

As I was also doing everything in my power to avoid another pregnancy, Paul decided he'd had enough, and wheeled out the big guns: he called a family conference to discuss my case and try and put me back on the straight and narrow path of motherhood and conjugal duty. We all assembled at Joseph's with cousin Prywes, the clan's medicine man and highest intellectual and moral arbiter ... the best man in the world. He led the debate and drew conclusions: I had to get a grip on myself, become more serious-minded, more housewifely. Easily said. In short, I was in the wrong not wanting to be a good bourgeoise and a real Jewish mother. Joseph listened distractedly to all this: he knew of course that you could never make a silk purse out of a sow's ear, as my directrice had said six years before. But my cousin said there were attenuating circumstances: notably Paul's long absences from home. He would have to spend more time with me. Given the way things were between us I didn't think much of this idea, though I didn't say so. At this point, Paul, who didn't want to leave the diagnosis there, made a suggestion. I needed some psychoanalysis! Where on earth did he get that idea from? It was pretty unheard of at that time. But analysis appealed to me ... It was very chic so I was all for it. My cousin approved, saying that he believed in it, and that in any case it could hardly do any harm. That's what they always say.

The sessions started with an analyst my cousin had found. I was very impressed, non-plussed even. At least to begin with ... But when he asked me to talk about my childhood, there was no holding me. There was plenty to tell. What I chose to miss out, I made up for with some highly unlikely yarns which clearly didn't fool him. It went on for two months, three sessions a week, and cost an arm and a leg. At the end of it, he got Paul to come in and explained it all to him, in front of me, something like this: I'd been traumatized by my childhood; I was suffering from the loss of my father and my mother; the problems of adulthood had been heaped on me during my childhood and adolescence, which had greatly perturbed me; I needed to sort myself out and it would take time. He also explained that, in searching for my lost childhood, dancing was my way of compensating for the parents, the tea-parties and the dolls I'd never had. It was frustration that made me dance ... He concluded: 'Everything will all settle down gradually. Your wife needs another baby, that would be very good for her: unless she has completely different ambitions, in which case nothing will stop her from realizing them.' He seemed to have understood that I danced to forget what I never had, but also that I danced to think about what I would have one day; in other words, for the moment at least, I had no ambitions to play at happy families. I wanted to find what I'd never had, but not that way.

Life picked up. I felt calmer, but not radically transformed. I did try to play the game and Paul, full of good intentions, decided that we would have another child. He came back every Friday morning so we could spend the weekends together with Lionel. To stave off boredom during the week, I played my favourite records over and over again; Yves Montand and yet more Yves Montand. I listened to 'Le grand plombier-zingueur' so often that Lionel was stamping to the rhythm in his playpen. And I listened to people who'd started their careers before the war, and were still singing: Trenet, Rina Ketty, Chevalier, Suzy Solidor and Tino Rossi, whose songs I had played at full volume for the neighbours' benefit back in 1939. Our efforts at being the model couple were just a series of meaningless gestures, a sad comedy which had to come to an end sometime. When he came back on Fridays I tried to pay attention to what my heart and body were telling me, but they weren't speaking to me at all. So almost unnoticeably, irresistibly, my mind started working in reverse: I wasn't trying to make the marriage work any more, but trying to work out how to end it. It wasn't easy to get a divorce: who should I go and see? How to explain? But the words just went round and round my head: 'I must get a divorce, I must get a divorce'. I was now convinced that if I remained a married woman I'd never be 'Régine'.

That's when things started speeding up. I was round at Monique's one day, she lived opposite the *France-Soir* offices on the corner of rue des Petits-Carreaux and rue Réaumur, just near us. It was four o'clock, and I was just getting ready to go dancing at the Mimi Pinson (I'd thrown all my good resolutions out the window). Monique's brother was there, who introduced me to his fiancée and then came over to talk to me quietly. He told me he was very happy but that it hadn't gone down too well at home because his fiancée was a Catholic. I reassured him: 'You'll see, it'll all work out fine. Things like that don't matter any more. The most important thing is to be happy.'

As I spoke these wise words, a handsome blond boy arrived, the fiancée's brother. His name was Yves. He was really good-looking. Monique suggested I celebrate the Jewish Easter (Pesach) with them, that same evening: I was particularly glad since Paul was away, and I was still out of touch with Joseph. I would be spending Easter with a real family after all, not all by myself.

After a couple of hours dancing at Mimi Pinson alone amidst unknown but familiar people, I went back to Monique's. We sat down to dinner; Yves was next to me. He was a good talker, if very slightly pretentious. He offered to take me home at the end of the evening. A discreet 'yes, please', and there I was sitting in an open-topped car. Better than the metro any day. While we were driving, he explained that he was a painter, and told me about his father, who was an auctioneer. He mentioned his surname, but I didn't pay much attention since he obviously wasn't related to any celebrity, band-leader or even writer I might have heard of, like Hemingway for example, whose novels I was reading voraciously. The 'man whose name wasn't Charles Trenet or Hemingway' pulled up outside the flat and asked to see me again. Being a virtuous married woman, I replied that I wasn't really free, but that I'd be delighted if we bumped into each other at Monique's. There I left him, and climbed the five flights of stairs to the ill-fated flat.

One day shortly after, I thought I'd dress all in black: a tight sheath dress, laced-up shoes, and big wide-brimmed hat. I was headed for the Champs-Élysées. I thought I looked great, and wanted to show the rest of the world. Before I caught the bus, I popped in to see Monique. Yves was there; he'd been round every day to find out how I was, and on the off-chance that I might just happen to be there. He grabbed the opportunity and offered to take me. I gave up the idea of going by bus (although I always caused a bit of a stir in my various outfits) and settled into his Hotchkiss. By day and with the roof open, the machine impressed me almost as much as its owner. Yves asked me: 'Do you mind if we stop off on the way to see a friend who's not well?'

'I'm in no hurry.'

I'm sure he didn't doubt it! I can hardly have given the impression of being pressed for time. He added: 'I'll call at home and collect a bottle of champagne.'

Quite right too: much more sparkling than cherry-stalk tea. I said I'd wait in the car while he went up to her flat, but he told me to come up too, saying she was nice, I'd really like her.

I've met lots of 'nice girls', but none quite like this one. A very thin young woman opened the door. We were introduced, and the usual enquiries were made about her state of health ... They started chatting and I just observed. She lay on the sofa, diaphanous and lanquid, about as wholesome as a wraith. Her work: decorating glasses! If she'd said she painted stained-glass windows I wouldn't have been any more surprised. (Thirty years later and she would probably have been a china-restorer, it was all very much the same: the height of good taste, delicacy and fragility.) I wanted to be just that sort of invalid, too, who got visited by handsome young men bearing gifts of champagne. But unfortunately I have an iron constitution and tend to break glasses, not repair them. I couldn't have been more different. I drank a couple of glasses of champagne to get over the disappointment; just enough to feel pleasantly bubbly and a little ethereal, like my hostess the convalescent Ophelia.

We took our leave and Yves drove me over to the Champs-Elysées. He waited in the car while I did a little shopping. I was in seventh heaven: for the first time, I was playing the real little Parisienne snob. Sadly I still had to go back home to rue Réaumur, although no one was going to be there. Paul was away and I'd just sent Lionel off to Villard-de-Lans to a children's home for the winter holidays.

And when Yves asked if I'd like to have dinner with him I gave in and accepted. He suggested going to Les Halles. It was the first time I'd been out to dinner alone with another man since my marriage.

We ate upstairs in a fashionable bistro. I was thrilled but a little embarrassed, and told him about my husband and our situation. I also told him something a colleague of Paul's had said to me shortly before: 'He doesn't get bored, you know.' I understood what he meant and felt all of a sudden that I'd been over-cautious. If Paul didn't 'get bored' then why shouldn't I have some fun too, and why did the idea of a divorce continue to worry me? The wine relaxed me and I started thinking about how I could use this evening to make the divorce a bit easier to come by. I've only got to get this boy back to the flat, I thought, and then when Paul finds him tomorrow morning we can both come to an agreement. QED. My little alcohol-befuddled brain tried to work out how I'd play the scene, and the more I drank, the clearer and simpler things seemed to be. At one in the morning we went back to the flat.

About eight the next morning, knocks on the door. I'd sobered up by now and suddenly realized what was going on! In a complete panic I woke Yves up: 'My husband! It's my husband!'

He yawned and smiled: 'Oh yes! You should never joke about things like that, you know!'

'I'm not joking! He sent a telegram to say he'd be back this morning!'

'Why on earth didn't you tell me that yesterday?'

I stammered out any old thing: 'I ... I ... I've no idea, I thought you'd be leaving, I'd had too much to drink.'

'But hasn't he got a key?'

'No, no, I've got to let him in. What am I going to do?'

'Going to do? How should I know?'

I got up, pulled on my dressing-gown, and — why I don't know — put the one-night stand's socks in my pocket. I went to the door: 'Who is it?'

I heard Paul, obviously in a good mood, say 'It's the postman!'
'Wait a minute, I can't find the key, hang on!'
I was frantic, and near to passing out, when I got the door open.
'Are you all right?'
'I'm fine.'
'You don't look fine ...'
'Yes, yes. I feel a bit sick but I'm fine ...'
'No, there's something wrong.'
'No, no ...'
I leant against the wall to let him through, my arms dangling. He went straight into the bedroom and saw the two glasses on the floor.
'You're drinking now, are you?'
He saw the bed all disarranged: 'Been having nightmares?'
I didn't have an answer.
'Sort of ...'
He looked at me and said: 'Whatever is the matter with you? And why have you got your hand in your pocket like that?'
One arm was still dangling, but the other hand kept pressing Yves's socks down into my pocket, no doubt in case they jumped out of their own accord.
Yves wasn't in the bedroom. Had he gone into the kitchen while I was talking to Paul? Impossible. I no longer had any idea what was going on, and then I saw Paul go out onto the balcony and say: 'Do come in, you look ridiculous out there like that!'
I poked my head round the door and saw Yves on the balcony in his trousers with his shirt open.
'I know it looks ridiculous,' he said, looking at Paul. 'Please excuse me. I'm very sorry about all this.'
'Not a word, not a word, there are even more ridiculous positions to be caught in,' Paul said with a knowing smile.
Was he thinking of himself or me, with the socks stuffed in my pocket?
I'd gone white, and felt completely drained.
They were talking quietly, not even looking at me. I stayed out in the hall wondering what part I had to play in all this. I heard Yves say something I didn't really understand, then Paul called me: 'Régine, make us some coffee, would you?'
I was on my way to the kitchen when I heard Yves, now with his tie on, say: 'How stupid, I can't find my socks anywhere.'
I pulled them out of my pocket and said with a sob, 'They're here'.

Paul wise-cracked: 'What a funny idea, hiding the socks! You're supposed to hide the lover in these situations!'

I didn't reply, I was so used to big scenes, I'd much rather something had happened: then I could have shouted and cried and threatened. But nothing happened. I wandered into the kitchen without a word, listened to them, quite in control, having a polite conversation.

While I poured the coffee, Yves passed a comb through his hair, and slipped a bit of paper into my hand: 'My phone number, call me.'

Once he'd gone, Paul said: 'You're full of surprises, aren't you? I sent you the telegram saying I'd be back early so I could surprise you with the engagement ring you never had.'

I burst into tears: 'I only did it because I don't want to be married any more, I don't know the boy, he doesn't mean anything to me. And you seem to do that sort of thing quite happily, so I thought I'd do the same.'

I saw him twitch a bit but he said he didn't have time to talk about it right now, he'd come round and fetch me at lunchtime.

He left, and after he'd gone I had a chance to calm down and think about what had happened. What's done was done. There was no going back, and while I put on my make-up I rehearsed my arguments. We ate at the café on the ground floor of the block. I chose the tomato and cucumber salad, the dieter's favourite dish. But Paul still wouldn't talk about it: 'To be quite honest, Régine, I haven't come to a decision yet; I still don't know what I'm going to do. We'll talk about it this evening.'

I said nothing, and waited for him to come back in the evening. Seven o'clock, eight, nine, still no Paul. I was getting very nervous, and started crying again. Where will it all end? I thought about Lionel, whom we were going to see next weekend at Villard-de-Lans. Paul didn't come home until morning. It was wrong of him not to come back, he said, but he'd come back this evening, he promised. (I learnt later that he'd taken advantage of that day to consult a lawyer, and to try and put all the blame onto me. And the lawyer had strongly advised him not to spend any more nights away from home ...) I felt completely helpless, and rang Mademoiselle Hubert.

'Mademoiselle Hubert, I must be completely mad, look what I've done ...'

And I told her the whole story. She punctuated my narrative with: 'My poor little girl! My poor little girl!'

It was a habit of hers: she always called me her 'poor little girl', and at every turn asked, 'But what's to become of us?' When I'd finished my tale, she promptly came out with: 'But what's to become of us?'

'That's just it, I don't know what's to become of me and I want your advice.'

'But I've never been in a situation like that, Régine my dear. What do you expect, my poor child, I don't know, I really don't know. Perhaps you should talk to your father about it?'

'Certainly not! I don't want anyone else to know about it, swear to me you won't tell anyone else about it.'

'I promise ... I swear ... But what's to become of us?'

My stepmother or someone must have come into the office because Mademoiselle Hubert cut short the conversation, and I was no nearer a solution. All I'd learnt was that Mademoiselle Hubert had bever been in my situation. What a surprise. So I phoned Yves.

'Hello, it's Régine ...'

'You've phoned at last! How are you?'

'Not well.'

I was so sad right then that I wished he'd call me 'tu', but he wouldn't, he insisted on addressing me formally.

'What's happening?'

'Can't you imagine? What's happening is that I don't know whether I'm coming or going, and I can't even manage to have a proper conversation with Paul. And I really need to.'

'I understand perfectly well, but what can I do about it?'

'You've got to come and explain to him that we don't know each other, and that that was the first and last time. I don't want to have all the wrong on my side if we start divorce proceedings.' (Naïvely, I'd completely forgotten that Paul didn't have any legal proof of my 'indiscretion'.)

By now he was getting a bit annoyed.

'Look, I told him all that yesterday morning, while you were making coffee. And I don't really know what you're after any more. You kept on telling me you wanted to get divorced and now you want to try and put the pieces back together again. You're putting me in a very difficult situation.'

'What about my difficult situation then?'

And I hung up on him shouting, 'You're just a coward!'

I climbed back up the five flights and cried all day long. Paul came in at about seven, very relaxed, and said: 'Régine, would you please make me up a bed, here on the sofa. I'll sleep there from now on.'

'Yes, all right.'

He talked to me while I was making the bed.

'I think the first thing is to separate for a few days. I still need time to think. It would be a good idea if you went to see your son on your own.'

'But I want to know now what you want to do, and what's to become of me.'

'I told you, I haven't decided yet, and in any case I won't do anything at the moment. I'm going to tell your father what's happened, or rather, no, you will go and tell the family, calmly and collectedly, the whole story.'

I let the pillow drop and shouted: 'I'm not telling them anything, do you understand? Nothing!'

'All right then, I'll tell them instead; it's quite simple.'

Second family pow-wow at the rue Villiers-de-l'Isle-Adam, again with cousin Prywes. Paul ran through what had happened. When he'd finished my father got up and cried: 'Daughter! Daughter! Is this what you do, is this how you dare to behave, after all that good education I gave you?'

I watched the tears roll down his cheeks. I thought this was a bit much and it made me want to defend myself. While I tried to put my side of the story, Mademoiselle Hubert wept copiously ('Dear God, what's to become of us?') and Ettie cried triumphantly: 'I'm not surprised! I'm not surprised! I'm not surprised!'

The atmosphere was getting heated, and cousin Prywes tried to calm us down, but in vain. The family reunion broke up in complete confusion.

Paul got up and left. My morale couldn't have been lower, and I phoned Yves, who sent me some flowers. He called me again, and told me not to let myself dwell on such dark thoughts, that it wouldn't make things any better. I accepted his dinner invitation. The next day, I went round to Monique's and told her the whole story. She shook her head, and pursed her lips saying: 'How complicated things get in your family!'

'Look, I've come round to confide in you, is that all you've got to say?'

And I left, more disheartened than when I arrived.

There was a knock at the door next morning. It was Maurice, with the intransigence of youth, come to pass judgement: 'I've come to tell you that there's no reason to be proud of what you've done!'

And off he went! I see! So now I'm angry with my brother too!

That evening Paul, sitting on his sofa, advised me to spend a week on my own at Villard. When I got back, I was to find myself a job. I agreed. He repeated that he still hadn't reached a decision. I believed him ...

The day I was leaving, Yves offered to take me to the station. I said no at first, then changed my mind. On the platform he promised to write. I told him not to. I so much wanted to forget the whole episode ...

When I reached Villard, I hugged Lionel close and cried. I took a room in a small family hotel close to the home where Lionel was. I spent part of the day writing tear-stained letters to Paul.

On my third day there, a young man came and sat opposite me at dessert.

'Hello.'

I didn't respond, and engrossed myself in a crème caramel. He persisted and I said: 'Please, leave me alone, I want to be alone, and I don't want to talk to anyone.'

After dinner, I went into the little sitting room to drink a tisane. I sat at a tiny desk in one corner and wrote yet another letter to Paul. When I'd finished I went up to bed, wishing a vague good-night to my fellow residents.

I ate lunch alone the next day, but at dinner found another place set at my table. They usually do put people together to eat in small hotels. The boy I'd seen the night before smiled at me and asked if he might eat with me. Of course I had to accept: rather him than someone else.

'You do look sad,' he said. 'Have you got problems?'

'Yes.'

'I thought so. What's happened? Tell me about it; it helps to talk ...'

'I'm in the middle of a divorce, and it's a painful business.'

And so I told my story yet again. And he told me a bit about himself: he lived on the Riviera, had a fashion jewellery business, loved winter sports, and was trying to mix business with pleasure. His name was Jacques.

He seemed very nice, and his concern was very touching. He was tall, dark, elegant: his ski outfits were superb, and I thought to myself that the jewellery business must be quite lucrative. I wasn't exactly the height of elegance, however. I had no desire to ski, so I was dressed as I would be in town, and felt a bit out of place with all the fantastic-looking girls who arrived at the bottom of the slopes with tousled hair, laughing, in their beautifully cut ski-suits.

I spent the afternoons with my son, who was two years old now. Whenever he smiled at me I had a twinge of remorse and felt like crawling into a corner somewhere. And I was cold, too. If you're not happy you always feel the cold winter-sporting. And Jacques kept appearing too! One day he saw me sticking down a letter for Paul, and offered to post it in Grenoble, where he went every day. He said it would get to Paris much quicker. I gave it to him, and he confided to me that he was only staying as long as he was in Villard-de-Lans in order to see me. The day after, I had quite a nice letter from Paul. It put me in a good mood and I let Jacques take me for a drink. We went to the Escale, where they knew him because he came every year. He bought drinks all around.

So I owed my only moments of relaxation to my son and to my jewellery merchant. Jacques took me to Grenoble one day to buy ... sequins! More fun than medals, and I asked him excitedly what he wanted sequins for. He told me they were for a friend who made costumes for shows. My eyes lit up. We bought packets of the things, red, blue, yellow, white, and ribbons the same colour. I tried to imagine what his friend was going to do with them all. I told myself that one day I'd be arranging shows with gold, sequins, and balloons ... On the way back from Grenoble I felt almost happy, believing that my dreams would come true one day. He had to leave for Switzerland that evening, and as he couldn't keep his room over the weekend (it was Friday) he asked me to look after his trunk. He'd collect it on Monday. I agreed, and that evening I dined alone. As he left, the jewellery man stole a kiss, furtively, as if in friendship.

Over dinner, spent intimately with my plate, I spotted a man I was sure I recognized. He was sitting alone at a table near mine. Yes! It was Monsieur S., the man whose three little girls I'd looked after in Lyon. I was pleased to see him, and so much had happened in between ... He asked how I was and I gave him the happy, fulfilled woman bit, whose life left nothing to be desired.

'And your father?'

I told him rather pompously that he'd been reinstated, and had a big factory now, and was married too. He brought me up to date on his wife and children, then looking me straight in the eye said: 'I'm really very happy that things have worked out, and that the scars of the war have healed for you.'

I mumbled an incoherent answer, but was ashamed of myself. If only he knew ... How alone and trapped I felt at that moment, and how I was almost regretting having been helped by such a good man during the Liberation.

After dinner I went back to the Escale and struck up a conversation with the barmaid, a girl about my age. We were chatting and she said to me all of a sudden: 'Do you know, you look just like Silvana Mangano ...'

She'd said just the right thing: she was my idol of the moment, I copied her as much as possible, and I was mad about her film *Bitter Rice* and had just dyed my hair auburn. My eyes sparkled at the compliment and the conversation really got going: 'Here's someone I can talk to!' I confessed to her that my ambition was to own my own nightclubs or else to be a famous artiste. When I see her these days she always reminds me: 'You've done everything you said you would.'

That's as maybe, but we're not quite there yet. She asked me if I'd known Jacques long. I told her that I hadn't, that we just happened to be staying at the same hotel, that was all.

'Oh, I see! Because, between you and me, he looks as if he's fallen for you ...'

I was surprised; he'd hardly made it obvious ...

But he soon made amends, and on Monday morning when he got back, the way he started speaking to me meant I had to throw him out ... The friendship would never have lasted long and I was on my own again. Three days later, I got a letter from Paul asking me to come quickly back to Paris, 'so we can talk'. Ever hopeful, I presumed he must finally have 'thought about it'.

I had to catch a bus to get down to the station in Grenoble. I missed it, and started to panic. 'And Paul's waiting for me in Paris! What's he going to be thinking now!' So I stuck out my thumb and a little Citroën pulled up:

'Where are you going?'

'Grenoble.'

'That's where I'm going, too . . . Hop in!'

There was a stack of big dictionaries on the back seat: he was a
Larousse salesman. That obviously didn't stop him having the odd
pint or two, as I realized when we came to the first bend. He was
clearly quite drunk and only just missed slicing a road-sign in half.
I didn't think we'd ever get to Grenoble in one piece and asked him
to let me get out. He looked at me surprised and befuddled:

'Are you scared or something? I've been coming along this road
for thirty years. I could do it with my eyes closed, asleep even.'

At that point the car skidded off the road and we ended up three
metres below, in a river. I left my Larousse salesman to his bewilderment and opened the door. The car was sinking slowly and I
splashed through the water in my baby seal coat, which now weighed
at least three tons. I clambered up the bank and got back onto the
road. That's when I felt the effects of the impact. I didn't seem to
be hurt, but my head was buzzing horribly. Several cars stopped,
and one took me back to the hotel, soaked through and half unconscious. A doctor gave me a camphor injection and I came out in a
nasty nettle rash from shock. It was incredibly itchy and they had
to give me quite a powerful sedative to help me sleep. My new
friend Corinne, the barmaid, had said to me, 'You keep wearing
those black scarves; it's unlucky.' I heard her speaking in my
delirium and answered out loud, 'But black's my favourite colour.'

She was at my bedside when I woke up. That same evening,
instead of resting, I took the train for Paris. What a journey it was!
Tired and discouraged I did finally fall asleep. And a few minutes
later, the train arrived at Gare de Lyon, Paris. That week went by
like a nightmare in slow motion. Paul, who was sleeping on the
sofa, decided he'd go down to Villard the following weekend. When
he got back, he reported all the 'follies' I'd committed while I'd
been there, and a few days later I received the divorce petition . . .
It would be better to get it all over with now . . . to suffer some
affrontery for the sake of a little peace. Peace . . . Joseph took me to
see a friend's lawyer, who asked me in a very informal way: 'Have
you got any furs?'

'No, I do have a baby seal coat, but it's in a very sorry state.'

'What about jewellery?'

'Well, I should have had two diamonds, but I've not set eyes on
them as yet . . .'

'Okay, you'll have to borrow a fur coat and some jewels.'

'What for?'

'To wear to the court for the settlement of course. There's no need to think about the past any more. The most important thing is to concentrate on the future. On the maintenance you'll be getting. Your husband, as far as we know, is going for "irretrievable breakdown". It's better for everyone that way. You'll have custody of Lionel, but you'll need a decent amount of maintenance. You must come to the hearing immaculately dressed: the judge will be able to see that your husband's got a bit of money, so he'll have to award you more.'

When I got out of the lawyer's chambers I started thinking about it, and decided that he must be completely mad. If I went to court dressed like a star, he'd think I was rich and award me nothing. So I went to the court hearing dressed like a pauper. I was awarded custody of Lionel, as expected, and monthly living expenses, but only forty thousand francs: a pittance. The lawyer had been right. For once, Joseph had done me proud: the man he hired was one of the best lawyers in Paris.

8

Rue de Beaujolais

I became a shop assistant on rue de Rivoli, selling men's underwear, socks and shirts ... Ettie got me the job. It was just round the corner from the flat. Paul had moved out of course, and only called once a week to see Lionel.

After the ordeals I'd been through I didn't last long selling underwear. I became unwell and went to stay at Joseph's for a few days. The doctor advised a rest somewhere warm. Ettie, who was having a good phase, suggested I went to Nice for a holiday with a friend of hers, Marie-Louise, and her two girls. She ran a hotel somewhere in Paris. I met her and she agreed to take me with her.

The four of us assembled at Gare de Lyon. Her girls must have been about twenty-five and quite striking in their way. They were clearly of mixed parentage (had Marie-Louise been married to a black, then?), very showily dressed and heavily made-up. In the corridor they cleared the way saying to the gentlemen, 'Move over a bit, darling!' And I noticed they didn't 'move over' quite as much as they could have done.

Nice meant sea, palm trees, sunshine and, above all, freedom. We were staying at the Hotel Napoléon, which seemed only fitting given that our party consisted of two girls with Martinique origins (like Napoléon's first empress, Josephine) and a Marie-Louise (namesake of his second!). One of the girls shared a room with her mother, the other one shared mine. I asked my roommate the first evening:

'Is Marie-Louise really the mother of both of you?'

'Yes, to all intents and purposes, yes.'

'What do you mean, to all intents and purposes?'

'Look, goodnight little girl, I'm really sleepy and I want to get up early tomorrow for the beach.'

When I got back to Paris, Maurice filled me in on the finer details of the story: in actual fact, Marie-Louise ran a brothel in the eighteenth arrondissement and 'her two girls' were really 'two of her girls' ... Some connections Ettie had!

While the little family was taking a well-earned rest, I wandered about Nice. I've never liked the sun very much: like a true baker's daughter my skin is happier under artificial light. In the course of my wanderings, I stopped in front of a shop selling ladies' underwear where they had some strapless bras in the window. I went in to buy one and asked the lady whether or not I could find the same thing in Paris. She told me I couldn't: she made them herself, and hadn't got an agent yet to sell them in Paris. I offered my services, we chatted for a bit, and she agreed to give me a suitcase full of strapless bras.

I gave up the job in rue de Rivoli and come autumn I was tramping the hard Parisian streets, suitcase in hand. No flashy dressing for me: I wore trousers, a jacket, beret and plimsolls. I had left the unlucky flat in rue Réaumur and was back at Porte Dorée where I'd lived just after the war. With my maintenance and the bras I just about managed. I'd put Lionel back in a boarding school in a château near Sens. He had his dose of châteaux too ... In addition to his teaching duties, the directeur read the cards. When I went to see Lionel, by train or by car with friends, he told my fortune for me. While I was hawking my wares near Palais-Royal, I met a very pleasant woman who happened to own a dress shop. She was Madame de Jarcy, an aristocrat and businesswoman, who made raglan-sleeve jackets in a workshop on rue Lecourbe. She suggested I be a representative for her too. So there I was with two suitcases.

An Italian film-producer friend had bought the business for her, and she had a super daughter called Roselyne. We got on really well. She was the same age as me, flirtatious and funny, tall and blonde. The following spring her mother suggested I went with them to Juan-les-Pins, where they had two boutiques. I would look after the smaller one, Roselyne the larger. What decided me was that I'd be right near a very fashionable nightclub called the Vieux Colombier which had just opened, and not far either from Cannes or Antibes, magical places if ever there were. I'd been to see Claude Luter and Sidney Bechet at the Paris Vieux Colombier and I expected to have a lot of fun at the one in Juan-les-Pins.

In 1951 Juan-les-Pins was still a big uncrowded village, with its own institutions: the Vieux Colombier and the casino ... I happily settled into 'my' boutique, dressed the window, and went to help Roselyne do hers. I lived in a studio-flat with another sweet girl who was also a friend of the Jarcys. We got ourselves organized, and were happy and carefree. I'd never lived like that before, and after all I'd been through these last months, I thought I'd make the most of it and live life to the full. One day Roselyne and I met the woman who ran the Vieux Colombier, and I plied her with questions about it.

'But why don't you come?' she said. 'Be my guests. It won't cost you anything.'

We accepted her invitation and quickly realized that all she wanted us to do was dance and have fun, to get the evening off to a good start. The summer season hadn't begun yet, and they needed something to pull the crowds. So, decked out in tight black sweaters and flared bebop skirts (they were selling like hot-cakes in our two boutiques), we worked overtime every evening in the Vieux Colombier. To begin with we didn't stay too late, but gradually as the season got into full swing and the crowds arrived, summer madness got the better of us. By July they had to open up the other room, which quickly got packed out too. I used to get home at dawn, and then get up again two hours later, feeling terrible. But by evening, miracle of miracles, tiredness vanished and my legs took off: I went dancing, I always went dancing.

I started a diet of hard-boiled eggs and salad, didn't lose an ounce, but it didn't seem to matter; I had my admirers, amongst them two musicians whose style of courtship was as funny as it was brazen. But I wasn't about to do anything stupid: I was scared stiff of getting pregnant. So I was very sensible all summer, and the following winter in Paris too, without having to try too hard.

That's when my night-life began in earnest: the little red-head was a great dancer and everyone was asking who she was.

I danced to everything, but tried not to dance just any old how, and to make people laugh, keep upright, and to liven things up a bit, I started dancing with a glass on my head. That's when I really got noticed, and when people came into the shop it was as often to discover if I was going 'out' that evening as to buy swimsuits.

I started to get known. Some evenings I danced with a boy called Jean-Pierre Cassel, who was doing a stint at the club to earn a bit of money. His ambition was to be an actor.

I was sleeping less and less, but that was the least of my worries. The waiters and the band at the Vieux Colombier had jokingly named me 'la frigide', because I rebuffed all the wandering hands. But that didn't bother me either, because I had another, more flattering nickname: 'spinning top'. When other dancers were exhausted and, one by one, dropped out, I carried on, as if I'd been wound up like clockwork for the night. I talked to everyone: some were broke (I'd end up buying them a couple of eggs at the Pam-Pam at the end of the evening), others were loaded, and yet others were struggling journalists like Yves Salgue or Philippe Charpentier. I met a young reporter from *Paris-Presse* called Jean-François Devay, who became very well-known and founded and directed *Minute*. We remained friends until his death, despite our differences of political opinion. I wasn't deliberately trying to form a 'clan', but even then, when I was no one in particular, I was choosy and selective: with those I liked it was instant camaraderie, uncomplicated yet demanding; those who didn't meet my requirements were swiftly excluded from my mind. I'd started doing what everyone has to do in life, but I did it with a passion and a rigour which was out of the ordinary.

We always ended up at the Pam-Pam at dawn, and that's where the evening usually began too, for aperitifs. We'd sit there watching the succession of Rolls-Royces, sports cars, handsome young men and rich people who cruised up and down between the two chic poles of the Côte d'Azur, Cannes and Antibes. From our own key position we heard talk of nothing but big houses, yachts and fabulous parties ... But it didn't bother me, sitting there with an orange juice and three sous in my pocket: I watched and listened with perfect calmness, unenviously, because I knew that soon enough I'd be joining in the round, and that one day they would be dancing to my tune.

At the Vieux Colombier, the show took place on stage of course, with Eddie Constantine, Henri Salvador, Moustache and his future wife Simone, and Jean-Pierre Cassel, but there was quite a show on the floor too: Aly Khan and Florence Gould came, neither of whom could possibly have heard of Belleville, and Darryl Zanuck and Bella Darvi, though she would have done because her father had been a baker in Belleville like mine; and then there was the diminutive Piaf with her urchin's cap. They said Zanuck lugged a suitcase full of money round with him for Bella to use at the casino ... People said all sorts of things, and I started realizing that 'rumours', true or false, got about much quicker at night than they did in the daytime. I observed all the waitresses' tricks too: they did all they could to earn tips, but if they weren't big enough they'd pocket the bills instead. The girls were pretty good at getting boys and girls together, too; and not always at the behest of the boys! It all made me laugh and I didn't miss a trick. Even on the dance-floor I was watching to see what went and what didn't, who was who, and who created what impression. With my long red frizzy hair (tied back in a knot) I was a zany, bubbling, fun-loving twenty-year-old. My long scarves were a sensation: they trailed behind me like the snatches of conversation I caught while I danced: 'Have you had that Régine yet?'

'No, what about you?'

'No luck, old chap.'

'Is she a lesbian or something?'

They criticized me for not sleeping around enough, and Madame de Jarcy criticized me for going out too much and not working hard enough. She was right, and I was rather afraid she'd send me packing at the end of the season.

It worked out all right though, and she kept me on to work in her new 'shop' on rue de Choiseul in Paris. It was a very special sort of shop: it was on the ground floor of what was once a famous brothel (the Chabanais), and we sold dresses without ever showing a single one to the customers! We showed them samples and described the styles ... Our 'stock' consisted of a few sad sweaters and jackets.

Roselyne had met a smashing boy who was generous too, and we used to go out together in the evenings. Sometimes he took us away for the weekend to the sort of little inn where I'd spent my 'honeymoon', only better. In Paris, we usually went over to Saint-Germaine-des-Prés, to La Libraire (where the amazing Jean-Claude Merle was MC) or to Le Fiacre, which was the equivalent of Carol's for men. There we met all the smartest gays in Paris, and with a bit of luck some pretty smart heteros too. Ex-hairdresser and brother-in-law of Roger Hanin, Louis, ran the place, and the show was strictly on the floor. The food was excellent, the wildlife amusing, the men handsome, and the women were delighted to be courted gallantly, but not too excessively.

I remember a crazy evening, whose after-effects were quite striking. I'd bailed out a waitress at the Vieux Colombier in Juan-les-Pins by lending her some money for a dress. She was supposed to pay me back at the end of the season. Back in Paris, I tried in vain to get back in pocket. One day when I was really penniless, I

126

thought I'd go round to the club where she worked, Carol's, to get my money back. I was with some friends, and suggested we all go. But they said: 'Go on your own, we'll be at the Whisky à gogo.'

So there I was at Carol's trying to retrieve my money. I waited an hour, two hours; I danced to while away the time, but by three o'clock in the morning I was beginning to get a bit fed up.

'Hand it over, or I'll smash the place up!'

Terrified, the poor girl coughed up my two hundred and fifty francs . . .

Ages afterwards, at Jimmy's, boulevard du Montparnasse, a smart man said to me one evening: 'I haven't seen you for ages. How's it going with the girlfriends?'

I gave him a piercing look and answered: 'What do you mean, girlfriends?'

'Sorry, but I was at Carol's one evening and I saw you having a set-to with a girlfriend. It looked like a real domestic row.'

For a few seconds my mind was a complete blank, and then I remembered the occasion. I turned quite surly and replied: 'Is that your idea of a joke? I was asking for some money back, that's all.'

I became a little perturbed that evening, at the thought of that man telling everyone for years that I was a lesbian. If I had been, it wouldn't have mattered, but since I wasn't . . . That's how people get reputations.

The famous Whisky à gogo where my friends waited the whole night for me, was the one-time Plancher des vaches. That's where they started the practice of marking the whisky bottle with the customer's name. Roselyne's friend had his own bottle, in a numbered locker which he opened like a strong-box with a little key. I'd finished with the 'dancings' like the Mimi Pinson and La Coupole: now I only went to fashionable places, like the ritzy bars on the Champs-Elysées such as Le Val d'Isère, L'Ascot or Le Silène, where I often saw Henri Vidal and Daniel Gelin.

At the Porte Dorée I'd taken on a charlady for a couple of hours a week. Her name was Suzanne; she was from Brittany. She soon became my confidante. I told her everything that was going on in my mind, including the ambitions I had for the future.

'Suzanne, you know, one day I'm going to have so many pairs of shoes that I won't know where to put them all.'

I don't know whether she thought I was too crazy to contradict or whether she really believed what I told her, but she burst out laughing: 'Why not?'

I'll have more to say about 'Suzon' later on. (She stayed with me for thirty years, and it took me twenty to understand her. She was my nanny but I should have made her my accountant as well.) As for shoes, it's true I've still got a thing about them. I think about flowers and cars and furs, but at night I dream about shoes.

I hardly ever set foot in the flat: the night-time was too good to waste at Porte Dorée. There were so many fantastic places still to discover, and so many magical nightspots ... That's where 'real life' was, through the looking glass, with the coloured lights and non-stop music.

It was at this time that Paul Pacini moved his Whisky from rue de Beaujolais to the rue Robert-Étienne. In his luggage was the famous juke-box, the first imported into France. For the first six months people flocked there, it was absolutely crazy. The wildest, and the most fun, were a group of kids known as 'the dogs' because they were for ever chasing pretty girls. Perpetually on the prowl, they led completely chaotic lives, going to bed at ten in the morning – like I did, except I also got up early (or didn't go to bed at all). They had money, youth, intelligence, wit and generosity on their side. You can never have too much of a good thing, I've always thought.

I was everyone's pal at the Whisky, and I became a pillar of the establishment – albeit a slightly fragile pillar, though not lacking in humour or, when called for, acidity. Plump as could be, with my dresses cut as daringly low as possible and my belt so tight it almost killed me, I danced away with my glass on my head and paste jewels round my neck. If I didn't like something, I said so, and people started making choice remarks about me. It didn't make me less popular, it made me more so: people asked me out to dinner, or to dance, because at least they knew they wouldn't be bored. I had an affair with a pressure-cooker salesman. But after a few months we reached boiling point, let off some steam and cooled off. Just then, Madame de Jarcy, delighted to see me having a good time, but a bit worried about my work – or lack of it – told me she was very sorry, but she couldn't keep me any longer. She said her expenses were too high. I was fond of my pressure-cooker man, and of Madame de Jarcy too; two setbacks together ... Never mind, I told myself, I'll become a rep all over again.

But I wasn't really looking seriously, and I recalled what my pressure-cooker lover kept telling me: 'You're made for living at night, why don't you find a job which starts at eight in the evening and finishes at six in the morning? Talk to Pacini about it.'

It was then that I realized I absolutely had to make the most of the incredible physical advantage I had over other people: I never got tired — and especially not at night. And even in the daytime I felt good because I only needed a very few hours sleep.

I was quite good friends now with Pacini and his wife. He was a small man of Italian origins from Marseille, and had some funny habits (he kept fiddling with his nose, and touching everything, and then sniffing his fingers), and some good qualities: spunk, plenty of fun ideas, and a feeling for a good gimmick. But I was convinced that the best customers were drifting away from his club, and being replaced by others who, whichever way you looked at it, weren't so good. But why? Because his club was very 'private' on popular nights, but much less so on empty nights: they let anyone in, and that changed the whole atmosphere. It was good that some clubs were like that, but in my opinion you had to choose one way or the other. The door had either to be open or closed: it was no good half and half. Things just weren't going right and finally I said to him: 'Listen, Paul, I'm sure it would work if you re-opened the rue de Beaujolais club.'

'Do you think so? People'll never go back to Palais-Royal. That part's all washed up. Look at La Paella; it was doing really well, and now it's finished.'

La Paella had actually just been taken over by the proprietor of La Péniche, a floating restaurant by Saint-Cloud bridge, a crazy place we often went to as a group. We queued up to eat there and hear the epic rows between the patronne and Albert, the waiter. They had their act down to a fine art, and we absolutely screamed with laughter: 'You're just a rotten old bag, a stupid, idiotic ...'

'If that's how it is, Albert, out you go!'

'All right then,' Albert would answer, 'I'm going!'

And off he'd go, complete with his tray, out of the room, up onto the safety rail, and then he'd throw himself into the Seine!

Pacini was none to keen on Palais-Royal, but I insisted: 'Paul, I'd love to take over the rue de Beaujolais for you ...'

'Do you really think it would work?'

Every night, I sang the same old song: 'Give it a try, you won't regret it ...'

'All right, let's try,' he said in the end.

It was a moment of triumph. I was over the moon to be able to announce to my friends:

'I'm re-opening the Whisky à gogo at Palais-Royal next week!'

I could lay my hands on a barmaid, disc-jockey, cloakroom attendant and bouncer right away, no problem; I did it all myself. No staff problems. I had a dozen hands, six legs and four eyes. I was a Jack-of-all-trades; I welcomed people in, gave them a drink, put the records on, and chucked out undesirables. My domaine? A cellar on three levels. As you came in there was the bar, where ten people could get a drink, provided they trod on each others' toes. Down five steps to the second level where there were four tables and a banquette. Five steps further down was the dance-floor, which also served as a bottle-store. With more than forty people in the place you got asphyxiated. I can only suppose that asphyxia has something to recommend it because all my friends came along on the first night, stayed late, and came back the next night too. Among these veterans, Jean Poniatowski, Kim d'Estainville, Maurice Siégel and Bobby Barriet, who was to become my manager. Most of them weren't even twenty years old but were happy to look older. They were good fun and well brought-up, and only mixed with similar people; it might not sound much, but it counts for a lot.

By the end of the first month, I had thirty or so regulars, and by the end of the second the place was bursting at the seams. On peak nights they were packed into my little kingdom like sardines: only the oil was missing. After three months, we extended into the cellar next door, and I took on a barman and a waiter, who've both got their own businesses now. Habitués from the Milord d'Arsouille (a very famous club where Francis Claude, Gréco, Annabel, Gainsbourg and Jean Yanne all sang) and from the Grand Véfour, the well-known restaurant, came to see what the Whisky á gogo was like, and often didn't leave till dawn.

Sacha Distel came too, a gorgeous-looking boy with an angelic smile who sang and played guitar, and Zanuck, Guy d'Arcangues, Barbara Warner, Zsa-Zsa Gabor, Louis Malle, and above all Claude Terrail, who remained a faithful friend. He was the proprietor of the Tour d'Argent; Monday night was party night and he really used to let his hair down. He always had fabulous women with him and ended up at the Monseigneur or Scheherazade. I was one of his untitled accomplices, and got on particularly well with his great friend Prince Rachevski. We had a contrasting mixture at the club, but it was effective. We danced the cha-cha, the meringue and of course rock'n'roll. I'd bought some rock records before it became fashionable, and when people started talking about it I got them out and everyone went wild. Everyone was doing it: François Perier,

130

Marie Daems, Jacques Charron, Robert Hirsch. All the theatre people came round to my place and let rip, rolling and diving and spinning and leaping about dangerously. To launch the cha-cha, I opened a dance-school at the club on Sunday afternoons. As soon as someone could prove himself competent, he got a medal and then taught the steps to someone else. News of it spread all round Paris, and a journalist from *France-Dimanche* came round and even wrote a full page article about it!

The cha-cha: everyone line up! One-two, one-two-three, one-two, one-two-three. No, no, not like that! You're out of step. One-two, one-two-three, one-two ... Quite different from every other dance, one long giggle, but not as easy as it looks to start with ... It was the first time couples had to separate, and this new departure proved most disorienting.

Then one night, the door opened. In came a stunning man whom I recognized immediately because his picture was always in the papers: Porfirio Rubirosa. I already knew all about him. He was a great friend of Aly Khan's; they both came from the same world. That fairy-tale world of international millionaires, for whom money had strictly no importance because they were certain of having plenty all their lives. But Rubirosa's style of millionaire was quite special. He was the son of a rich landowner, and began by marrying the president's daughter in his own country, the Dominican Republic. His marriage to Flor Trujillo didn't last long, but he remained a friend of his father-in-law, who later made him the Dominican Republic's ambassador to Argentina. Launched by the Trujillo family, he lived in great style and then met Danielle Darrieux, with whom he spent the best part of the war. As soon as they parted, he got a telegram from the famous American million-airess Doris Duke saying: 'If you're free, I'll marry you'. No sooner said than done. He did marry her, and then became the lover of Zsa-Zsa Gabor, the Hungarian blonde everyone was talking about, who also never seemed to stop getting married and unmarried. That's when I met him: he was living mainly in Paris, in his house on rue de Bellechasse, and on fine days he let the press photographers take pictures. His photo was all over the papers.

Later he married the eccentric Barbara Hutton, and the only woman he was to live with who had no fortune of her own was the last, Odile Rodin, who still lives in Brazil.

Porfirio Rubirosa was without a doubt one of the most seductive men of his time. His life was one long party, and he gave the impression of having no cares in the world. He was a man's man as well as every woman's dream lover. He was a great polo player, loved racing cars, was a tennis champion, and had everything going for him. He married several of the world's richest women, and contrived to make it appear that he was doing them a service ... and it was true.

That evening, he came down the steep staircase of the Whisky à gogo with Pierre and Ingrid Smadja. It was his first visit. He usually went to L'Elephant blanc, the smartest and most celebrated club in Paris (it was in rue Vavin, and later became François Patrice's Saint-Hilaire) or to bars like the Florence or Jimmy's, which used to be run by Jimmy, but was taken over by his wife Suzette after his death. Just looking at him, I could see why he had such a reputation. A charismatic figure, he had magnetic fascination.

When he came up to the bar and saw people rising to greet him he said: 'Don't get up!' It was amazing how magical a banal little phrase could sound, and as he spoke he pressed his index finger hard on the arm of one of the women there (just in the crook of her arm). That's what he always did, and whenever he did it to me I experienced something like a violent electric shock (lots of men tried to imitate him, but only succeeded in causing an excruciating pain ...).

He asked my name, and how I'd come to be there. I was surprised how easily and how volubly I could talk to this man everyone either wanted to know or was so proud to have met. I didn't feel embarrassed, or hesitant, and I had the impression that I was talking to an old friend. We danced together a long time; he danced as he moved — beautifully.

He invited me to go for a drink with him somewhere else. We went to Jimmy's in rue Huyghens. Downstairs, in a little room, there was a bar which stayed open all night. Upstairs, it was sumptuous. The walls were painted black, table cloths and tables bright red. A black dance band was playing and Henri Salvador sang there every night. Everyone looked so happy and on the dance floor couples were entwined or leaving together. I'd have been terribly impressed if I'd gone there alone or with a friend, but going there on Rubirosa's arm made me feel like I was stepping into the history books!

I realized I wasn't really dressed for the occasion ... My orange skirt, charcoal cashmere sweater and spool-heeled shoes (1955 style) didn't exactly look 'high fashion', but I didn't care. I danced and talked and laughed: I walked tall on my little heels, and in my sweater I felt more chic than a marquise in crinolines. We were going round to his place for one last drink. On the way, he explained his art of living: 'Don't ever waste your time with people you don't like, it's just not worth it and it won't get you anywhere. But waste as much as you want with people you do like.'

'But you can't always see just the people you like!'

'Of course you can, that's exactly what I do!'

I thought to myself that he was one of the few who could ...

At eight o'clock in the morning, we arrived at his place, going in through the kitchen door. Between the office and the lounge we went through the linen store and then down a long corridor lined with a multitude of boots and shoes, all standing to attention, waxed and polished. A real guard of honour. Rubi rang the bell, and a footman appeared: 'Monsieur?'

'Bring us some rice and pimento.'

We ate our rice and pimento and then finally at half past ten we went to bed. He said to me: 'You should live it up for four consecutive days, and afterwards take twenty-four hours complete rest.'

Since he'd slept the day before, our party really did last for four days; we rose at five in the evening and went to bed at ten in the morning. The fifth day, I left him taking some exercise in his boxing ring, which was fixed up in one of the lounges, and returned to my everyday life ...

He stuck by me faithfully until his death, and we were to share an exceptional closeness. He brought the Parisian smart set to the rue de Beaujolais, then to the rue du Four, then to Jimmy's, and I had only to remember the lessons he'd taught me to know how to keep them there. I never stopped learning from him, and when I told him about my various plans he'd always tell me: 'Do whatever you want, but remember it's the quality that counts, whether it's people or things.'

And how often I heard him say to friends who wanted to drag him off somewhere else: 'Go on. I'll wait for you here.'

Of course he didn't spend his whole time in my clubs, but he did open lots of other doors for me, always as a friend, and with great delicacy of touch. I often saw him chatting to lonely, unattractive women, giving them a moment's sense of being courted and desirable. I'll always remember one particular evening when, faced with a club that was practically empty, he calmed my anxiety with these simple, true words: 'Don't move, don't change. If you remain sure of yourself, and if you always give your best, you'll end up eclipsing all the others. Don't follow fashion, become a classic.'

He advised me not to go anywhere else in the evenings, and he gave me a feeling for mystery, a feeling for perfumes and the sense of how to create a party atmosphere, and how the mix of perfection and transience worked. He was my Pygmalion.

'With charisma like yours, you could go international,' he said one day. 'The foreigners I bring here want to see more of you. One day you'll go to their countries too.'

'Why don't we go into partnership?' I suggested quickly.

'No, no, my job's to pay for it.'

And it was true that no one else was ever allowed to pay while he was there. I could never treat him to a bottle of champagne.

Thus, Rubirosa played a very important role in my career, and it was partly due to him that I understood what my own character was to be, and what my ambitions were; to make the night sparkle and to become, as far as I could, a sort of high priestess of the here and now. The best thing is surprising people, knowing that tomorrow it will all be forgotten. The moment, the sparkle, the glamour, the sensation: tomorrow I had new things to think about, and happily, so did everyone else.

Like his friend Aly Khan, Rubi was to die tragically. At eight o'clock one morning in the Bois de Boulogne his car smashed into a tree. He had won his last polo cup the evening before.

Rubi came into my life only shortly before Françoise Sagan. Her affection and her presence were to make a deep impression on my life at the rue de Beaujolais, and later at the rue du Four and Jimmy's. She was already a legendary figure, having published *Bonjour, Tristesse* at the age of nineteen. The press hounded her wherever she went. When she came in with Philippe Charpentier, whom I had met in Juan-les-Pins, I was immediately intrigued by her and quickly won over. She walked shyly, without a handbag, her head slightly bowed, fragile and melancholic.

'Regine, do you know Françoise?'

I'd just finished her novel and I replied: 'Bonjour, Françoise.'

She said hello very gently, with her head on one side. She stayed for an hour, two hours, and left as she came, smiling, with her head on one side. She came back again the following night with a group of friends, and the night after that, and almost every evening for a long time afterwards.

We became very great friends, and always got very emotional when we remembered our first meeting. At that moment, we had both found something far far better than any ordinary amusement or pleasure in each other's company. What we had found was a shared space, a refuge against the knocks (there would be plenty), a real unbreachable little fortress. Many years later, she talked about that moment during an interview I did with her for *Paris-Match*: 'You said hello, and I knew at once that I belonged to your family. It was like finding a sister. I felt at ease. No harm could come to me with you. That was very important at the time, because people were driving me crazy with their photos and their autographs ...'

The sense of calm and of being protected that she'd felt near me encouraged her to ask me a little favour: 'Do you mind if I bring the photographers here? They want to do an interview, with pictures, and I think the best place to do it would be here.'

So the journalists came, they grilled her, they took their pictures, and then spread the word that the only place Françoise Sagan liked to go was *Chez Régine*. Soon everyone knew that the author of *Bonjour, Tristesse* had made friends with me and made her nest at my club.

One day at seven a.m. I asked her to help me in return: Eddy Barclay wanted me to write the recipe for dancing the cha-cha for a record called 'How to dance the cha-cha'. So there we both were, pens in hand, noting down in the best French, and in the minutest detail, how the steps went. That night, we ended up at the Tabou, eating chips.

It was a fact that people didn't say they were going to the Whisky à gogo any more, but *Chez Régine*. No one could dispute it (including my boss), and I was not a little proud of this almost overnight success. It didn't stop me, like an idiot, still being on a fixed salary: fifty thousand francs a month, not a sou more. So I asked Pacini to put my wages up. He didn't see why he should: he had too many expenses, he said. The only presents he gave me were a few train tickets for Cannes. André Saunier, the manager of the Carlton, gave me a discount. In short, the rue de Beaujolais had been first and foremost a moral victory for me.

My purse may not have been very full, but my heart was quite empty, and my bed crowded. If they took me home as far as Porte

Dorée, why not stay? I was having a good time too. Suzanne, who came to clean two or three times a week now, thought me very fast, but actually she quite liked it. Finding someone new in a lady's bed each morning when that wasn't her chosen profession set her imagination running riot and soon we just roared with laughter over the succession of similar yet subtly different breakfast times.

I kept up my acrobatics with Jacques Charon, Robert Hirsch and various other actors from the Comédie-Française who came next door to dance the cha-cha or the mambo after eating at La Régence. I still danced with a glass on my head, and some evenings I managed my *tour de force*, which was to lie down on the ground and pick up a handkerchief with my teeth. This circus trick impressed everyone.

Summer came and Paris emptied. In August, Pacini asked me to go down to Cannes and look after the Whisky à gogo there. It was the first real discothèque in Cannes, and it hadn't taken off at all. It was a disaster. Even Cannes residents preferred to go down to Juan-les-Pins. I went down. I stayed with Paul and his wife in their villa above the club, and not far from Palm-Beach. It was tragic to see their beautifully appointed club (one part outdoors with a garden, bar, tables and chairs, and the other part traditional and indoors) doing so badly. I got an idea.

'Listen, Paul, we've got to do something. Let's invite lots of friends for two or three consecutive evenings, to fill the place up and make a lot of noise. But let's keep everyone else we don't know out — whoever they are. We've got to make a hell of a row to pull the crowds, then turn them away.'

'Do you think they'll ever bother to come back? They'd be too discouraged!'

'What have we got to lose?'

We had nothing to lose. So I invited all my friends from Plage sportive (it was the fashionable beach then, and still is now). We packed them in, and I closed the door. I more or less locked it too. Very quickly, other people started turning up. I opened the spy-hole.

'Can we come in?'

'No, it's a private club, and in any case we're full up.'

'How can we get in?'

'I don't know. You'll have to come with some friends who are members.'

'But listen, just tonight, let us in, just for tonight.'

'No, it's impossible.'

I put on this act for several days. More and more people came to the door and soon there was a real queue outside.

The Whisky in Cannes took off, and now it was the crowd from Juan-les-Pins who came to us. The summer was wonderful, bathed in the glow of this unexpected success. I kept an eye on Pacini, who still didn't offer me an increase, and looked after the garden bar all through August; at the beginning of September I went back to Paris.

The rue de Beaujolais was going well, but we had competition from a new club, the Black and White, run by a handsome young black called Samba. He'd been a waiter at the rue Robert-Etienne, and was to have a long career himself. As for the club in rue Robert-Etienne, it had well and truly folded.

Needless to say, Pacini was now delighted with the rue Beaujolais. We opened up another cellar, which doubled the length of the second one. We put loudspeakers in every corner, to make the sound carry, but left the lino dance floor as it was. There was a bit more room for dancing between the tables, which meant they didn't get knocked over quite so often: they were light wooden tables which did a legs-up display the moment anyone jogged them.

It became impossible for me to serve even a small number of customers, and I let my waiters do it; there were now three of them. I concentrated solely on creating the right atmosphere, letting people in and keeping people out: I carried on throwing out trouble-makers myself, dishing out the odd punch as occasion demanded. I always did that job myself, never asking a waiter to do it. It was more efficient that way: when I got angry, the barmen said, there was no one in the world who could get rid of people faster than I could.

Pacini and I weren't so close now. He couldn't stand hearing 'We're going to Régine's', everywhere he went: he didn't feel he was his own master any more, and with good reason, because as far as everyone was concerned his club was really mine. Later, after we'd parted company, he said: 'And to think she was once just a cloakroom attendant at my club!'

And he believed it!

But after leaving the rue de Beaujolais and before starting at the rue du Four, there was a crazy, crazy chapter in my life called Jean-Claude.

9

Jean-Claude

Summer 1955. Paris to Cannes in twelve hours flat was quite a feat for a novice, especially in a Renault Dauphine ... I had just learnt to drive and I'd bought the car with the insurance money from an accident I'd had in a friend's car. Having hardly stopped *en route* I arrived completely exhausted at Plage sportive, where I'd arranged to meet some friends, including Charron and Hirsch, and a whole happy band I was sure of having fun with during my two weeks' working holiday.

Desperate for a rest (it was about five o'clock) I flung myself on a mattress under a parasol — to protect my pale, sensitive skin, which turns lobster-pink in the sun. I was just drifting off when I heard someone whooping like a savage to the accompaniment of a throbbing outboard motor. All around me people started running, women were screaming. The boat had ploughed straight up onto the sand, scaring the daylights out of everybody. I looked, and saw what appeared to be a madman on the boat, roaring, a real he-man. Just near me, the redoubtable Madeleine, who ran Plage sportive, shouted: 'Knock it off! Where do you think you are?'

A man near us bellowed over to the fellow: 'Enough, Jean-Claude, you understand, that's enough! I'll burn that boat of yours, do you hear, I'm going to burn it!'

He completely lost his cool, while a child with him, in tears, was begging him: 'Calm down, papa! Papa, calm down!'

The young hulk, an Elvis Presley lookalike, was having great fun, as were the other boys and girls on board the boat with him. It was very funny, as far as they were concerned. Soon the Adonis jumped down from the boat and started singing and clapping, kicking up sand in time to the beat. Of course everyone, including me, got showered with it. That was the last straw. Fuming, I charged over to the big show-off and slapped him hard, twice. He stopped dead, went rigid, and I saw a wild, murderous look in his eyes.

'When you've quite finished annoying everybody, you lout! I came here for a rest, not to get myself killed by an outboard motor.'

This Jean-Claude was dumbstruck: a woman giving him an earful like that! I later learnt that no one had ever dared say anything to him for fear of the consequences. A crowd gathered round to see what sort of mincemeat he'd make of me. But instant reprisals seemed to be beneath him, so I took the chance to retire to my corner and dropped back onto my mattress.

My little performance was greeted with loud approving noises from all around me and once our Jean-Claude had departed on his boat I said to Madeleine: 'If you want to keep your customers, you'll have to watch out for yobs like that.'

'He's a crazy fellow, terrorizes everyone, but he doesn't mean any harm; he's great fun, a real live wire. The poor baron's scared stiff . . .'

'I tell you he's a thug. And who's this baron?'

'Baron D, the one who shouted that he was going to burn the boat.'

That evening I started work at the Whisky and I saw this Jean-Claude again, giving me extremely unfriendly looks. He came to the club every night of the two weeks I was there, and each time I saw him I thought to myself: 'That's someone I never want to bump into on a dark night . . .'. I saw him on the beach, too, where his silence was very much appreciated . . . In actual fact he was plotting his revenge, gleaning various bits of information about me from the girl he was going out with at the time, who knew me vaguely.

Without suspecting a thing, I returned to Paris and shortly afterwards the same girl turned up at the rue de Beaujolais with three fellows in dinner jackets.

'Hello, Régine. I'm waiting for my fiancé, he's meeting me here.'

'I didn't know you were engaged.'

'Oh, yes, to a divine boy, I couldn't begin to tell you, he's so funny, he's . . .'

You know the sort of things girls say in these situations. I answered, non-committally: 'Oh good, as long as he's nice, that's the main thing.'

In case she missed her betrothed in the vast premises she waited right there at the foot of the stairs. Shortly afterwards, the door opened and someone came in. I heard the girl say: 'But Jean-Claude, I've been waiting for over an hour. Where have you been?'

Astonished, I turned round: it was none other than the show-off from the beach!

'Régine, do you know Jean-Claude?'

I did what I always do when I don't want to know or acknowledge people: I made no reply. Leaning towards me slightly, he said: 'Bonjour, Mademoiselle.'

I still didn't answer. He was in a dinner jacket, smiling, handsome, and it was all extremely irritating. He ordered a bottle of whisky and wrote his name on it. There was absolutely nothing I could do. He was behaving quite perfectly, and I could think of no reason whatever to sling him out. But I had a quiet word with the girl and told her what I thought about her 'fiancé' coming to my club. She replied: 'He's told me all about that day on the beach, and I know you don't like him. But he'd had far too much to drink that day. You know, he didn't want to come, he thought you'd throw him out. He knows what you're like. But I've been going out with him for two months now and I can assure you that he's a very quiet boy.'

Quiet ... In Paris maybe, but not in Cannes. In the end he came to the club every other night for a whole month, with some friends and his girlfriend, and they drank bottle after bottle. Even so, each time I told my waiters (discreetly) to put them downstairs. (That's what I did when I didn't want to see too much of someone during the evening.) His girlfriend asked me twice if I'd teach her 'fiancé' the cha-cha. Both times I told her she could teach him herself. And he only had to watch, after all; I spent the whole night dancing.

They both became regulars, Jean-Claude was always very polite, very nice, very quiet ... I didn't try to find out who he was or what he did. I simply noticed that occasionally he was with some attractive and amusing homosexuals. One night, I was close to his table when he got up and said, as if he wanted to have done with an old quarrel: 'You know, I am terribly sorry if I upset you that day, but I beg you to forgive me and stop hating me for it. I really would love to learn the cha-cha, and I'd be so happy if you'd teach me.'

140

By now it was a habit. I told him I wasn't a cha-cha teacher and advised him to enrol at the Beraduc School, where shy people who didn't dare take the plunge without knowing all the steps went for lessons.

He wasn't a bit pleased, needled even. His fiancée tugged at his arm, but he brushed her away, and I went back to the bar.

About an hour later, I went to La Calvados, where I'd arranged to meet some friends. It was one of the restaurants where night-clubbers met in the early hours to eat dishes from all over the world and to have one last drink. We listened to tunes on the guitar and also to the marvellous pianist who, thirty years later in 1985, was still playing there . . . It was one of the great places to go in Paris and, what's more, has remained so. I was sitting with my friends (eating my habitual diet of ham and salad, drinking tea) when the waiter brought over a bottle of champagne and said: 'It's from the gentleman at the bar, Mademoiselle.'

I looked over at the 'gentleman' at the bar and told the waiter: 'Take the bottle back, please.'

He obeyed. Jean-Claude asked him to try again with the bottle. I sent it back yet again. The poor bottle went back and forth several times. The waiter (Luciano — he worked for me later on) said with his Italian accent: 'Look, I'm not walking up and down with this bottle all night! What have you got against the fellow? He looks nice!'

'Oh all right, leave the bottle here then. But I'm not drinking it.'

At a distance, Jean-Claude was smiling and toasting me. Was he doing it just to get on my nerves or what? My friends were leaving, so I went too, and he barred my way: 'Come on, don't you think this has gone far enough? You're not going to hold it against me for the rest of your life, are you? I've been on my best behaviour, you must admit.'

Looking at him I started to feel that I'd be ready to admit anything he liked. But I made do with a rather frosty: 'All right then, we've stopped being angry . . .'

'Can I take you home, then? Your friends have gone, I think . . .'

'No, thank you, I've got my own car.'

'Take mine, and I'll take yours. I'll bring it back tomorrow.'

I laughed and said no, but because it was just the sort of silly idea I liked I probably didn't sound as though I meant it. We walked a few steps towards his famous orange-and-cream open-topped Chevrolet. It knocked spots off my Dauphine.

'How on earth am I supposed to drive that thing?'

It was eight o'clock in the morning.

'A doddle, it's an automatic.'

He saw me pull a face and threw in some bait he knew I'd rise to (not difficult to do in those days): 'I bet you wouldn't know what to do with it!'

I swallowed it, of course: 'You must be kidding. I can handle anything!'

I switched on the ignition, and the engine turned over, but the car ground to a halt after a few yards and was impossible to get going again. Exasperated, I left the bloody machine where it was and ran back to my Dauphine. Gone! He'd already driven it off! And I didn't even know his address ... I hunted in the car and in the glove compartment. Nothing. Did I feel stupid! All I could do was jump into a taxi and go home, furious to have been trapped by my own pride.

Three days went by, no Jean-Claude, no car. And I still had his keys. Eventually he reappeared.

'Where's my car?'

He smiled: 'I don't know why you're so worried about your car, I'm not worried about mine ...'

'Well, you should be! It's been on the zebra crossing by La Calvados for three days now!'

'How come?'

'Because I didn't feel like driving it.'

He didn't seem very pleased and said: 'But I've brought yours back intact, it's right outside, washed and cleaned ...'

'The Chevrolet ought to be pretty clean by now too, because it's been raining non-stop and I had no idea how to put the roof on. You should have explained ...'

I laughed and so did he. I went on: 'I wanted to tell you, but I didn't know where you lived.'

'Yes, and I should have given you the papers for it, too.'

'Well, yes, exactly, and if I'd been stopped?'

And then I started berating him! He cut me short: 'You're utterly impossible, quite odious, and you wholly deserve the reputation you've got!'

'I beg your pardon. What reputation's that?'

'Everyone says you're a prize shit, and they're absolutely right!'

'What a little jerk you are! Cretin!'

We tried to shout each other down, but our hearts weren't in it.

In the end, it made us both rather sad, and we ended up talking all night instead. At dawn, he said he'd take me back home in my car.

'No, why don't you go and get yours?'

He went off, and came back with one very wet car, the upholstery saturated, its windscreen covered in parking tickets ... It didn't seem to worry him: he had friends in high places who could get him off. Then suddenly he came out with: 'I'm in love with you, you know. At first I only wanted *you* to fall in love with me and then when I'd got you where I wanted you, I was going to give you the boot — to pay you back for Cannes, of course.'

'Who's telling me you've given up the idea?'

'You'll have to believe me.'

I did. For a whole week he took me out to all sorts of places, sent me flowers, the works. After all my trumpeting about being independent, I let him spoil me. He confessed to me one day that he'd been on drugs for five years but had completely kicked the habit all on his own. It was true. He was twenty-four; I was twenty-five. He was in love; so was I. People started telling me: 'Be careful, he's the wrong boy for you!', but I took no notice of what they said. Our love affair was destined to be stormy and passionate.

Six foot three, thirteen and a half stone of solid muscle, beautifully proportioned, with pale violet eyes, chestnut brown hair with blond highlights, an irresistible little mouth, that was Jean-Claude. Some of his friends nicknamed him 'Dimples', because of his smile. Other people thought he was a hoodlum because he got into fights so often ... To my mind he seemed to be trying to prove something, but what I didn't know.

I knew that when he was sixteen he hung around Saint-Germain-des-Prés, then he lived with an actress and mixed with a very 'in' crowd. After he'd finished with drugs, he started drinking. His parents were quite old when he was born and they had spoiled their surprise son, giving him a free rein. They lived in Guadeloupe for many years.

For three or four months, I thought I knew all there was to know about him. He used to say: 'Do you need money? Here ...'

And he'd give me some. He seemed to have plenty. He took me to the most expensive places, bought me expensive dresses. He gave me his American car. No one had ever given me presents like that before. What's more, he assured me that he craved a well-ordered, quiet life, and that he wanted to help me cope with my professional responsibilities, which were more and more pressing.

He announced our engagement to his parents, and took me to meet them. They had a beautiful house on the banks of the Marne, near La Varenne. His father was sixty-eight, small and slight. His mother, who was younger, went into raptures when she saw her son. They were well-bred, distinguished, upper middle class people.

He was such a madcap, so spontaneous, whimsical, and charming, and he loved me so much that he couldn't bear to be parted from me for a moment. When I took a bath, he washed me, and was forever making up new gags to make me laugh. He had a violent temper, and insisted that everyone respect me. He monopolized me; everything became larger than life, out of proportion, and absolute. I started rather neglecting the rue de Beaujolais. The dream lasted for four months.

His pals (Baron D was still among them) turned up at the club now and then. I didn't particularly like them. Jean-Claude didn't much like my friends either, but he knew how to be pleasant to the men and considerate to the women. As soon as his friends appeared, I noticed a change in him, as if he was on the defensive. He arranged it so I wouldn't have to spend too long on my own with them, and then when we did sit together with them, a heavy, unnatural silence fell between them. As for Baron D himself, he never said a word.

One day Jean-Claude said: 'I'm in the throes of selling an antique shop with a friend of mine, you know, and I'd like to go round and collect the stuff which belongs to me.'

'When?'

'Right now.'

'But it's six in the morning!'

'It doesn't matter, we'll go straight away. It'll be a laugh.'

I was used to his hare-brained schemes and went with him, unconcerned. We went over to rue de Miromesnil in his car. There was a grille over the front of the shop.

'Shit,' he said, 'I've forgotten the keys! Never mind.'

He took a tool of some sort out of the boot and forced the lock. (Did I mention he was a handyman?) He did it all so naturally that I didn't ask questions. I simply said it was a shame to break it when we could come back next day.

'No, no, it doesn't matter!'

We went in. Three minutes later he'd moved an enormous rug and a sofa out onto the pavement.

'That's great, we'll put them in your flat. They'll look very nice.'

144

'But they won't go with my flat at all.'

I'd swapped my conjugal Louix XVI for modern furniture.

'Yes, yes. We'll change the whole lot!'

Just as he started loading the rug and the sofa onto the car, it started raining.

'This is stupid,' I said. 'We'll ruin them. We can't close the roof.'

'It doesn't matter! It doesn't matter!'

He seemed to be having such fun, and I thought, well, after all it's his problem, not mine, and we departed, leaving the shop door open: he didn't even pretend to close it. I knew he'd had rather a lot to drink that night, but even so I thought he'd gone a bit too far: 'You shouldn't drink so much, you know!'

'I know,' he said with a big grin, 'but I'm celebrating something, you wait and see. Things'll be great from now on.'

Completely euphoric, he drove at top speed towards Porte Dorée.

'You know,' he said, turning to me at a red light (one of those he didn't jump), 'there are some people around who don't like me. So if you hear any nonsense about me, tell me, won't you?'

'Why do you say that?'

'Oh, just because ...'

I could feel that something wasn't quite right, but I didn't try to find out what. He had become so much a part of my life that I could not imagine anything that might be serious enough to come between us. He even got on well with Suzanne, which was not easy at the best of times. They had lived in the same area at one time, and shopped at the same grocer's; it was something they had in common, and she absolutely adored him. She still laughs every time she talks about him. People who make you laugh are so rare; people for whom life is one long gag, and a harmless one at that ... Jean-Claude was one of them ...

We unrolled the rug and moved the sofa in. It didn't look very good: 'You see, Jean-Claude, it just doesn't look right ...'

'It doesn't matter, they'll come in useful later on; we'll get a flat on avenue Victor-Hugo, buy some more furniture, and then we'll get married. You don't fancy getting married next month, do you?'

We had little conversations like that from time to time, but didn't talk about it very seriously. I wanted to marry him, he knew that, but he also knew I wanted to wait a bit.

'That's a bit too soon, we've only been together four months.'

'I know what I want, and I know we'll be happy. Anyway, I'm going to sell the house in the country.'

'Which house?'

'The one at La Varenne. My mother decided to sell it, and I'm getting half the proceeds. I'll be able to buy a flat. I'll give you the money tomorrow, you keep it for the moment.'

'All right.'

And indeed, next day he gave me a million francs. It was a huge amount of money. I looked at all those banknotes with a certain surprise.

'Take it,' he said, 'it's yours.'

'Listen, why don't you keep it yourself? Put it in the bank.'

'No, no. It's for you.'

I did keep the million, and used it partly to finance my club in rue du Four, with Jean-Claude's agreement of course. It didn't stop people saying I was keeping him, though, which on my meagre salary would have been difficult.

After he'd given me the money, he just disappeared, as he sometimes did, for the whole day. He would say, 'I'll be back in a couple of hours,' and then he'd come back six, seven or eight hours later. When he got back this time, he sat down on the carpet in his suit and told me the following story: 'I have been having a long discussion with my parents. You know, as well as the house, they're sorting out the inheritance problems. There's some land in Guadeloupe ... banana plantations ... Let's go there for our honeymoon, shall we?'

I let myself be lulled by his stories. What could be more romantic than banana-trees by moonlight, when you're stuck with noise, smoke and little flashing lights? He told me I should leave the Whisky à gogo and start up a club of my own: since people came to see me, they'd come all the more when I was captain of my own ship. I knew it too, and I'd been thinking about it for a long time, but I was happy to have him tell me and sound enthusiastic about it.

Four days after he'd given me the million, and ten or so after the trip to the antique shop, the doorbell rang. Jean-Claude wasn't in; I opened the door. It was Baron D!

'Régine, my dear, how are you? I haven't seen you for ages ...'

He treated me to a bitter little smile which wasn't worth having. I really did not like that man.

'Hello. Do you want to come in?'

'Yes, please, I've come for a little chat with you.'

'That's very nice. But what do you want a little chat about?'

I had decided not to make myself agreeable.

'I wanted to talk to you about Jean-Claude. You know I'm very fond of him. He's like a son to me.'

'That's very nice ...'

'Oh, what a lovely rug,' he said admiringly.

'Do you really think so? I can't stand it myself.'

'Really? I can see you don't know how much it's worth,' he said with a pinched expression.

'No, I've no idea how much it cost, and I don't really care. Have you come here to discuss carpet prices or what?'

'I see, if that's the way you want it, I'll come straight to the point: everything you've got, the rug, the money, the car, all of it, it's me!'

'What do you mean, it's you?'

'I mean it's mine! The inheritance, the house they're selling, the banana plantation, the whole lot!'

His aggressive manner got on my nerves and I said: 'Get out before I kick you out!'

He got up and snapped in his high falsetto voice: 'What a nasty little bitch you are!'

Here we go! Before I could come back at him he fired a volley of choice little phrases, and they hurt: 'I can tell you a thing or two about your perfect romance, your grand idyll! I'm not the only one in the race you know, there are others, especially Marc, whom you certainly know, whom you smile at and then stab in the back. All the dresses, and everything else that Jean-Claude gives you, it doesn't come from his family at all. I'll tell you where it comes from ...'

It all came pouring out any old how, and it left me dumbstruck. I wanted to kick him out, but at the same time I wanted to know. It's true that I'd been puzzled ever since the episode at Plage sportive, and now, deep down, I knew that what the baron was saying was true. That explained the way Jean-Claude kept contradicting himself when he talked about his family. So the money all came from the baron and from this guy Marc whom I vaguely knew ...

When he'd had his say, I pushed him towards the door.

'Now you can go! And you can take your carpet and your sofa with you, I don't want anything to do with them.'

I was foaming with rage and he started to look scared. He fled shouting: 'It's too bad, I've told you everything and now we'll see what happens. Jean-Claude said he'd kill me if I told you anything.'

I shut the door on him and cried.

Jean-Claude didn't come home that night. He phoned next morning and said sadly: 'I know the baron came to see you. I hope you didn't believe a word of what that idiot told you. He's in love with me, that's true, but I've never had anything to do with him. He only came to see you because he's jealous of you, it was nothing to do with the money really.'

'Listen, I'm not going to see you for a bit, because it's all given me a bit of a shock and I need time to think ...'

'I promise you there's nothing between us. He's in love with me, and he gave me some money, that's all.'

'You're lying, Jean-Claude.'

He carried on trying to salvage what he could. But I was no longer listening. When he told me that the baron only wanted to 'look' at him, I wanted to hang up. I told him again: 'Don't come to the club any more, and don't come round here either. I don't want to see you at the moment.'

'I'll kill those two ...'

'You're not going to kill anyone.'

And I rang off.

For several nights in succession, he drove past the club and sounded his horn. It was instantly recognizable and every time I heard it I'd pause between smiles while my heart missed a beat. When his friends came they treated me to comments like: 'Jean-Claude's in despair; he wants to kill himself ...' Stupid remarks like that had such an effect on me that I realized then how deeply I must have been smitten. I started finding all sorts of excuses for his behaviour. I'd tell myself: 'You accepted the idea that he took drugs, why not accept this too?' Some people said to me with an air of complicity: 'You're not the first one it's happened to, you know ...' Another friend said to me frankly one day: 'You're not telling me you never realized that Jean-Claude was a bit peculiar and completely nuts.'

After a month, Jean-Claude decided that thinking time was over and he turned up at the Whisky and planted himself squarely before me: 'Well?'

We talked a little, I held back a moment, and then said: 'I don't mind starting again, on condition that you tell me the whole story.' And so he began.

When he was eighteen, just after he'd kicked drugs, Jean-Claude found himself utterly lost. He fell into the clutches of this Marc person, who took him in but, although he had a great influence over him, didn't really convert him. After I turned up they neither of them had any hold on him any more, except financially. They were both terrified of him, and for the baron to have come to see me that day, he must have conquered considerable fear. Forking out the whole time without ever even seeing Jean-Claude evidently gave him the courage he needed.

Effectively, Jean-Claude's parents, I later learnt, had no money at all. His father, a high-ranking civil servant now retired, had never had enough, even when he was working, to live in luxury . . . The house at La Varenne wasn't his, but belonged to some cousins, and since they had to move out, Jean-Claude made up the story about it being up for sale.

Then he swore to me that he now wanted to live a normal life, and asked me to have confidence in him.

The days went by, and everything seemed to be settling down. He did seem extremely uptight, though. A boy only had to look at me a bit too closely, especially at the club, for Jean-Claude to intervene. He had it in for everyone, for himself too, and for me. He kept making appalling scenes, for no real reason. He arrived in a fury at the club and shouted in my face: 'I don't know why I've sacrificed all this for you, you don't understand a thing!'

An atrocious scene followed.

Other times he'd say 'Ciao' and disappear with his car. Did he find it hard having less money than before? I'm sure he did.

It was 1956, just before the summer holiday, and I'd just quit the rue de Beaujolais. A friend, an inspector with the drug squad, told me about L'Arlequin, a club in rue du Four which was to let: 'Why don't you go and see the proprietor of La Pergola, the café upstairs: L'Arlequin belongs to him too. You should move over towards Saint-Germain.'

I went to see him and we came to an agreement, on one condition: the customers from La Pergola (quite dangerous types) wouldn't be allowed downstairs: 'I want it to be a members only club.'

'That suits me fine, I won't even come down myself.'

And in fact he only ever came down once.

But there was one problem: the café licence covered the club as well. Since this most picturesque of cafés was closed down sometimes because of trouble with the police, I had to dissociate the two . . . That's where my inspector friend came in useful: he told me not to worry and we came to a sort of gentleman's agreement that I wouldn't get embroiled in the problems at La Pergola. Actually, the café was closed down twice while I was at the rue du Four and my club stayed open both times.

To get the club done up as cheaply as possible I hired Jacky le Marin as foreman; he was a well-known figure round Saint-Germain-des-Prés. A Jack-of-all-trades, he'd shown how well he could work at Jean Castel's. He was never without his pipe, and always wore the same clothes: clogs, bib and braces, sailor's hat — though he'd never set foot in a boat other than Le Bateau Ivre. I spent Jean-Claude's million on doing the place up, and Jean-Claude himself said he'd like to help Jacky with the work.

We took one other workman, and set to. I fetched bags of cement in the Chevrolet, and Jean-Claude, in blue overalls, mixed it. He found an Italian mason called Giovanni from somewhere or other and together we cleaned the walls, painted them white, then midnight blue. It made a change from the original colour, a sort of goose-shit green. We put railings along the walls and at the end put up a little bandstand like they have in parks where a band plays on a Sunday. But we weren't going to play military music or classical concertos of course: it was to be the cha-cha and very soon the twist ...

After his last escapade, Jean-Claude had told me he was going to work at the club, but that he wasn't going to live with me. Of course, after four days, he started coming home with me ... I was quite happy, because we were getting on well: he really got stuck into the work, and wasn't touching the drink either. He took the whole venture to heart and promised he'd run the bar right from day one. But you have to let your hair down occasionally, and that's what he did with his pal Giovanni, who was a real clown too; they got on like a house on fire. They had both caught the painting bug: before they'd even finished on the club, they decided they'd paint the sitting room and the loo at the flat bright red, to keep their hand in.

I had the flu one evening. Jean-Claude told me to go to bed and take it easy. 'We're going to work on the sitting room tonight. So when you wake up tomorrow the room will all be finished.'

I left them and went to bed, delighted with this good news. I woke up again at four in the morning. Not a sound. I got up and went into the sitting room: it was as beige as ever, and completely dead. The wine bottles scattered about on the floor were all dead too: the sheer numbers bore witness to an enormous piss-up. 'Swine!' I said to myself. The phone rang. It was Jean-Claude, or what was left of him.

'You've got to come and fetch us because we haven't got any money. We went out without the keys: they were in your room and I didn't want to wake you. Come quickly.'

He spluttered all this out between two drunken bouts of laughter. I asked him to explain. After swilling down the bottles in the sitting room, they had gone off to buy some more. As everywhere else was closed, they'd gone right over to Gare de Lyon, where they'd found an all-night bistro. They'd decided to drink it there, and had stayed till dawn. Pissed out of his mind, Jean-Claude yelled down the phone: 'Listen! You've got to bring some money because we've found a bloke on a bike and we told him, "there's ten thousand francs for you if you'll take us back to Porte Dorée". I got up on the front, Giovanni got on the back, the bloke was in the middle. Splat! The bike's as flat as a pancake. A real pancake, I mean it,' he insisted, screaming like a monkey. 'Kersplat! So the bloke wants to call the police and they're going to take us down to the station for sure.'

'Go to hell, I'm not coming, I'm ill.'

'But they'll take us to the station!'

On second thoughts, I couldn't afford to have any trouble with the police when we were just about to open the club. The satisfaction of letting them stew for a couple of hours down in the cells wasn't worth the risk. I threw on a coat and went to pick them up.

The man with the bike was just leaving for work when they stumbled across him. It was partly for the ten thousand francs, and partly from sheer terror (Jean-Claude could be very disagreeable when he was tight) that he'd let them get onto the bike. And then 'splat', as Jean-Claude put it. It was hard not to laugh when I saw the result: one Daliesque soft bicycle.

There were discussions about the cost of replacing the bike, I gave him the necessary, and took my two hijackers back to the flat. I left them to sleep it off in the sitting room, and when I woke up around midday, Jean-Claude said: 'You know, we only went out for some fresh air, the smell of paint was getting to us ...'

'Weren't the bottles of wine getting to you too?'

'Oh, don't take it so seriously, when you work hard you sweat, so you need to drink ...'

'I see, well, for your trouble, you can go ahead and paint the loo, right now.'

I shut him in the loo with only a pot of paint for companion, and pushed the furniture across the door. From time to time he'd implore me to let him out, because he said he was going to faint!

151

'Not until it's finished.'

While he was suffocating in the paint fumes, I was telling myself how wonderful he really was, so good-hearted, so mad ... Of course, he *had* promised me he wouldn't drink any more, but that wasn't the end of the world. You can't change your whole lifestyle from one day to the next ...

Two days later and I was still in bed with this wretched flu, when the phone rang. It was Jacky.

'Is everything all right, Jacky?'

'No, it certainly is not! I've had enough, I'm leaving! I'm leaving the whole crazy lot of you!'

I panicked for a moment because if Jacky went now, then the club would never open on time.

'But what's gone wrong?'

'I'll tell you what's gone wrong all right! You know that pipe you gave me, the one I'd seasoned, the really perfect one?'

'Yes, yes, what's the matter with your pipe?'

'I'll tell you what's the matter ... I left it on site yesterday, and got here a bit late this morning because we worked so hard yesterday ...'

'Yes, I know, Jean-Claude was worn out ...'

'Don't mention that boy to me, or the other one either! So I get there this morning, fill my pipe with tobacco, light it, I suck on it ...'

'And then?'

'Then, I suck, and I suck, like an idiot, and nothing happens! They'd blocked my pipe up, the bastards! And you know what with? With cement!'

Next to me, Jean-Claude had taken the receiver and was now choking with laughter. I desperately wanted to do the same but absolutely had to stop myself. I clenched my teeth together and managed to say: 'But that's terrible!'

The more I thought about Jacky with his eyes popping out, sucking to save his life, the more I wanted to laugh. I exclaimed in shocked tones: 'Jean-Claude, was it you who put cement in Jacky's pipe?'

'Me?' he replied loudly, outraged, 'you have my word, it was nothing to do with me! Giovanni did it! I told him not to, but he took no notice!'

Jacky heard it all and then said to me: 'Yes, well, I was going to say, it would have surprised me if a boy like Jean-Claude had done it. Only the day before yesterday he'd been complimenting me on

my pipe; he'd even said what a pleasure it was to smoke a good
pipe. Yes, I'd be very surprised if it was him, really!'

Jean-Claude, still listening, couldn't bear it a moment longer,
and neither could I. But I just had to stop myself from laughing:
'Listen, Jacky, I've still got flu, but I'm going to get up and go and
find that Giovanni and get rid of him!'

'No, no, poor boy, don't do that; he hasn't got anywhere else to
go, don't do that ...'

'You know I really need you at the moment, so I'll do anything to
keep you. You can't just dump me now, Jacky, you know they're
just a couple of jokers, those two ...'

'Yes, yes, I know ... and then there's Arthur, I couldn't leave
him ...'

Arthur! Another of Jean-Claude's little follies! He was totally
mad about animals, and we had creatures all over the house. He'd
bring back hamsters, mice, dogs ... And one day he bought a
monkey, a very unhealthy-looking chimpanzee, which I took an
instant dislike to. There wasn't much in life that scared me, but
Arthur did. Since I refused to have him in the flat, Jacky adopted
him, and treated him quite differently from Jean-Claude: no more
whiskies, but endless bananas instead! Jacky's wife had even kitted
the chimp out like a footballer.

'All right then, I'll stay, I've got Arthur to look after and you
know I'm very fond of you.'

'Jacky, you're a sport ... I'll buy you a new pipe!'

Jacky, his pipe, the monkey and me ...

After begging Jean-Claude not to fool about again with anything
quite so vital as Jacky's pipe, I bought him another one, at vast
expense. We gave it to him the following day and, true connoisseur,
he stroked it lovingly, with a broadening smile.

'I'll try it out tomorrow,' he said, as if to delay the pleasure.

Work got going again. We dug and plastered and painted with
new-found camaraderie. A carpenter joined us, and everything was
going well. The following day, Jacky sat down for a break and got
his brand new pipe out: 'I've got to season this one too,' he said.
'All that work to do all over again, ah well ...'

That's when I noticed my two comedians stifling their laughter.
What was going on now? Jacky was filling his pipe and started off
on one of his speeches: 'You know, Régine my dear, I think you're
very brave launching into all this. It's not easy to get a club going,
but you're right, you've got to take risks in this life ...'

He struck a match, lit the pipe and BANG! A great flame leapt

153

from the bowl, making a noise like firecracker. Jean-Claude and Giovanni had lined the pipe with match-heads! This time I just burst out laughing, and couldn't stop. If Jacky left us now, it was just tough luck.

Looking at that face and that pipe, it might have been the end of the world for all we cared, we were laughing so much.

Fortunately, even after that little tragedy, Jacky still stayed. But the other two hadn't finished playing practical jokes on him by any means.

As it was so cold, Jacky had scrapped his clogs in favour of some good solid crêpe-soled shoes. One day when he was perched up on a stool, putting in some electric cables, Jean-Claude nailed the very edge of one of his shoes to the stool, and then suggested they went for a drink.

'Come on, Jacky, down you come, you've done enough for today.'

Jacky had had his head up inside the roof-space and hadn't noticed a thing.

'Yes, you're right, we've done bloody well! I'm just coming.'

As soon as he tried to move, he was caught off balance, because his other foot refused to follow. Jean-Claude shouted to me to come (I was in the next room).

When I got there I saw Jacky, his foot stuck to the stool, rolling his eyes in utter bewilderment.

We did finish the work in the end. And despite a couple of minor relapses, Jean-Claude behaved himself, and sobered down. He'd worked with a vengeance, knowing how much this club meant to me, to both of us. I was glad of this relative calm, because with all the problems we had in store, I was going to need a clear head and unshakeable optimism.

When I took over the Whisky à gogo in rue de Beaujolais, it was private, but people knew where it was. I was running it, but I wasn't involved with the purchasing side. At the rue du Four, it was different: I had to publicize the place and organize the stock and the accounts as well. With this particular boat I helped to build it, launch it and maintain it. I made contact with representatives of the various brands of whisky (we sold very little champagne), I calculated how many glasses we'd get from each bottle; in short, I took sole responsibility for the financial success of the club.

So, except for the walls, the club was all *mine*. People came in through a terribly narrow door, figuratively speaking too, complete with a spy hole. The door opened for those I chose, and was shut tight against others. The first 'ordeal' over, it was single file, no passing places, because there wasn't space to do otherwise. There was a small landing (where a curtain concealed the dustbins), and then you went down an extremely steep staircase, and into the main room. The décor was rather disconcerting, almost magical as night-clubs went. The room was done up to look like a city square garden, more realistic than the real thing. Instead of upholstered benches, there were real curvy park benches (moulded to fit the human body). They were painted green, as were the railings on the walls and the little bandstand. Rather surrealistic branches stuck out of the walls, branches we'd picked up in the woods and which Androuchka, a friend of Charles Aznavour, had with immense patience stuck leaves to. It had taken hours, but the result was superb. We'd thought about the lighting very carefully, to create just the right mix of intimacy and mystery.

Everyone came on the opening night, all my clientèle from the Whisky. I'd sent invitations out to the four corners of the city and they'd all come to pay their respects to the *genius loci*. It was a great party. Jean-Claude, in black trousers, tartan waistcoat and black tie, took care of the bar. I'd engaged one new waiter, Giovanni, and one familiar face, Touré, a handsome black man who'd worked with me at the rue de Beaujolais. Odette was on the door, and she knew who was who and only to let friends in. She used to roll cigars at Carol's, and had a real gift for 'picking' the right people; she set the standard for others who were to follow her.

As the days went by I noticed that Jean-Claude's transformation wasn't actually quite complete, and that his bugbears were back. He started scowling again at people he didn't much care for. And because people knew he had a bit of a temper they steered clear of him and I could feel a heavy atmosphere building up. Afraid that trouble was about to erupt, I found it increasingly difficult to be natural, which only made matters worse. I tried to reason with him, calm him down, dispel his suspicions. Whether I was adopting the right approach or not I don't know, but my efforts met with no success. He was jealous, quite pathologically jealous. Some evenings he used to roll down his sleeves and desert his post at the bar saying: 'I'm fed up, I'm off.' Later on, I'd hear, usually through a friend, that he was in such and such a place, blind drunk, or smashing the place up. I'd go and fetch him. I usually found him, unless he'd gone on somewhere else — to one of those dirty or dangerous places he knew — where he'd be brawling. I used to go

155

in all on my own and fetch him back by the scruff of his neck. Sometimes it worked, sometimes it didn't. Our early morning homecomings were not of the most joyful. I'd shout, he'd shout, things went flying round the flat. One day, I was even threatened with expulsion from the flat by the residents' association ... We sorted that one out, but I couldn't bear it any longer and asked myself where it was all leading to.

I don't think I always made it easy for him to apologize. I knew what an attractive and warm person Jean-Claude was when he was sober: everyone adored him. And then sometimes I blamed myself for not being indulgent or flexible enough. It's true that I overlooked some things which other people would not have forgiven, but also that I could really overreact to jokes or trivial remarks. Instead of staying cool, I'd fight back. In some ways, I detested myself for having lost none of the aggressive/defensive mechanisms I'd had as a child, and which still made me behave so irrationally on occasions.

Anyway, the jokes and horseplay multiplied (he still adored practical jokes) and so did our little fights: one night at the Escale in Saint-Tropez, we didn't come to blows but ended up throwing lobsters at each other instead. It was a draw. We were starting on the cutlery when the patron, Félix, cried out: 'Not the knives! Not the knives!'

The problems were exacerbated because I was worrying about the club too. After the triumphant opening night, I realized that I hadn't quite retained all my clientèle from the rue de Beaujolais. It was tough going at the start of the week. Other new clubs had opened at the same time, and not as many people went out as they do nowadays. But thanks to my vitality, my 'dancing lessons' and my 'intellectuals' (Sagan, Bernard Frank, Louis Malle, César the sculptor), things started looking up after a few weeks. People got into the habit of coming in very late for a drink, after they'd been at my great friend Jean Castel's Épi-club. The idea caught on, perhaps because things at the Épi went off the boil a bit. Whatever the reason, the most hardened nightclubbers started coming *Chez Régine* for their last drinks.

Being open on Sunday helped too. It totally exhausted me, but at least people knew that, thanks to me, Paris wasn't quite such a vale of tears that day.

Jean-Claude's escapades and rash impulsiveness were really grinding me down now, and soon there was no avoiding the obvious: it was him or me. One particular evening triggered it off. Jean-Claude had gone off a couple of hours before, and I was wondering

156

when he would come back. It was about the time he usually did return, invariably with a 'Here, meet my best friend'. He had 'best friends' everywhere, who mainly existed as alibis: I wasn't to think for a moment (he was a real stickler about this!) that he might have been hanging about with a girl. And in fact there were no problems in that respect: if a girl gave him her number (as often happened, unsolicited), he'd show me and we'd have a laugh and phone her together.

That particular night, I was getting ready to leave the club (it was five o'clock by now), and just saying goodbye to a friend, when I saw Jean-Claude coming. I looked at him and said simply: 'What are you going to do? I'm off home.'

He didn't answer straight away, but muttered: 'Yes, that's it, we'll go home ...'

I got into my new car (a turquoise Simca 8 convertible) and he got in beside me. I started the car, put it into first, and as I was revving to pull away, he quietly pulled a revolver out of his pocket, pointed it downwards and fired! The bullet just missed my foot on the accelerator. There was no one about at that time of night, except the cabbies waiting outside the club.

'What's the trouble? Anything wrong, Madame? We heard a shot!'

'No, no, it was the car, something must have blown ...'

'Oh, okay, do you need a hand?'

'No thanks. I'll just leave the car here, I'll pick it up tomorrow, thanks.'

Before they came over, I'd had time to snatch the gun out of Jean-Claude's hand and put it under the seat, shouting, 'Where the hell did you get that?' I wasn't so much surprised that he had a gun, because he often wandered about with a shotgun or a rifle. He was a crack shot, and loved hunting. But I was extremely surprised that he'd shot at me! I didn't like his gun-toting habit at the best of times, but being cast in the role of rabbit was downright sinister.

I got out of the car, grabbed the keys and took a taxi to a hotel. I went back home again at about midday, and Jean Claude phoned me at about six p.m.: 'I must have been mad, I was jealous, I thought you were kissing the guy at the door. But you weren't, were you ...?'

'Look, Jean-Claude, enough's enough. Things have gone too far, we're through.'

'But no, listen, you'll see ...'

'I'm not going to "see" anything, and it's all over now, finished.

I'm leaving at the weekend for three months on the Riviera and I'm shutting up the flat.'

'I see, so you're throwing me out?'

'Take it how you want, but in any case I'm leaving.'

I'd decided I'd had enough heartache.

Two very pleasant young men had suggested I take over a club of theirs in Saint-Tropez for the summer. We'd sorted out the fundamentals: they owned the place, but while I was in charge it would be my club and I would run the show my way. After the shooting incident, I hoped that getting away from it all would sort me out and help me decide on a final break. I left Jean-Claude in Paris. I was soon to learn that he'd immediately started seeing his former friends again and was in Cannes with them once more.

It was purgatory going to the beach. I was enormous and unrecognizable. I weighed thirteen stone: the result of three years with Jean-Claude. I started work. A fortnight after opening, one of the proprietors punched a customer. I didn't like it at all and told him: 'Listen, if you've got scores to settle, you can do it outside. You're *chez Régine* here, so no fighting.'

'It's my club!' he retorted.

I replied: 'You're dead right it's your club ... all yours, you can keep it.'

I stopped the music, retrieved the float, took hold of my barman, announced that I was going to L'Esquinade (the club which was then going strong), and walked out leaving the boxer out for the count.

But it wasn't enough to make me quit Saint-Tropez. On the contrary: for the first time in years I thought I'd hang out quietly for a bit. The club in Paris had stayed open and was being looked after by Touré. The only problem was that I was sharing the 'furnished' flat that I'd rented with hoards of cockroaches and lizards, which weren't in the original contract!

I was so glad to be alone at last that I flatly refused to share my solitude with cockroaches, so I moved. I rented a converted garage out in the country, with a double bed and a shower. A most charming painter called Bernard Lignon, with whom I got on very well, lived in the house next door. I decided to relax and enjoy life for the two months I had left. It was about time. I went out every night and danced, and very gradually became my old self again, no fears, no hang-ups. I listened with half an ear to the news people gave me of Jean-Claude, but very soon I had fresh, first-hand information: the door-bell rang, I opened it, and there he was! I looked at him. I looked for a little too long. He had a contrite air, and was breathless as though he'd run all the way from Cannes. We got back together. We split up. In between times, bad scenes, rows, shouting-matches, all over again. My poor neighbour couldn't sleep for it all; no one had ever broken quite so many plates in one garage before ... Since Jean-Claude thought he'd stay on in Saint-Tropez, I decided to leave, and I went back to Paris a bit earlier than planned to get ready for the new season.

The people I'd met over the summer came to the club, bringing new customers with them. Everything came together very well and I had no cause to regret my long vacation. As soon as he got back to Paris, Jean-Claude announced he was going to go it alone in a club of his own. I didn't for one moment think he could possibly make a success of it, and I knew that, in turn, it would widen the gulf between us. So much the better.

In the early days, he phoned every night, around three or four, to find out when I was expecting to get back home. I'd tell him and he'd come and sleep at the Porte Dorée. But little by little, he 'forgot' to phone me, and wouldn't get back home till midday or early afternoon. Of course, I didn't say anything, hoping that it would all end quietly, like that ... I listened to what people told me about the stupid things he did at his club (in rue Sainte-Anne, it later became Le 7): he sank whole bottles, chucked customers out, fired shots at the ceiling ... A kindly soul told me one day that he was often seen around with a celebrated stripper. 'She goes and joins him every morning.' I still played dumb, only too glad to feel his vice-like grip loosening after so long.

One evening, some friends dragged me round to his club, and I found him with his usual bunch of friends, the stripper clinging round his neck. As he'd told me a thousand times he'd love me forever and that there was no one else, etc ... he looked a bit put out, and said: 'Let me explain ...'

'There's nothing to explain, we've just popped in for a drink.'

Non-plussed that I didn't say anything, even though it was the first time I'd seen him actually kissing someone else, the boot was pretty soon on the other foot, and looking at my friends he said nastily:

'And who are these blokes then?'

'If that's how it is, we'll go elsewhere.'

And we left.

Shortly after, he announced that he was planning to live with this girl. I gave him my blessing. All this while, my club was doing very well, and I'd taken on Luciano, the lovely Italian barman from La Calvados. He'd suggested it himself, and his boss had 'agreed', that's to say he wasn't angry with Luciano or me. Luciano and I worked together for twenty years — the perfect partner.

I discovered one day that Jean-Claude was getting married the next morning. The following night, Odette, who was monitoring the door, came downstairs to warn me that Jean-Claude was upstairs and wanted to come in! He was alone. I watched the young bridegroom come down the stairs; white shirt, fitted overcoat, navy blue suit, impeccable tie, very handsome indeed. When he got close to me he said: 'It's all because of you, this bloody mess! I've got married! You should have stopped me! You don't realize what a stupid bloody thing I've done!'

He started drinking, and decided he was going to spend his wedding night at the club, and come home with me afterwards! I told him he'd made a decision (that's the very least one could say) and that he had to stick to it. There I was trying to persuade him not to desert the conjugal nest! I would never have imagined myself saying something like that ... We talked at length and sadly, and in the end he went. I felt utterly drained and would never forget that night.

It was 1959. Jean-Claude had his destiny to follow, and I had mine, each retaining an immense tenderness for the other. During the first few months, I saw him from time to time, and we'd often spend the whole night talking together. He got divorced very quickly, then remarried, and had a little daughter. But by then he was already seriously ill, and one day I had a letter from him saying he was in a sanatorium, penniless. I arranged with his mother for him to have access to the income he had always pretended to have from Guadeloupe; I sent it, without his knowing. For three years running after he left the sanatorium, he sent me a big bouquet of flowers every Christmas. The last time I saw him, he looked monstrous, with his face all swollen up and the end of his nose torn off: he'd jumped out of a window during a fit, disfiguring himself. He died exactly six years after we parted, on an operating table at the Sainte-Anne hospital. He ended up drinking meths, having sunk to the depths with a vengeance. I offered his wife my help. She refused, but added that Jean-Claude had often talked about me. He always said he'd be dead by the time he was thirty.

10

Chez Régine,
rue du Four

I insisted on there being no gaps between the records, and there were to be none elsewhere either: no errors in the accounts, no give-or-take-a-bit over the drinks, no lapses in good behaviour. I was responsible for everything, so everything had to be perfect. From customers I demanded the same high standards I demanded of my waiters, and my staff had to be as classy as my clients. At the first slip-up I simply made a mental note, the second time I'd say something; if it happened a third time I'd take action: the culprit was almost always a client, hardly ever one of my staff.

Everything falls into place, like a child's puzzle. Doing my job is like doing a tricky jigsaw, with similar moments of contemplation, doubt and hesitation. And then suddenly you get it right, find the missing piece, complete the puzzle. Then you can get the show on the road, again.

One night in 1961, two good looking boys arrived at the club, one of whom was currently playing to a packed house night after night at l'Olympia. He was eighteen, wearing a blouson jacket and open-necked shirt. His name? Johnny Hallyday. Hallyday or no, I told him I didn't let people in without a tie. He insisted, but nothing doing: I asked him to leave (in the nicest possible way). I thought it rather a shame because, bar the tie, both of them were appealing and nicely turned out ... An hour later, the two of them came back for a second try, but wearing the most appalling suits: to say nothing of the ties. I sent them away to change yet again, and they came back in their original blousons. Since then, Johnny Hallyday has been allowed in without a tie: beneath his 'hard' exterior he's a real sweetie, with a soft heart. Marc Doelnitz and I made him the star attraction at the party at the Eiffel Tower restaurant to celebrate the thousandth performance of *Patate*, Marcel Achard's play. He met Sylvie Vartan at my club, and she's a great friend of mine too. Both of them became firm favourites and we were all inseparable for the next ten years.

The number of couples who've met in my clubs, then subsequently married, is incredible, there are dozens of them. That's why it's good to make people show the best side of themselves ... and if others can't see what they might be hiding beneath their bow ties or their tiaras, that's their lookout! They'd be just as likely to miss it beneath an apron or an anorak.

Luciano, Giovanni and Bernard kept the revelry under perfect control, they were attentive, smiling and efficient. Louis Malle, Françoise Sagan, and Bernard Frank always came, and so did Rubirosa, Jimmy de Cadaval and their friends, among them Gérard Bonnet who now lives in Marbella. The friendship we all shared by night developed into something life-long. Bernard Buffet was telling me about his first exhibition, just after the war. The day before the private view an ex-deporté, who'd had his entire collection of paintings stolen during the Occupation, came to the gallery, looked round and said: 'I like them all. I'll take them.'

'Which ones, monsieur?'

'All of them, mademoiselle.'

Next day, at the opening, there was not a single picture still for sale. The private view had become a retrospective.

I was under fewer and fewer illusions about the world, and about people in general, but was becoming increasingly interested in both. Thanks to my animal instinct, errors of judgement were rare, and my natural dislikes hardly ever proved unfounded. I was never tired, kept a sharp eye on everything, and listened with both ears. When others wilted I carried on, without missing a moment. And I mean physically as well as mentally. I could sail calmly through the night and always keep my bearings.

In the *Paris-Match* team was a young man I really liked called Paul Chantrel. He was a marvellous horseman and was also to make a brilliant career for himself in publishing. He was handsome, witty and cultivated. He had his leg in plaster the first time he came to the club in the rue de Beaujolais. He was twenty-four, I was twenty-three. It was one of those evenings with 'atmosphere'; I had already ejected a fighting-drunk parachutist who'd forced the door.

162

The para lurched out, defeated, the army in retreat. Paul had watched the scene, every bit as astonished as the para. I didn't want him to leave with too severe a first impression, so I invited them both to dance, him and his plaster-cast, that is. So we struck up a friendship despite a stiff leg and a drunken paratrooper. He actually lived in rue du Four and often came to those memorable all-night parties, which went on till seven, eight or nine in the morning. In that cramped space we danced and danced and danced. In any case there weren't sufficient chairs (by a long way) for everyone to sit down. It was total delirium and the sun, shining brightly outside, was left out in the cold!

I'll have to explain what *Paris-Match* meant in those days. It was a hot-house full of brilliant young people and a Scott Fitzgerald fantasy rolled into one. Huge expense accounts and exclusive, heroic reports from Budapest and Algiers (some journalists died there); a seductive kind of insolence, sports cars hurtling along at full speed à la James Dean, ravishing 'fiancées' (models and socialites), the smartest haunts in Paris; that just about sums up the *Paris-Match* gang. Nothing that could touch high society playboys like Aly Khan, though: the latter really were extremely wealthy, the former just behaved as though they were. But they did possess that magical quality, which is worth millions, called charm. They all helped each other out, and all adored each other, went on café-crawls and binges together (and with me), and got up to all sorts of crazy and grandiose capers.

It was these two or three groups that made Paris the most exciting city in Europe. For these people, in contrast to a Rubirosa, luxury was essentially something you read about in books or acquired on your expense account; so the need to enjoy it, or to mock at it, was doubly pressing. The life of someone like Rubirosa was highly organized, cushioned and, on the surface at least, serene: theirs was totally disordered, sometimes dangerous, often anxious. They were putting on the show entirely for their own benefit. Racing from Castel to Régine, and from Régine back to Castel, they themselves would get lost, as in a hall of mirrors, and would emerge, stunned, at nine o'clock in the morning to catch a plane to New York or take a taxi to Tobruk.

But whether for the dandies or the princes, the Paris we all lived in bore no resemblance to the Paris of today. Can you imagine Rubirosa leaving some Russian bar in Montmartre these days, at eight in the morning, surrounded by musicians who then accompanied him and his party through the streets, collecting tips at every lamppost, with six chauffeur-driven cars following behind! Can you imagine two young men racing their cars at midnight from la Muette to the rue du Four — in reverse gear! That's what a friend of mine did, and it makes you realize just how much of a change has taken place in thirty years. No one used to be ashamed of having money then, or of going out on the town, no one was afraid to leave tips that were bigger than the bill, no one thought it at all strange to eat in a dinner jacket nearly every evening.

Festive occasions are always more sparkling at night than in the daytime, and at my club, as Paul Chantrel put it, the night is more night-like than elsewhere. I try and force people into making the most of themselves. I want people at my club to be better than they are anywhere else, more proud of themselves and the people they're with. I want to make the creatures of the night more beautiful, more glamorous, more deserving of the luck or talent they were born with. There are strictly no drugs, deals or thugs in my club. Of course it could never be just angels who fly by night, but I do ask mine to make sure they fly high enough not to disturb people or involve them in their business. I don't want to change the world; I just want the good times to be really good. That's how they were at the rue du Four.

Why did people have more fun at my place? Because I'd got the mix right: people were quite different from each other without clashing. Or if, occasionally, they did, they managed to hide it. If they couldn't hide it, I showed them the door. Which left me with the people who amused me or pleased me. But they came in all shapes and sizes. One Sunday night, Louis Malle and Bernard Frank were deep in conversation. In came a regular called Maller, who was very rich (or appeared to be) yet hard to place. On his arm was a dancer from the Lido who Louis Malle started eyeing up in such a way as to leave no doubts about his intentions. Wanting to chat up the lovely lady, he asked Bernard Frank to engage this chap Maller in conversation. Bernard, being a good pal, did so, and Louis Malle started talking to the lady from the Lido. Things seemed to be going well when all of a sudden I saw Maller throw a punch at Bernard, who fell backwards off his stool! I came over and berated him. He bit me savagely on the finger, grabbed me by the hair . . . and pulled off my wig! My hair goes incredibly curly and I couldn't get to the hairdresser on a Sunday, so that day I was wearing a superb wig from Alexandre pinned onto my chignon. The wig went flying and landed under a bench. Fortunately a girlfriend of mine, a transvestite in a Chanel suit called Zsa-Zsa Diors, happened to be sitting right there. I shouted out: 'Grab my wig!'

The confusion spread, the table tipped over, the transvestite scrabbled under the bench on all fours. She brandished the wig victoriously and we got rid of the fighter with a little help from the police, who then took us off to the hospital for a tetanus jab.

Bernard Frank, who always took his dog to the club with him, dragged the animal into the van with us and then half way to the hospital asked the police to stop and let it out for a pee. Things were already getting a bit beyond them, and they agreed.

My ex-husband, whom I still saw from time to time, was of the opinion that I was not surrounded entirely by friends (as if I didn't know) and he had been thinking for a long time now that I was neither able nor willing to look after Lionel. From the start of the rue de Beaujolais, he had made up his mind to take custody of him and relieve me of all the expenses: as he never stopped telling me, he now had a good job (he became a brilliant businessman) and wanted to look after his son on his own. I didn't agree to it to start with, and he went to the courts to get Lionel removed from my custody. He won his case and for a whole year I saw my son only once a month.

During that period I embarked on diet after diet, but at that stage these were really nothing more than 'trial runs'. It was after the opening of Jimmy's that dieting really took off. I became quite addicted. As for my customers, I continued offering them whisky cures, straight or with Coca-Cola. No one put Perrier or still mineral water in their whisky as yet. Johnny Walker Red or Black Label was in fashion, ditto Dimple and Black and White. At the rue de Beaujolais it was Vat 69 and Ballantine's ... Never champagne, or very little ... It was not at all the club style.

The way the club was going I was able to indulge my weakness for shoes (I bought pairs by the dozen and in case of fire they would be the first things I'd save). My feeling for shoes was such that I could tell a great deal about people at the club just watching them come down the stairs. The staircase was so steep that from below I saw their feet first and from the way those feet came down the steps I knew what sort of person I would be dealing with:

someone decent or not. I must confess that the system worked better for men than for women: women are more difficult to judge. I've come across harpies with delicate little feet, fine ladies in clogs, and witches in glass slippers.

11

The Twist

Something happened at the Paris Alhambra in April 1961 which was to have enormous repercussions on my career in particular and on the life-style of the French more generally.

With very little publicity, and very small audiences, almost clandestinely, a musical with an American cast had just opened there. I had been brought up on music-hall, and was obsessed by the musicals of Gene Kelly, Fred Astaire, Cyd Charisse and Ginger Rogers, so I made a bee-line for the Alhambra. It wasn't the sort of thing you usually saw in Paris. The show was brilliant, and I was furious (though not in the least surprised) that Parisians hadn't come to see it in greater numbers. So I got myself introduced to the cast and invited them all for a drink that same evening, *Chez Régine*. They duly came, we all had a fantastic evening and I was hardly ever out of their company for the rest of their stay in Paris. And I took a dancer from the cast home with me every night (the same one!) His name was Michael Bennett; later he became very famous and produced two of the best musicals on Broadway, *Dream Girl* and *Chorus Line*. I became like one of the cast. My English was dreadful then, but it didn't seem to matter. I dance, they dance, we dance: dancing is the best language there is, and you don't need an interpreter. I spent almost every evening backstage and never tired of the show, however many times I saw it. By the way, I'm talking about *West Side Story*. There at the Alhambra we were the advance guard of the tens of millions of people who flocked into cinemas the world over to see the film of the same name. Many saw the film as often as I saw the play . . .

I noticed that to warm up before going on stage my friends performed some curious movements. They explained what the movements meant as best they could, but I didn't really understand. My dancer-boyfriend, who spoke a little French, explained it better: 'It's called twist.'

'Twist?'

'Yes, in New York, when kids are fighting and the police come, they turn the fight into a kind of ballet, where they hold back their punches, and make sort of twisting movements. They carry on swaying their hips, with their fists up, as if they're fighting, but they don't hit each other.' My twisting friend went on: 'It inspired a dance called the Twist a couple of years ago, but it wasn't very popular.'

'So there must be some records, mustn't there?'

One of the dancers told me that Chubby Checker had made a couple. I ordered them, and a week later received 'Let's twist again' ...

I could not have envisaged the epidemic that swept the world. If I'd known, and especially if I'd known then what I know now about the music publishing business, I could have made myself a huge fortune in the twinkling of an eye. But I simply wanted to start a fashion and make use of the fantastic opportunity that the *West Side Story* dancers presented. At the club we started dancing to the records. I could see straight away that people were a bit thrown by this new dance, yet, as if pulled by an irresistible force, they kept getting up and having a go. A few days later César, the sculptor, said to me: 'Your gimmick's brilliant. It's going to really catch on. You'll change the world with it.' He was exaggerating a bit, I thought.

In May, I went down to Cannes to open a *Chez Régine* during the film festival. I took the twist with me ... André Saunier introduced me to Georges Cravenne, one of the organisers of the festival. He thought the dance was great too, and every evening he brought me or sent me film stars to teach the dance to. Photographers would be waiting outside the club and everyone started talking about *Chez Régine* and about the twist: the two went together. The first picture and article devoted to the twist appeared in *Nice-Matin*. The article, by Mario Brun, started like this: 'Régine has launched the twist, the dance which is going to take the world by storm ...'

The bush telegraph worked brilliantly, and Cannes night-clubbers twisted the summer away. George Hamilton, Tina Onassis, David Niven, and lots more came in their dozens from Saint-Tropez or Monte-Carlo to find out about the dance 'they couldn't do but had heard all about'. I was fetched in Rolls-Royces to teach the twist to guests on yachts ... Back in Paris I taught Sophia Loren and Anthony Perkins while they were filming *Aimez-vous Brahms*, the Litvak film of the book by Françoise Sagan.

I got my son back all of a sudden, when he was twelve years old. He looked just like me. In fact he looked so much like me that I decided he'd have to go on a diet. I should have been dieting too, but I wasn't bothered. It didn't matter whether I was fat or thin, what mattered was success ...

When I got back to Paris, things had started happening: the twist had taken off and 'Let's twist again', which Eddie Barclay had bought, was selling like hot cakes. Rolls-Royces queued up outside *Chez Régine* and the club was under siege. Everyone had to take their jackets off to dance, and their shirts got all wrinkled ... Jacques Chazot came every night, and he and I performed a much-appreciated little number: we managed to whirl and twist at the same time, and the opera stars that Jacques brought along were all stunned ... The craze spread all over France. Two or three very fashionable night clubs, however, decided that it wasn't 'fashionable' after all, and resolutely refused to play twist records ... It was a fatal mistake: their customers deserted them and went elsewhere to hear the electric guitar chords of the kings of twist. This mania lasted for two whole years.

The longest night I spent was during the filming of *The Longest Day* (in Normandy). Over the Easter weekend, the actors had a four-day break, and they all wanted to spend it in Paris. The stars had all arranged to meet other American actors who were passing through the capital. And they all came and spent the evening and night at the rue du Four. Among them: Robert Mitchum, Robert Wagner, Natalie Wood ... Big John Wayne was there too, and when he kissed me it was one of the most emotional moments of my life. Others included: Liz Taylor, Warren Beatty (who later lived with Natalie Wood and often came to Jimmy's), Shirley McLaine, Eddy Fisher (with whom I spoke Yiddish), George Hamilton ... No director had ever had a set like it. It was as if the whole American film world were appearing as extras *Chez Régine* ...

I had another prestigious but less successful visitor shortly after this, in the person of Ava Gardner, who was brought along by

Claude Terrail. After he left, she stayed at the bar (still in her camel coat despite the heat) drinking beer and whisky. In those days, no other woman would have dreamt of sitting at a bar drinking.

Eventually a waiter sat down with her and they talked together all evening. I saw Ava Gardner again at Françoise Sagan's. Once again she was in an advanced 'beer and whisky' state, and when I started to tell her that we'd met once before she raised her hand at me, furious ... Françoise told me later: 'Ava can be a little aggressive with people she doesn't know very well ...'

Plenty of other, more voluble folk came to the club too: Mel Ferrer, Gene Kelly (the greatest dancer of all!), Audrey Hepburn ... I even danced a tango with Charlie Chaplin.

Not to mention various princes, kings, dukes and consorts, nor Rubirosa, back in Paris after a year's absence and now married to the beautiful, light-hearted, divine Odile. My cast-list was a happy mix of Hollywood, international jet-set and *Who's Who*, unceremoniously crammed together. Above these famous and crowned heads a cavalcade of rats paraded in the false ceiling. The heat was atrocious (there was only one air-conditioner) and drips of water sweated from the ceiling. But people found it all very amusing. Reaching the loo was a major expedition when the club wasn't crowded, but now that journey became a real ordeal. You had to negotiate a cellar passage which was fusty and smelt of coal, avoid bumping into the person making the return journey, climb three steps, open a little door, turn round, go up three more steps and, having got there, it just remained to contemplate the return trip, and with justifiable apprehension.

The proper 'society' blessing was given one night in the person of the Duke of Windsor, ex-King of England, accompanied by his Duchess. I was seven years old when Edward VIII, having hardly mounted the world's most prestigious throne, abdicated in order to marry his mistress, Mrs Simpson, an American divorcée. This new version of an old fairy tale had caught the world's imagination when it happened and by now the Duke and Duchess were living happily ever after in Neuilly.

Both of them were very sweet, uncomplicated, and amusing. They returned to the rue du Four on several occasions and one evening when I was twisting with the Duke a photographer snapped us and the picture appeared in papers the world over.

One day the Duchess invited me to her home for coffee. I told her that people usually invited me for lunch or dinner, and only rarely for coffee. I didn't go, but remained on the very best terms with them both.

So it was that the smartest, most fashionable people deserted their usual luxurious haunts to spend the night in my overheated cellar, sometimes until ten in the morning, sometimes going straight on to the office without a moment's sleep. The phone never stopped ringing with requests to welcome some celebrity or other who was passing through Paris and who wanted to dance the twist with me at my club. Each evening, before opening, we checked under the benches in case the celebrity in question sat on one of the OAS bombs which were going off everywhere in Paris at the time. The twist was to be the only explosion at my place!

It's hard to be as successful as I was without discovering that you have an impressive list of friends. Nothing makes your ratings go up more in the night-clubbers' charts than hosting the Duke and Duchess of Windsor for twist lessons. People whose loyalties wavered between two clubs let the other fall by the wayside in favour of mine, and I gained numerous new 'faithfuls', many of whom were not so very durable. But I didn't have to sift them; time would do that for me. While I was waiting, there was plenty of 'give and take': they were cultivating me for the free whisky at the 'in' club, while I benefited from their wit, gossip-column ratings and style.

Twist-mania reached the States and reporters turned up almost daily to photograph the epicentre of the phenomenon: my legs.

Everything was fine apropos my head and legs, though I was still very overweight. But I was much too excited to follow a diet at all seriously. And anyway, as a gynaecologist friend said to me: 'Stay fat, don't burn up all your calories and you'll never get tired!'

So instead of me getting a complex about it, my body was getting quite a reputation.

Having tried lots of different hairdressers over the years, including Alexandre, I finally decided to get my hair done at home. It made a huge difference, especially with all the phone calls. And for me it was almost as great a blessing as having the ex-King of England come to the club.

In spite of the success, I didn't want to be a slave to fashion or to one particular way of doing things. I knew it wouldn't last for ever, and I began to think about how to keep my clientèle. Because of the twist, people didn't seem to worry about the lack of amenities in the club, but I couldn't keep them much longer in a miniscule turkish bath with one miserable loo for two hundred people. Once the enthusiasm for the twist waned, how was I going to prolong my success? Quite simply perhaps by removing all these people to more chic surroundings where they wouldn't have to take their jackets off to dance; in short, by replacing the cramped craziness of the past two years with something more permanent, solid, elegant and organized.

The problem was all the more urgent because I had competition right on my doorstep, in rue Princesse. Jean Castel had left L'Épi-club in Montparnasse, and I now found our neck of the woods a bit crowded. What's more, the regulars at La Pergola upstairs were getting restless. Because the café stayed open late into the night, there were sometimes 'little' misunderstandings at the door, and a few fights with Odette ... Without asking anyone's advice, on the throw of a dice, I decided to move.

I heard about a strip-club which had closed down a year before, called the Vénus, situated just next door to the old Épi-club: it was a curious coincidence, this criss-crossing of paths with Jean Castel. The proprietor was interested in my proposition and immediately asked how I was going to go about it. I explained and described the club as I imagined it. He liked the idea and we signed a contract which was to last ten years. I rented the flat above the club too. (He also owned the Jockey, a cabaret on the other side of boulevard du Montparnasse where girls dressed as jockeys kissed and whipped the customers. Pretty strange!)

In memory of my evening with Rubirosa at Jimmy's, the club in rue Huyghens, I decided to call my new place New Jimmy's and to decorate it, like the old Jimmy's, in art deco style: Lalique lamps, tinted mirrors and black lacquered walls, to make things sparkle all the more ... and so you'd forget there were any walls at all. The end result was a kind of immense black and gold bathroom, the whole master-minded by François de Lamothe, the great theatre and cinema set designer. It was my first 1930s décor; François did me ten more.

After the short-lived craze called the twist, the long-lived craze called New Jimmy's was about to begin ...

12

Jimmy's Montparnasse

The night before our official opening, a friend, Dick de Surmont, and his wife hosted a private party at the club, which was a great success. The décor met with approval all round: it reminded older guests of the old Jimmy's and the younger people were delighted with the luxuriousness of the art deco style, where faces were reflected in all their beauty. The theme of the evening was 'Black Tie and White'.

The following night it was my own friends' turn (some of them had been at the party the night before and were thrilled to be coming again). Guy Laroche had made me a red chiffon dress. My hair was short with feathery bits over the ears. The Rolls-Royces began pulling up outside, disgorging crowds of people all dying to see the new club. There wasn't room for them all inside, so I had champagne served outside. A journalist happened to notice some members of the Rothschild family waiting patiently in line, glass in hand, and hit upon this detail for an eye-catching headline: 'Rothschilds on the pavement!' The party was a huge success, though not without its tricky moment: around dawn, someone discovered that a mink coat belonging to Gunther Sachs's stunning German girlfriend had been stolen ... by one of this very select band. There were emotional scenes, a search, despair ... Fortunately the coat was insured, and so was I. There was such a crush that we couldn't tell who was coming and who was going.

They raved about it, I'd made it ... I was one step ahead of the music, one step ahead of the twist. Everyone who'd made the rue

173

du Four such a success (the Rothschilds, Kennedys, Guinesses and Patinos) came with me to the boulevard du Montparnasse where they no longer needed to strip off their jackets ... They were joined by the Greek contingent, Niarchos, Onassis, and Goulandris, and a whole host of actors.

I finally moved out of the Porte Dorée apartment and into the one I'd rented above the club, on the corner of rue Léopold-Robert and boulevard du Montparnasse. Just as Joseph had done in Belleville, I too now lived 'over the shop'. Ever since then, if people ask me where I live I always say 'above my means ...' They twig sooner or later, and it sounds good.

Before the move I'd said to Suzanne, my Bretonne housekeeper, who was every bit as clever as she was stubborn: 'Suzanne, it's decision time: either it'll be a success, or a total flop, but whichever, you're coming with me!'

Without a moment's hesitation, she gave up her other jobs to stick with me. Those other jobs must have been few and far between by now because I'd gradually been upping her hours from one a day to two, three, four, and finally five. She had become increasingly indispensable and she often said to me: 'When I'm dead and buried you'll be banging on my coffin asking where some particular pair of shoes is.' That's not to say that we didn't have a blistering row every six months or so ...

At that time, Marc Doelnitz and I were going out together, not in the physical sense, but we were never seen without each other. I'd say to him: 'Well, pet, what shall we do tonight?' And he'd say to me: 'Let's have fun, duckie!' We were genuinely very fond of each other. Whatever people say, friendships forged at night are often deeper than those made by day. Night people are a special breed, all a little lost, a little in need of human warmth, of intimacy, of the illusion of security. They are more tolerant of defects in others, things which by day might seem serious, seem less so at night, and they make fewer judgements about people and their way of life. They'll jump from one idea to the next, without having time to be too rigorous. They won't make a tragedy out of a misplaced word, or rarely so; and if someone's down they usually joke them out of it.

The *Paris-Match* gang, including Marc Doelnitz, whom I saw at least one evening in two, used to meet up at La Belle Ferronnière, the bistro over the road from the newspaper office, to decide where to eat in the evening. That's how I met Hervé Mille (the magazine's director from 1949 to 1969), Roger Théroud and Gaston

Bonheur, who wrote some of my songs, including 'La Rue des Rosiers'. My friends and I used to do the rounds of all the good bars, having endless discussions, making harmless and not so harmless jokes, making sure we always had fun. For five whole years from 1960 to 1965 we lived as a group, and it didn't matter if there were discordant notes, or if friendships sometimes didn't ring true, what counted was being together. Later it all changed. Some of them moved on and grew out of their prolonged adolescence. Some didn't want to change or couldn't. I still see some of them, some I can't be bothered with, and others I have no desire to see any more.

Even before I opened Jimmy's, there were certain things which had started to annoy me. It was the little *Paris-Match* group that coined the phrase: 'We're going round to Fatty's'. I knew it was more a token of our intimacy than malice but even so ... And what's more, some of them had taken up residence at Castel's at the time of the opening, playing the prophets of doom: 'She'll never make it work! She's mad! She'll get her fingers burnt!' Of course, if everyone had gone to Castel's and only there, then it would never have worked at Jimmy's! But as success took root at Jimmy's, I watched as they gingerly ventured back, but it wasn't the same ...
Among those from *Paris-Match* who did remain loyal, apart from Paul Chantrel, I must mention Honoré Bostel, an ex-lawyer turned journalist, a person with many gifts and great intelligence, who was also a real gourmet. He it was, as the name suggests, who invented the 'Bostella' one riotous evening. He hadn't a clue about dancing, and shifted from foot to foot like a bear, and then, bursting with laughter, threw himself at someone and knocked them over. We all started doing it; it was a knock-out!

With Marc Doelnitz and Luc Fournol, another night-and-day accomplice, I started developing my own personal style, mixing Napoleon III with 1900 and lots of 1930. In the flea market (where things were still incredibly cheap) we bought black inlaid furniture, Perzel standard lamps, Brandt boas, Bugatti animal sculptures, a chrome drinks trolley, some modern lithographs, Daum crystal lamps, Gallé vases, Ruhlmann mirrors and screens (with plenty of ivory and sharkskin), Lalique bottles. On the walls, perspective lines, paintings by César, Buffet, Kijno ... When people wanted to give me a present, they knew that bronze serpents rearing up ready to bite had the right effect on me. That sort of décor is almost commonplace nowadays, but in 1960 it wasn't at all, and the flat looked like a museum, lacquered and inlaid, black and red, gilded and silvered.

175

Then I decided to make my dinner table one of the most sought-after in Paris, both for the food, and for the company. We'd had 'sausage parties' at the Porte Dorée, then came the restaurant period, and now I was into meatballs. I launched into Polish cuisine, convinced my friends would love it. In small doses, yes; all the time, no. As they left I caught them muttering, 'Oh no, not more meatballs!' So began the 'palettes aux lentilles' period. Suzanne and I gave serious thought to the question of how to make this ultra-classic dish original in some way. As we gained confidence, the dish became more elaborate, as did the whole menu, and we grew more particular about the 'clientèle' too ... We started having literary or film dinners, with women who had led exciting lives and who had been the inspiration of their times. These people fascinated me and from them I learnt many things.

I moved heaven and earth to arrange dinner parties which were both brilliant and bizarre, where I mixed very different sorts of people, and more particularly those who went out a lot with those who didn't. Françoise Sagan said one day that if I'd lived at the time of Louis-Philippe I would have had a literary salon full of intrigues. In fact, the flat 'above my means' was a bit of a 'salon littéraire' ... and even if I didn't do any real plotting, other people certainly intrigued to get in!

Some evenings were more sparkling than others, but the guests were never disappointed by the meal. I certainly didn't stint on the food: all my money went on grub (and shoes!).

There were some marvellous moments, such as those with Louise de Vilmorin and Marie-Laure de Noailles. Some people thought they were past it, but I found them quite fascinating. One evening, I teamed them with Marie Bell. Each of them was absolutely determined to be the most brilliant. The perfect topic of conversation: lovers they had had or might have had in common.

Louise de Vilmorin hadn't yet made her revealing appearances on the Guy Béart show, which were to make her famous throughout France. It was then that people discovered her (although she had long been famous in 'salons' and châteaux, but had been thought of as past her prime), realizing what an extraordinary degree of refinement, common sense, and mystique she possessed. At long last people began reading her novels and poems, and the one-time fiancée of Antoine de Saint-Exupéry, the ex-Countess Palfy, became famous in her own right. One day she remarked to me: 'The best friend one can have is one's husband.' (I wasn't yet quite persuaded of this.) She also said: 'One never looks quite as good in other people's mirrors as in one's own. Before I go out, I make sure I look beautiful in my own room, then I needn't look at myself for the rest of the evening.'

Marie-Laure de Noailles had been one of the greatest patrons of her time (she and her husband had financed Buñuel's *L'Age d'or* and Cocteau's *Le Sang d'un poète*. She gave me something she'd made and decorated herself, a papier mâché ball which had been exhibited at the Salon de l'Objet. It was covered in strange vampire-like designs, and I hung it in my drawing room. Marie Bell was amazing and when she talked about actresses of her generation she used to smile broadly and say: 'And she's fifteen years older than me . . .' Marlene Dietrich also came to dinner. She was supposed to come with Paul Giannoli, but he got delayed so she arrived alone, in rather a bad mood, and then refused to speak to him all evening. I'm glad to say they were swiftly reconciled.

The great love of Louise de Vilmorin's life at that time, as everyone knew, was André Malraux, with whom she lived at the Palais-Royal in Paris and the Château in Verrières-le-Buisson. Malraux was Minister of Culture, having given up being spokesman first of the left, then of the right, for the role of commander-in-chief of French culture. He was devastated by the death of Louise de Vilmorin in 1969. I met him a year later at a dinner given by Ludmilla Tchérina, in company with Jacques Rueff, General de Gaulle's pet economist, the gold-standard man. Next day, I was mulling over the evening's entertainment, thinking what a fascinating man Malraux was, when I got a phone call from Carmen Tessier, who was the toast of Paris with her gossip column 'Potins de la Commère' in *France-Soir*. She told me Malraux had greatly enjoyed talking to me. I thought it would be nice to give a dinner-party for him. I called him up: he accepted, with the proviso that the evening start at half-past eight.

As usual, the guests were a diverse mixture. I had invited Carmen Tessier and her husband (André-Louis Dubois), Serge Gainsbourg, Jane Birkin, Jean Cau and Bettina Grazziani (the girl Aly Khan was about to marry when he died), and Louisa Colpen, Patrick Modiano's mother. André Malraux arrived first, early, at quarter to eight. I was still in my dressing gown, my hair in rollers. I pretended this was all absolutely normal, but it threw me completely. My hairdresser was still there, and not wanting to leave the minister all alone in the drawing room, I invited him into my room for a minute. I realized there was nowhere for him to sit, but he said it didn't matter and promptly sat down on the edge of the bidet and began munching peanuts and sipping his whisky.

Suzanne, whom I'd coached in these matters, asked: 'Would you like another drink, Minister?' He said yes, and then suddenly reached for his handkerchief, and put it into his mouth, whence he retrieved a tooth — victim of the peanuts. Wanting to make him feel at ease (although he clearly already was) I said: 'It happened to me too, only last week. Don't worry: you'll get a present tomorrow.' (I sent him one of the little boxes I collect, which he had been admiring.)

The other guests arrived, and after a drink we sat down: foie gras, *chaud-froid* of chicken, Berthillon ice-cream. No meatballs for the Minister of Culture. With his tooth in his pocket, Malraux, who had drunk a great deal and eaten very little, talked and talked, jumping as was his wont from Vietnam to Russia, from Stalin to Mao, from the war to de Gaulle. Jean Cau interrupted him constantly, but he always had the last word. Gainsbourg and I listened intently.

Carmen Tessier and her husband, incorrigible early-nighters, left at one in the morning, which was a record for them. Malraux stayed, and at about three his chauffeur came up to see if 'Monsieur le Ministre' was still in the land of the living. We gave him our assurances, and the Minister took up the thread of his story. He didn't finally leave until five o'clock, leaving me exhausted but delighted. Malraux may have lost a tooth, but my little dinner parties had gained in prestige.

I entertained Henry Miller too. His wife and I had met in a Los Angeles night-club. She was a gorgeous Chinese girl. We had an instant rapport, and she told me she would be in Paris the following month. 'Henry's coming too,' she said, 'they're filming *Tropic of Capricorn*.' She arrived a month later, on her own, and we had dinner together. Then she phoned to say that her husband had arrived, and the following night they both came round. I hadn't let anyone else know, to give my friends a little surprise. And that's what they got. There was a bunch of everlasting flowers — those daisies which look like chrysanthemums — on the table, and over dinner Henry Miller said something extraordinary: 'It's funny, but looking at these flowers has made me think about death for the first time in ages.' He was eighty-two years old then.

Apart from the Malraux and Miller evenings, one of the most

amazing was the party to celebrate the reconciliation between Annabel Buffet and Juliette Gréco, after an unfortunate misunderstanding. The fairy godmother in all this was Françoise Sagan, while I was the means to the end. The two ladies in question were there of course, plus Bernard Buffet, Françoise Sagan, Paul Chantrel, Georges Cravenne, Hélène Lazareff, and Carmen Tessier and her husband. On the menu: vodka, caviar and gypsies. At half-past eight we were all kissing each other, and by eleven it was general and total drunkenness. We could hardly stand up and I was practically crawling. At midnight I said: 'Let's all go down to the club!' Suzon tried to stop me and put me to bed instead. But to no avail: I threatened to get out by the window. I went to powder my nose in the bathroom and got handfuls of it all over my face and clothes. Down we all went. It was Carmen Tessier's first visit and she certainly wasn't disappointed. Françoise Sagan recounted later how, when I arrived, Prince Alexander of Yugoslavia wanted to kiss my hand, but I didn't recognize him. All I remember is dropping a bottle of whisky which rolled over Hubert de Givenchy's feet while he was dancing with an American girlfriend. I had always admired him greatly, but I wasn't really in any condition to express my feelings. (I sent him a little note next day thinking: he doesn't come here often, what on earth must he have thought of me!)

I don't know how the evening finished, but I do know that I woke up next morning lying in the kitchen minus my dress. The doctor was called and gave me a camphor injection and a couple of days later I discovered my dress stuffed down behind the loo. We'd all been in such a state that Bernard Buffet was convinced there must have been some dope in the food. But actually, there was no great mystery about it: with eleven bottles of vodka between eleven people (three of whom hardly drank) some damage was inevitable.

One important detail: the whisky which had rolled under Hubert de Givenchy was J&B, a brand which Georges Cravenne had just made the 'in' drink, after noticing that his American friends always ordered it. I was as much of an Americanophile as he was, and followed suit, giving pride of place to this brand at Jimmy's. Ever since then, J&B has been *the* elegant whisky to drink. (Later, Cravenne borrowed the Americans' Oscars, turning them into Césars . . .)

At the time, Georges Cravenne was a very close friend, or more than that because I very nearly became Madame Cravenne. He was known as 'the father of public relations', and had grasped the importance of such things with the American army during the war. Each unit, however small, had its own officer exclusively in charge of public relations. He realized that there was scope for developing PR for shows and cinema too. He was in charge of public relations for the Cannes film festival and ended up as the agent for prestigious film producers like Litvak and Zanuck, as well as for big French stars like Chevalier, Enrico Macias, Yves Montand, Gilbert Bécaud, Fernand Raynaud ... As he said to the Americans in Cannes: 'Come and dance the twist at Régine's', so he also said later: 'If you want to know Paris go to Jimmy's'. He organized all the biggest galas and the most spectacular premières at the Lido, the Alhambra, the Moulin Rouge. I was one of Cravenne's 'magic circle', people he singled out because of their talents, wealth, birth or importance, and brought together. He knew how to focus people, how to make things happen. So did I.

He was one of the mainstays of my dinner parties, and he dined (often more than once) with Louison Bobet, Maurice Ronet, Tino Rossi, Arnaud de Rosnay, Saint-Laurent, Aznavour, Simenon, Rubirosa, Nureyev ... There was a rush on places, and people weren't always lucky. Once you got over the first hurdle at the club door, and after you'd joined the select band who could claim early morning spaghetti in the basement, that just left an invitation to one of the dinner parties on the first floor and you'd be at the top of the tree. It was a bit like the famous colour-graded cards that Cravenne used: pink for people in the public eye, white for traditional, sacrosanct Paris society and blue for the *crème de la crème*.

Jacques Chazot was a great habitué of both club and dinner-table. Our friendship was deep and we never quarrelled — except just once for three minutes and a few seconds when I was having a dig at one of his friends. Friends were as sacred to him as to me, and he couldn't bear to hear them criticized — though it didn't stop him, or me, being sharp-tongued. Like me, he forgave some people everything, yet others weren't allowed to put a foot wrong.

He was a real hit one night at Jimmy's. It was a Jean Harlow evening: women had to look like her and men had to come in spencer jackets. Jacques had a Eurovision broadcast to do in Brussels the night before, and the next day he just put on the same suit, bought a top-hat, got a blond wig from Alexandre and came round to Jimmy's in the evening dressed as ... Marlene Dietrich! (Callas was there in a blond wig! And Marc Doelnitz came as

Shirley Temple). The funniest thing was that a week later an American newspaper printed some photos of the evening, with the following caption beneath the picture of Chazot: 'Jacques Chazot dressed as Marcel Marceau'. His comment: 'Why did I bother?'

He loved coming to dinner and greatly appreciated the kitchen banquette which he judged 'très snob' because I'd had it covered in fur ... We had a lot of shared memories, and two or three shared lovers, which is why he often said that we were 'related'.

The press regarded Françoise Sagan as one of the pillars of Jimmy's, which she was. Like everyone else, she danced a lot and forgot her worries, such as the time the OAS booby-trapped her apartment because she spoke out in favour of Algerian independence.

She loved the mix at the club, which, apart from the real artists and businessmen, included some brilliant failures, dossers who passed for high flyers, unconventional types who didn't just contemplate their navels, unrepentant good-timers, slightly *passé* society people, and professional followers of fashion — the people who didn't miss a trick, and whom new tricks didn't miss either ... She talked at length on the banquette (the prime location by the door) with Bernard Frank, Antoine Blondin, Pierre Bergé, André Oliver ... She thought it all, despite appearances to the contrary, very 'democratic', and she wasn't mistaken. One night she came in and during the course of the conversation she said, without changing her tone: 'I've done something really silly. Can someone lend me five million francs?' I got the money for her next day. On another occasion, she got involved in a scrap between her husband Bob and a mad Hungarian, who was later killed by Mickey Rooney in Hollywood. I rapidly got rid of the ill-fated Hungarian, and the club reverted to its normal cruise-liner rhythm. I agree that she didn't always like the show-biz side of things, but she was always there, quick, incisive, smiling. (Later after I was married and Roger thought I was getting back from the club too late she wrote me 'excuse notes' for him.)

Philippe Junot was another regular: his sense of fun and taste for parties was already well known. Aristotle Onassis was much more sedate ... He came with La Callas and they'd sit there sipping Coca-Cola by the dance floor. They only had champagne when they came with friends after dining at Maxim's or somewhere. He married Jacqueline Kennedy in 1968, and came to Jimmy's with her, and then later to Régine's Ponthieu. The first time he set foot in the place he said: 'It smells of oil in here!'

181

'Of course, we're over a garage!'

He looked at me a bit surprised and explained: 'I meant there's the sweet smell of success around here!'

'I agree!'

With meatballs, palettes and vodka, there wasn't much chance of slimming. In any case, my boyfriends seemed quite keen for me to stay as I was. Whenever I mentioned it, they protested: 'If you get thinner you'll just be like everyone else!' So I was quite simply 'Fatty'. But it wasn't as easy as all that. Whenever I met a girl who'd lost a spectacular amount of weight I would always ask how she'd done it, and then throw myself body and soul into some new diet, which never failed to disgust me after the third day, but which I pursued for at least two or three weeks, with a will of iron. After the diuretics I'd taken while I was with Jean-Claude, I worked my way through appetite-suppressants, carbohydrates, protein powder, caviar-vodka (breakfast, lunch and dinner), zen macrobiotic (brown rice, grapes, courgettes ...) cottage cheese with fruit, Scarsdale diet (foods of the same chemical composition — the inventor's mistress went mad and killed him), not to mention the pills, purgatives, sweat baths, paraffin, acupuncture, ionization and other electrical devices. I was forgetting grapefruit-*paillard de veau*, a diet I still follow now and again. But a word of advice: there's only one way to lose weight — don't eat.

I might have let dieting run away with me, but I always had my work on a tight rein. To my employees I was 'la patronne'. Nothing went unnoticed, and everyone knew it. I never wavered in my belief that each one should take his share of responsibility if he was to have his bite of the cherry. That's why I've always avoided amateurs. To work with me, you have to love the job, and not be content just to wait for pay-day. And it's evenings too ... And I must confess that I've been spoilt. I've always been able to count on all my waiters being there till the end, without them working shifts: they all stay. One of my strengths is the team I've got behind me, people working towards one goal over and above their immediate duties, supporting my efforts so that my clubs are special, and remain so.

And when I started out on my singing career, and refused to do long tours, it was for them, for the club; for me, for us. I did not desert them and was amply rewarded with their loyalty, even — especially — at difficult moments, as there always were. Apart from the fallow periods whenever a new club opened and our customers dwindled, we endlessly had jealousy and malicious gossip to contend with. Some people were pathologically jealous: they had no reason to be envious of me, we weren't even in the same business, but no matter, they were still jealous. As for spiteful tittle-tattle, that was just part of our daily fare and I didn't mind being the subject of the conversation: if I'd had no enemies I'd have had to invent some, because my enemies have made me every bit as much as my friends have.

With zany evenings at Jimmy's and my passion for assembling prestigious 'casts', I got to know 'le monde', as they say. Evenings à la Proust were many, which probably explains why I've always had such problems reading him. I was constantly arguing about Proust with Françoise Sagan. She gave me his complete works and though I never got further than page ten of the first volume, I often felt I'd read it from cover to cover. The New Jimmy's period coincided with a thirst for titles (now assuaged). (My barmen have always called everyone 'mon prince'.) Whenever I meet a real prince I conjure up stories of romance and mystery, fabulous wealth and great misfortune. And it all absolutely fascinated me (except for the châteaux, because I had already had my fill of those during the war). Of course that period of history is long past, circumstances are different, fashions have changed, but the people are the same, so are their problems and their way of behaving. Ejecting a duke from the club reminds me that among the 'well-born' there are those who are pleasant, charming, and well-mannered, and others who think they can have carte blanche. In such cases, even if I feel my barman might not be completely in the right, it's still the customer I ask to leave. Once he's gone, I then sort things out with the barman and demand a full explanation.

You wouldn't believe what extremes of pettiness and meanness I encouter. Penny-pinching, all sorts of bad habits and little defects which people hide in their everyday lives, get given free rein with night-club barmen. We've had lots of laughs about that sort of thing. When a client is distrustful enough to mark the level of his bottle — invisibly he thinks — we have great fun topping it up. Next time he comes in we watch his reaction ... In my experience, no one has yet complained of having too much whisky! The real skinflints replace what they've drunk with water, so their bottles last longer. When very rich people do it, it's rather sad, but funnier too! The only type of tease — even so — which I allow my waiters is to serve such people very generous measures from their own bottles, for the pleasure of hearing them protest: 'No, no, thank you, just a drop, just a drop please!' By contrast, if someone's been over-generous when flush, I knock a bit off the bill when he's feeling impoverished. Lots of people have their 'highs' and 'lows' . . . and then there are others whom I've been keeping in scotch for ever. Good whisky, good works.

I kiss people a lot, and they kiss me. They take a stab at me, and I stab back. That's life. I'm a great gossip, but I'm never nasty for the sake of it. There's always plenty to say about the dreadful people, the rest can remain unscathed. When I do speak out it's not just to 'have my say' or to play to the gallery. If the vulgar or the uninhibited get out of hand I always tell them what I think of them before I show them the door. I have the power to let them in or to refuse them entry. That's what a private club is all about. Some people I make it up with after a while, just like that, because they've got a good excuse, or because they're sorry, because I might have been wrong or simply because I like them and don't want to lose them. But there are others I never patch it up with. Those are the ones I turn into my 'living dead'.

The various 'outcasts', 'excommunicants' and 'living dead' get together elsewhere and spend their time saying vile things about me, providing me with plenty of free publicity! If by chance I meet one of them, it doesn't upset me. It's me they're afraid of, because they know I'm not a coward. Most people aren't really cowardly, but they'd rather 'let sleeping dogs lie', avoid scandal. People don't like getting themselves noticed. But I'm quite the opposite, a complete exhibitionist, by temperament and by design. I say what I think with a mixture of brutality and humour. You know the people who laugh are on your side and it also disarms the enemy. I never seek to destroy for the sake of it, but at the end of the day, since I've no vices other than work, it's the speed of my reactions which keeps me alive. I don't have time to be impressed by people − and certainly not by money.

Marc Doelnitz was one of the *Paris-Match* crew that I fell out with. Our feud started in 1967. Relations had already cooled somewhat because he'd fallen in love with a boy who had the bad taste to be more interested in me. It was one of those insoluble situations, both futile and fatal. But we all tried hard and kept smiling, more or less. I had given him a very expensive watch for his birthday, which was generous of me as I was pretty impoverished at the time. Three or four days later I got a call from a friend who told me I'd made a big mistake, and described something that had just happened at Castel's.

'I don't understand why you waste your time with people like Doelnitz. If you knew what went on behind your back ...'

At remarks like that I never feign indifference, so I asked him to tell me the whole story.

'You know that watch you gave him, well, he was a bit drunk, okay, but he put it in a glass of whisky and said, "That's what I think of presents from Fatty."'

I immediately phoned Castel's and asked for Marc.

'I know exactly what you've just done, and I'm never going to speak to you again as long as I live. I'm afraid you've gone too far this time.'

So our relationship foundered in a glass of whisky ... Some said that's how it had begun ... So it was all for the best. But it was a pity because Marc had been such a marvellous help with the famous dinner parties 'above my means', which now continued without him.

Night brings intrigue, sordid revelations perhaps, but also the delights of being with 'unconditional' people: the sort of people who will turn up at two in the morning and stay for spaghetti at sun-up. Spaghetti-time is the reward my late-night companions get for keeping the faith; it's happy hour, when we're at our most inspired and everything seems worthwhile.

A person's face is different at night, more relaxed than by day. My waiters and I can usually tell when people come to the club to forget unhappy love affairs or business worries because they behave out of character: we can tell by the way they move, the way they drink, the way they will suddenly claim 'their table' ... (I won't allow that sort of territoriality in my clubs: people should feel good, protected, at their ease, yes, but I refuse to let them 'possess' anything.) For the odd evening we don't mind, and don't say anything, and it's precisely that sensitivity to people's state of mind which gives Jimmy's Montparnasse such a family atmosphere. Someone might not come to the club for three months, or six months, and yet find his bottle, to his great amazement, exactly as he left it, as if it had been only the night before. That's what the job's about too. It's not just a question of opening a bottle and putting on some music. It's like politics, continuity is vital. It's less lucrative to start with, but promotes loyalty and, in the end, people come back to you. My clients understand that the money isn't my only or even my major concern. I don't open a club just for six months, a year or two years. When I open, it's for ten or twenty years. Most clubs want to see some return in the short term; I'm there to cater for one, two or three generations. It's an important difference. You have to merit people's loyalty. Because of it, parents let their children come to Jimmy's in all confidence, because they know it's a properly run club. Rising stars rub shoulders with old pros, and it gets beyond the stage of being fashionable and becomes more or less an institution. At Jimmy's, whole families get together to celebrate engagements. They practically ask if they can get married there too! And certainly plenty of wedding parties end up at Jimmy's.

During slack periods when for six, seven, eight months, a new club might set up and poach my customers, the barmen get nervous, but I don't. So the Privé or the Palace are all the rage? Well, we just bide our time. What you must never do is fling the doors wide open. Quite the opposite, I make it even more difficult to get in. There may be only a hundred people in the club, but I behave as though there are three hundred. I don't change a thing. I throw parties, I spend money, I invite friends, I take a gamble, and win. As I tell my barmen, competition is like a safety valve. 'Wait and see: they won't be quite so well treated after a couple of weeks at the other place, they'll decide the standard of service has declined, they'll find the new club a bit too crowded, the mixture wrong, and they won't feel they're getting their fair share of the action or the attention.' And I'm right, because they do all come back after two or three months. There's nothing like a bit of competition to keep everyone up to scratch.

When I set New Jimmy's up (and it was worse when I started singing a few years later), lots of people said there were powerful people with money behind me. I make a success of the club, a success of my singing career, so what's the secret? Well, apart from me and my eighteen-hour day, there's no secret, no personal fortune, no pennies from heaven, no sugar-daddy millionaire. I'm afraid you'll have to rule out any 'supernatural' explanation for my success.

Another thing which caused me a lot of heartache but which brought me much happiness was the Deauville club New Brummel. I'd just set up New Jimmy's in Paris when Lucien Barrière suggested I take over the running of his Brummel in Deauville. Lucien was no longer the very provincial young man I'd first met at the Cannes

186

Whisky à gogo, fresh from his native Ardèche, setting out in business. Handsome and charming he still was, but he had now acquired the aura of an accomplished businessman. Like the good peasant with his feet firmly on the ground who finds everything too expensive on principle, he made me a modest proposition. I accepted, because the prospect of 'seasonal work' was appealing. People had noticed that I prefer to spend my holidays working rather than doing nothing. So I went off to stay in a hotel along with rich jet-setters who were camping out in style to indulge their passion for gambling. I certainly loathe the casinos where I had to wait so long for my father, and I rarely set foot in gaming rooms, but even so, their grand buildings exert an undeniable influence. Love-hate relationships are second nature to me.

Brummel's was decked out in fairy lights, not terribly much to my taste, so I did it up my way and then took on the onerous task of attracting back the crowds and the young people who had long ago deserted Deauville. My job was to create something new and exciting in a town full of ageing, stay-at-home snobs. If I could make a wild Jimmy's evening happen despite the Normandy drizzle, then people might just come in to dry off and warm up. Fortunately there was a sound basis from which to work: August, the races and the polo ... I just had to extend my horizons, beyond the summer season.

'En route, we're all going to Deauville!' I'd say to my friends in Paris each weekend with the same confidence and enthusiasm I'd have had for Carnival in Rio. They grumbled a bit, moaning that the town was full of old fogeys, but I ended up laughing them into it along the lines of: 'I'm going to Deauville, and if I'm there, we're bound to have fun, aren't we?' Someone conceded and there was general assent. A motorcade of ten or fifteen cars assembled, and our caravan set off westward, loaded more with high spirits than luggage. Weekend after weekend, ever more girls and boys followed in my footsteps and made the wormeaten boards of the promenade vibrate to the rhythms of their youth and their imagination. There were the heroic midnight swims, the sarabands through the streets to the sound of drunken violins, the parties ending at nine or ten in the morning at the Vapeurs in Trouville, where they serve the best mussels and shrimps on the coast. The people who used to come now and again for the races and the polo tournaments saw us having fun and came more often. The townspeople themselves, as I'd hoped, got into the habit of going out once again. And young

Parisians were rediscovering the charms of their great-grandparents'
superb Deauville seaside houses ...

For the next two years, in the summer and at weekends, I lived
at the Royal hotel in Deauville, which I adored. But then, one day,
a friend told me about a ruin, a charming place he said, not far
from the town. 'You come here all the time, you need somewhere
like that. Come and I'll show you.' We drove about three miles,
then followed an overgrown footpath, clambered over a fence and
were confronted by 'the ruin'. It's name was Le Presbytère. I
started thinking it might be fun to own a priest's house ... I went
in. The floor was beaten earth but in the main room there were a
few fine floor tiles, some panelling and an old staircase.

'You're absolutely right, it is a charming place, I love it, I'll buy
it!'

The price was modest but, since my means were even more so,
several of us clubbed together to buy the lovely, uninhabitable ruin.
I left it exactly as it was for a year and a half, almost derelict, out of
self-defence perhaps, in case I discovered 'comfort' and became
hidebound. (Today I still avoid 'settling in' wherever I am. I've got
a flat in Paris, but it's more a flat-that-comes-with-the-job which I
happen to have decorated myself. As for my villa in Saint-Tropez I
have to re-learn where all the switches are every time I go there.)

One day, however, Françoise Sagan said to me: 'I've found a real
treasure to look after your house in Deauville.'

'But Françoise, it's not a house, it's a ruin ...'

'Exactly! Exactly! Listen, the caretaker in question is the man
who used to do my mother's feet and he's had a run of bad luck ...'

So I met the man who used to do Françoise Sagan's mother's
feet. A rather original old gentleman who had once run a beauty
salon. The first thing he said to me was: 'When my wife died, I
made a vow of humility.'

This made quite a change from most of the other people I knew,
and from me too. He explained that he'd just lost his fourth wife
and that he'd decided to lead a simple life and become a caretaker. I
looked at him in amazement, but was completely won over.

And it was first and foremost so that my footman shouldn't have
to sleep under a collapsing roof or on the beaten earth that I threw
myself into frenetic repairs with fast-depleted funds. Having said
that, I still carried on living in the hotel even when the work was all
finished. I sent my friends to sleep at Le Presbytère to christen my
bed. It was clearly going to be a problem getting me actually to live

in the house. The following year, 1964, I organized a picnic in honour not of the swimming pool, which there wasn't, but of the newly finished roof. Because it was so small inside, I decided to make it more of a fête champêtre, without worrying too much about the rain which had been falling constantly for a week. When the day came, fortunately it was brilliantly sunny ... The guests brought the drink, I laid on food. Accordions provided the atmosphere, and for once the party ended at sunset ...

For the next five years the Presbytère picnic became an annual ritual. People came from all over and in the weeks and days leading up to it the betting was furious: will it rain this year, or not? But no, every time Régine's Presbytère picnic took place under a blazing sun!

However, one year (I'd just met Roger), on the day of the picnic it was still raining at half-past twelve. People were coming at one. Consternation. I went out on the terrace, looked up at the sky and said: 'If it's still raining in half-an-hour I'm changing its name from Le Presbytère to La Synagogue.'

Quarter to one, the first rays of sunshine, and it was fine all afternoon! All the friends who had been so sure that this year Régine's picnic would be washed out were disgusted. And once again, the journalists could start their articles: 'Under perfect blue skies, Régine's picnic ...'

It was because of the picnics that I began to love the house, and started to settle in, to decorate it. Little by little we got used to each other. Spending all the summer weekends there, from July to September, I came to see how much my fears had diminished. I had difficulty sometimes in leaving the place, I felt so good there, I was having such a good time in Deauville, in this little priest's house which had come into my life by chance. But such abandon, which had nothing to do with what I'd dedicated my life to, ended up frightening me. And to such an extent that I used to force myself to stay at the hotel from time to time just to break the spell. I realized that (relative) lack of comfort, and the makeshift, are the only two things which will make me get up and do things. I understood that the deep-rooted yearning for houses had nothing to do with the desire to live there, but had more to do with a need for security. Because in the midst of the greatest pleasure there's always something missing: a lack of activity, lack of goal, lack of fight, which makes me feel nervous and unsatisfied. Houses are rather like shoes: having lots of them makes me feel calm. But to think of nothing else, to live for them, would be the beginning of the end.

On the whole, particularly counting my début as a singer, the Deauville years were happy ones. I cycled in the rain, the climate was good for me, I felt carefree, flirtatious, amusing, and much less 'regulated' than I later became. I even used to wear other people's shoes, for example, an idea which, twenty years later, seems inconceivable ...

But all things must come to an end, even carefree years, and when I announced to Lucien Barrière my decision to leave (I was dreaming of Monte-Carlo) he took the news quite badly, and his words reminded me of those of my ex-boss at the rue de Beaujolais: 'All right. Well, anyway, Deauville must have taught you quite a lot ...'

His tone hurt me and I replied: 'And the future will show what I can teach Monte-Carlo.'

We were a little chilly with each other, Lucien and I, but it was only the sort of minor Deauville chill which comes and goes quite quickly. Lucien Barrière is actually a deeply kind man, and that's a rare enough quality to make it worth underlining. As for the Deauville house, it was sold to François Nourissier, author of that beautiful book *Le Mâitre de maison*, then to Francis Perrin.

13

Party-time

Let's start with the most spectacular floorshow of all: El Cordobes in the bullring. In May 1961 I stayed with Jean Lafon, a rancher in the Camargue, for the Nîmes 'feria'. Days of 'pastis' and pleasure and flamenco guitars. I'm crazy about corridas and all things Spanish, and I was dying to see this promising young 'novicario' for myself. So one afternoon my friends and I took our seats in the Nîmes arena.

Released from the stalls into the ring, the bull was quickly brought to a pitch of fury by the picadors who stuck their banderillas into his flanks. Then, wearing a green costume embroidered in gold, the arresting figure of El Cordobes advanced into the centre of the ring, svelte, austere, like a masculine Bardot, mesmerizing and magnificent: the crowd gasped.

The bull charged. El Cordobes neatly sidestepped, and a most extraordinary ballet began. The crowd held its breath; there was total silence in the ring while the bullfighter went down on one knee, with the bull, foaming at the mouth, turning a semi-circle around him. The toreador stood up again, and carried on with his devilish dance for several more minutes. Having shown the crowd that the creature was entirely at his mercy, El Cordobes raised his sword dramatically into the air. The shout 'Olé' came in perfect unison from the crowd (rare in a French ring). Although the 'mise à mort' was not as spectacular as the passes had been, the roar of approval was no less immense. And I left the ring emotionally exhausted.

My friends and I went out to a restaurant that evening and found

El Cordobes was there too. That was our first meeting. Three months later, someone told me that he was in Paris and that Jean Cau was doing a feature on him for *Paris-Match*. But I also learnt that Marc Doelnitz, with whom I hadn't as yet fallen out, was organizing a dinner for thirty in his honour at Castel's, and hadn't asked me.

I was furious, and decided to organize a Régine dinner at Castel's the same night at the next table to the Doelnitz 'clan'. Thirty vs. thirty. I didn't breathe a word to Marc. The evening of the dinner I feigned ignorance and asked him who all the places were laid for. He said, 'It's a business thing, for the magazine. I'm afraid I couldn't ask you, you do understand, don't you ...' I understood only too well. Both dinners went extremely well. I was re-introduced to El Cordobes, and he said: 'I'd like to learn the twist.' We were constant companions for the next three days, and *Paris-Match* had real problems getting their article done.

During the course of those three days, we made ourselves understood through gesture, laughter and smiles: he spoke neither English nor French, and I spoke no Spanish. Even when there was no interpreter for us, I was still fascinated by his simplicity, his intelligence, his instinct — making him a perfect judge of people and things. He later became a remarkable businessman. I still see him now and again in Marbella where, between whiskies, he laughs and calls me 'the love of his life'. The son of poor people from Córdoba had known how to become a king.

The Rothschilds are kings too. I have wonderful memories of the evenings spent at the rue de Marignan (home of the Alain de Rothschilds) or at the hôtel Lambert (home of the Guy de Rothschilds). Over the years Eric Rothschild (Alain's son) and I have shared lots of laughs and good times; and I have a profound admiration for Marie-Hélène and Guy de Rothschild. They first met one another at the Grand Prix de Deauville, during the New Brummel era, and came dancing at the club together for the first time a few days later.

Like Marie-Hélène, I don't accept failure and I never give up. Like her, I have some things which really infuriate me and which I never joke about: racism, dishonesty, vulgarity. And Nadine de Rothschild danced with her future husband for the first time at Jimmy's Montparnasse. During the sixties, Nadine and Edmond were among those I called my 'never-say-die' brigade, and were often there for spaghetti breakfast. 'The baroness gets home at five o'clock,' read one headline ... Nadine used the title — *La Baronne rentre à cinq heures* — for her book, but with a quite different meaning.

If anyone might have been my financial 'backers', it would have been the Rothschilds. But let's get things straight. I met the Rothschilds during the twist era. Like the Duponts and the Durands, they just came along to see what the twist was. No reason not to dance just because you happen to be called Rothschild. They thought me funny, fat and good-humoured. And then, I was Jewish too. Elie and Eric were the first to come. One day, after we had got to know each other a little they said to me: 'You're well known, people talk about you, you could do a lot to help people.' Yes, it was actually them who asked me to help them in their work, and not the other way round. Thanks to them I transcended my lack of awareness and my frivolity. I came to realize what I could do to help Israel in a serious manner. Of course, up till then, if I'd heard anyone being called a 'dirty Jew', I used to get very angry and even, on occasions, throw the odd punch. But I didn't see what else I could do. It was the Rothschilds who brought the real nature of the problems to my attention, and I began working for the organizations which they supported. When I began singing and getting to know lots of people, I helped them in the same way that I helped other people who don't get talked about so often because they're not so well known. But the Rothschilds neither lead me nor follow me: we walk side by side. I have never asked them for handouts. When I needed to borrow money for a particular purpose they lent it to me, as bankers, at so many percent, because my business was sound and because I could provide guarantees. Outside of our business interests, we meet to work for the Jewish Social Front, and quite simply because we are friends. They love the arts, and beautiful things, they are cultured and pleasant, they try to do good and I get on extremely well with them. It is marvellous to see so much money in the hands of such remarkably generous people, who are as demanding of themselves as they are of their friends, and as faithful to their ideals as they are to their name. We each have very specific roles to play, and I think we all play our parts well. There has always been a girl from the backstreets who moves in the richest and smartest circles. Well, let's say that for the twentieth century I'm that girl!

The Rothschilds are too Anglophile to let you forget to have a joke with them, even a little black humour. When Elie lost an eye playing polo (that most expensive and smart of sports), one of his relations said: 'I always told you it would cost an eye!'

And I sent him the following telegram: 'If you want to look like Sammy Davis, all you need now is to turn black!' (As everyone knows, Sammy Davis is Jewish, black and blind in one eye.)

Later on, Elie and his wife asked if I'd go and sing at a charity ball at Château-Lafite − it's a sumptuous house, and the wine is sumptuous, too. The Count and Countess of Paris were among the guests. The house was full, and when Roger and I arrived (I was married by now), we realized that Liliane and Elie had given us their room and had moved out into a room in some friends' house which was doubtless much less beautiful and less comfortable too. We were very embarrassed but very touched, and we spent two unforgettable days there: extraordinary dinners, fireworks, visits to the wine cellars. There were four hundred people the night of the concert, and at the end everyone was singing 'Azzuro' ... We all forgot the time, and the party wound up at six in the morning. The most energetic of all were the Count and Countess of Paris. Liliane said to me that she didn't know who had the most energy, me or the Countess.

She adored parties and whenever I met her on my travels, wherever in the world it might be, she was always ready to go out, always ready to laugh. I think it must be her Brazilian blood.

I also have strong ties of friendship with Baron de Rédé, the inseparable friend of Guy and Marie-Hélène de Rothschild. The 'Rédé ball' in 1969 at hôtel Lambert (later taken over by Guy de Rothschild) will without a doubt be remembered as one of the best parties of the century. I was there: it was one of my first grand balls and I loved it.

Nicole, Duchess of Bedford is another brilliant hostess. I first met 'Nicole Nobody' in Cannes when I was launching the twist. The Duchess is a real personality; so is the Duke. He adores dancing and, between contortions, comes out with his own special brand of jokes and witticisms. And she has a very forthright and amusing side to her character which is quite rare in a woman.

She's very much the businesswoman, has great tact and good taste, and she never goes back on her word. Beneath her customary exuberance one can detect her serious nature and beneath her laughter one senses that serenity which comes of self-knowledge and of knowing others.

194

She once organized a big weekend house-party at Woburn Abbey for the competitors for the Miss Universe title, which was to take place shortly afterwards. I must say it was the craziest weekend of my life. In the Abbey, Nicole had re-created in minutest detail a dinner party of two hundred years ago: the food, the silver, the dinner service, costumes, lighting, the butlers, it was all historically accurate. Yet another meal, equally historical, was eaten farmhouse-style in the immense kitchen, at a plain wooden table out of plain wooden bowls, with honest food and the staff dressed as farm labourers ... The cook was called Mrs Cook — what else? (I had a cook in Monte-Carlo called Monsieur Cuisinier ...) One of the pieces of furniture in the kitchen at Woburn Abbey was very unusual: it looked like a safe ... and it was!

The tour of the house, with the family portraits and Nicole's commentary, was the high spot of the stay: we came out feeling faint from laughing so much ... and from all the murder stories we'd heard. We got the impression they'd all spent their whole lives killing each other. And when the Duke came and did his bit too, it was real 'noblesse oblige'. Splendid paintings hung in every room. One room in particular was dominated by an incredible Rubens. We christened the place Le Petit Rubens and turned it into our nightclub. Before leaving the drawing room in the evening, we asked for some whisky and continued the party at the Petit Rubens.

Paul Getty was among the guests. Reputed to be the richest man in the world, he was certainly not the most generous (having just installed a payphone for his house-guests). Nicole told me that if I wanted to get on with him I was to talk to him about the ghost in white socks. Next day, like a good girl, I thought I'd strike up a conversation with this 'poor man' who looked so sorry for himself. I dived in with: 'Did you see the ghost with white socks last night?' and he literally threw himself at me saying 'Did you see it?!' I said: 'Yes, I saw it.' I was a bit worried because he seemed completely overjoyed at this, and from then on he never left my side, and talked to no one else. It was clearly all a huge joke my friends had played on me: 'There's the future Mrs Getty.' He stuck fast, clinging to the ghost's socks, and mine! Nicole thought it was hilarious ...

On the Sunday morning, she announced: 'Well, children, we're not here to have fun, there's the guided tour to come yet' (Woburn Abbey being one of the most frequently visited stately homes). As the dining room was one of the rooms open to the public, we were wondering where we would be eating. Nicole said: 'Here of course, it doesn't matter, we'll eat as normal, but put the red velvet ropes round.' So there we were at one o'clock, cordoned off, with the visitors filing past. Each time a new group came in, we froze a little. It was a curious sensation, being looked at as though we were furniture ... (There's a very funny Anouilh play along the same lines, where after the revolution in 1917 a Russian family become living dolls, while the 'sovereign people' visit their requisitioned palace.) Nicole kept saying: 'Eat, eat ...', but we felt a bit uncomfortable ...

After lunch, one of the groups was being taken on a more detailed tour of the house, and Nicole suggested we all go round with her and her husband. I don't know whether it was the visitors who'd made us thirsty, but we'd all drunk far too much; by the time the tour started we were not a little tiddly. It was very amusing listening to the questions they asked, and even more amusing to hear the answers the Duke and Duchess gave. But after an hour of it I started to feel a trifle tired. Right on cue we walked into a particularly historic room (yet another...) while Nicole was saying: 'and this is the bed where Queen Victoria slept ...' On the bed, clearly displayed, some august white stockings, an ancestral nightdress, and a royal bonnet. The inevitable happened: I thought I'd just let the rest of the group go on and lie down for a few minutes on the bed. It was already time to think about getting up again (needs must!) when I heard someone coming back. It was Laurence Harvey, accompanied by Rex Harrison. Rex said to me: 'What are you doing there?'

'I'm having a little nap!'

'I'm knackered, I'm going to have a nap too', said Laurence Harvey.

So we both lay down, half laughing, half yawning. In fact, we must have been yawning more than laughing, because once Rex Harrison had gone, we were soon both sleeping like logs! The others came back to fetch us half an hour later, and found us there, dreaming of Queen Victoria. Fortunately we'd taken care to put her underclothes to one side, meticulously folded, on the most Victorian of armchairs.

A few years later, I was singing before the Duchess of Kent in London at a charity ball in aid of students. Nicole and the Duke took Roger on his guided tour of the house and told him about the ghost. Roger hates ghost stories. He's scared stiff of anything which might come through the door unannounced (he always double-locks it). Nicole told him one of her terrifying stories and managed to turn him to jelly ... And the same weekend some cosmetics that I was sure I'd brought with me disappeared somehow from our bathroom. Having no Hercule Poirot to hand, I said to Nicole: 'If you ever see a miraculously rejuvenated ghost you'll know he's been using my make-up.'

Among the other superb parties I went to, one in particular left me with painful memories.

It was right at the beginning of Jimmy's. At the time, I had an insatiable desire for fancy dress, pure folly and extravagance of all sorts. And one day, I got an invitation from Eddie Barclay to the 'craziest' party in town. Gold was currently à la mode: everyone was in gold dresses, golden tights, sequinned from top to toe. I decided I'd make a spectacular entrance. My idea was to go as something out of the Bengal Lancers, and to find three boys who'd dress up to accompany me, on my gold elephant.

I called up my friend Émilien Bouglione (who had a bit of a lisp) and said: 'Émilien, you've got to come over, I want to talk to you.' He came down to the club that evening, and I put my idea to him. He said: 'Ah! How annoying, our own circus is in Italy at the moment, and there's a German circus at our place right now. They're not our animals. And also the elephants are only fifteen years old, they're very young, and they've never been ridden by a woman before and it's not quite as easy as all that. You might fall off. And it's February too, it'll be cold ...'

A cruel let-down. I already had visions of myself jostling about in a kind of basket on a goose-pimpled elephant who would end up sending me flying! But seeing as I'd already found the three boys to be the lancers, I persisted: 'Okay, what other sort of animal can you offer me?'

'All I've got would be a camel.'

'A camel! They stink! And I've never ridden a camel in my life!'

'You've never ridden an elephant either!'

'No, I know, but they look more comfortable.'

'No, believe me! And anyway, the camel's auburn like you, and he's got magnificent eyes ...'

He described the beast to me as though it were a nubile young girl. He concluded by saying: 'Yes, but wait a moment, I'm not sure whether the ringmaster's prepared to lend the camel.'

But I'd already decided not to wait for the ringmaster's response, and was working on another new idea. Doing my Christmas shopping I'd noticed something on the boulevard Haussmann. The trees lit up with flashing fairy lights. So I said to myself: 'I'm going to get myself a blond wig all lit up with fairy lights, so I'll flash on and off, on and off.' I found out who'd done the lighting and was told it was a Monsieur Marseille and son. So I looked up the phone number of Marseille and son and called them: 'My dear Monsieur Marseille, it's Régine speaking. Look, I'd like you to illuminate a wig for me.'

They were more used to lighting up the Palais des Sports or the Boulevards and were a little reluctant, but I talked them round.

'All right then, we'll send a man over and have a look.'

When their man arrived I said: 'Look, this is the wig, I want you to create an enormous sauerkraut affair with very loose plaits and all lit up on the inside.'

'Right you are.'

And off he went with my wig.

I bought an exquisite gold dress, a gold necklace, which I still possess, some gold shoes, gold sequins, gold powder, and decided with Émilien Bouglione to do a seraglio scene. I told him: 'Émilien, we're going to make our entrance together; borrow your father's finest arab horses, get all the jewels out, and come dressed as an oriental prince.'

'Yes, yes,' he said delightedly, 'and if you like I'll bring you some acrobats: some little Moroccan fellows who climb up each other and make themselves into pyramids.'

He added: 'Do you want me to bring some snakes?'

'No, no, no, that'll be fine. If we bring the entire zoo we'll get under everyone's feet.'

On D-day afternoon a dinner-jacketed electrician took up his position at my place: for the party it had to be either fancy dress or dinner jackets ... He switched on my wig for me, and tucked the batteries under my belt. I've not got a wasp waist, and the dress was loose anyway, so it didn't matter. He filled me in on the details.

'The batteries will need changing every two hours.'

'That's all right, you just stay near the toilets and I'll come and find you every two hours to change the batteries.'

My make-up artist was there, my hairdresser busy with the gold powder and my brother too, who'd come for lunch. He said: 'Hey! It would really astound this friend of mine, he's the managing

My Thousand
and One Nights

Julio Iglesias: talent, quality and friendship.

With Prince Charles at Jimmy's Monte-Carlo.

I taught the world to twist ... including the Duke of Windsor.

Thierry Le Luron, one of the family.

1961, Mel Ferrer and Audrey Hepburn having a twist lesson.

Filming *D'où viens-tu, Johnny?*

With Pelé.

Liza Minnelli, Johnny Hallyday.

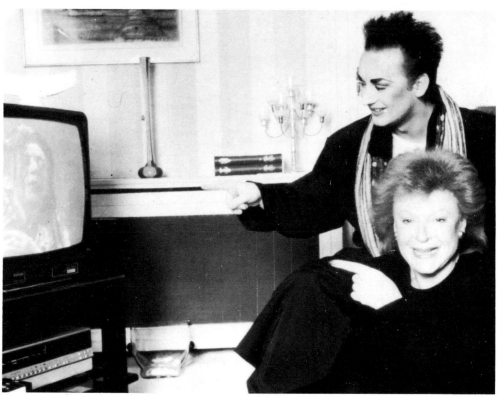

With Boy George.

My picture of perfect happiness . . .

director of a big textile firm, very serious; I'll ask him along this evening to watch your escapades.'

'Why not,' I said, 'he won't regret it.'

We set off, in high spirits, for the craziest ball in town. But meanwhile my act was threatening to run into difficulties: I got an excited phone call from Jacques Ary, a very well known comic, who said; 'I've had a stroke of luck and managed to hire the dromedary from the zoo, and if you like we can do a Lawrence of Arabia act, I can pursue you with rifle shots ...'

I called Émilien Bouglione to explain what Jacques wanted to do. He said: 'You must be mad! This camel's never heard gunfire in its life, do you realize how he might react?' I called Jacques back, who could not be wholly dissuaded: 'Okay, if that's really the case, I'll do a sabre attack instead ...' So we opted for the sabre attack ... I was peeved at someone else having the same idea as me, but since there were going to be two camels anyway, why not join forces?

I was scheduled to meet Émilien at half-past eleven outside the service entrance of the Armenonville pavilion in the Bois de Boulogne, where the party was to take place. I was on time, but there was no Émilien. I was shivering with cold, not yet 'illuminated', but I had the wig on, and round me were stationed the two Messieurs Marseille, father and son, and all the Marseille team in overalls, except the one in the dinner jacket ... My brother was waiting patiently in his very important friend's big Citroën DS. I needed a pee every three minutes because of the cold, necessitating arduous trips round behind the bushes, where I had to all but undress ... There was still no sign of Bouglione when Jacques arrived with his dromedary. I could see there would be problems mounting the beast ... I suggested he climb onto one of the outside broadcast lorries, which he did: they positioned the dromedary up against the lorry. Jacques jumped, the dromedary stepped sideways, and Lawrence of Arabia bit the dust. Hoots of laughter. Fortunately, with the snow, the soft ground beneath and all the people who rushed to pick him up he escaped unscathed. I was laughing so much that my make-up ran, which aged me thirty years in three minutes. But a little bit of powder soon fixed that.

Midnight came, the dromedary was still riderless, and neither Émilien nor my own camel had arrived. Finally, at quarter-past midnight, the circus trailers rolled up, and out tumbled the little acrobats who started jumping about in their dressing-gowns and slippers, trying to warm up. The horses came out of another trailer, the camel from the third: Régine's caravan was complete.

In the meantime, my friend with the dromedary had treated us to five or six action replays of his first stunt: every time, the dromedary leapt with fright at the noise and lights. I was starting to feel a bit jumpy myself, but there was no going back. Fortunately my own camel was a superb creature, ditto Émilien Bouglione, beribboned and bejewelled. I looked at him and said: 'Émilien, you know, I think you should tie my hands together, and I'll walk in all illuminated, like a captive.'

Yes! But I could see him blenching beneath his make-up.

'What? Can't we do that? Why not?'

'It's much too dangerous.'

He hesitated a moment, then added: 'And do you know why we're late? The only way to get hold of the camel was to send my two cousins along to get its German keeper drunk, but they failed miserably and ended up being brought home legless themselves, with the German thinking it was all a huge joke!'

'So what did you do?'

'Nothing, or rather yes! We had to lock him up and then pinched the camel!'

The long and the short of it was that if the camel went berserk there would be no one to calm him down! So I abandoned my ingenious idea and accepted that there would be no tying of the hands.

With considerable difficulty we got the beast down on his knees. It was quite a scramble but I finally got on. After a couple of minutes I felt very comfortable. They plugged me in, switched me on, and the camel got to his feet. But when he started walking it was ghastly. They shouted: 'Hang on to the hump!' I was sitting between the two humps and trying to cling on, but it was very difficult. The hump is made of cartilage, and its rather like touching an enormous nose, soft and quite disgusting. I was not at all happy up there, but had to put on a brave face: after all my brother was there, and the managing director, and there were lots of people watching ... My press officer started shouting to the police on duty outside the entrance: 'No cars!' (Émilien had said strictly no headlights, 'he' wasn't used to them!)

Émilien mounted his horse, the little acrobats swarmed round me. And inside the pavilion they announced (broadcast live on Europe Numéro 1): 'And now the spectacular arrival of Régine ...'

Everyone inside stood up to see me. I reached the main entrance, clinging on to the repulsive hump for dear life. 'Everything okay?' Émilien asked me. My brother said: 'Everything okay?' 'Yes, everything's fine!' I looked like a flashing lighthouse, my skirt was hitched right up because I was sitting astride the camel, but thanks to my gold tights I was not indecent.

As I started out on my fantastic entrance a car abruptly appeared from a side road, the driver obviously blithely unaware of the events taking place: at one in the morning, in the middle of the wood, he suddenly comes across a golden camel ridden by an illuminated lady. He was so flabbergasted that he started hooting madly and switched his headlights on full beam! That did it: my camel jumped and, unable to hold the hump a moment longer, I was thrown head-first, preceded by my illumination which touched the ground milliseconds before me. Everyone rushed over in a panic and from the ground I wondered what on earth I must look like minus my wig with my hair scraped back and my head all gold.

Then I realized that Jacques's dromedary was starting to trot a little too fast. He was shouting: 'But what do I do? What do I do?' The reply came: 'Carry on, carry on!' Seeing him do so well on his dromedary made me mad; I grabbed my wig, put it back on (back to front but still lit up) and tried to get up. As long as the others were holding me up I was all right. But as soon as they let go, down I went!

While the police were getting control of the camel, which was by now kicking at all and sundry, my brother said: 'Come on, enough's enough, we're taking you down to the hospital.' So we left for Boucicaut hospital in the friend's car. Between painful twinges in my hip, I said, referring to the camel: 'What can you expect, he's anti-semitic. I told him my name was Zylberberg, and he couldn't bear it.' Glad to see me so good-humoured after such a bad fall, my brother looked at me much reassured and smiled.

We arrived at Boucicaut hospital, they put me on a trolley and wheeled me into a white room to wait for my X-ray. I was lying on my batteries, which were starting to hurt, so I asked a houseman: 'Could you unplug me, please?'

He looked bewildered: 'Did you fall on your head?'

'Yes,' I told him.

He ran off and came back with my press officer, who had to explain the whole story to him. I repeated my request: 'I've got batteries sticking in my back, could you please unplug them!'

So he got some scissors, cut my belt and removed the batteries. The lights on the wig, by my side, finally went out. It looked like a severed head ... 'I've never seen anything like it!' And off he went to tell the entire hospital.

The most amazing thing was that while all this was going on, they were announcing on Europe Numéro 1 that I'd fallen off my camel, rolled under a car, that the car had hit a tree, and that both my legs were broken ... Seeing as the whole episode had taken place in complete darkness, and had all been over in a matter of two minutes, I imagined that no one would even mention it. But not only were people talking about it, there was no stopping them. Of course, various friends turned up at the hospital to see how the amazon was doing. And so did the circus, with Émilien coming in first, wailing: 'What's my father going to say? But what will he say? And the camel's keeper? And we weren't insured ... What are we going to do?' etc., etc. I was doing my best to reassure him when my doctor arrived. I told him the story: more insane laughter. His whole team were creased up. My ankle hurt and I was having terrible twinges in the side. The more I laughed, the more it hurt. They did an X-ray. Diagnosis: fracture of the pelvis. I wanted to go home. They wouldn't let me, saying the consultant wouldn't agree to it. I insisted, asked for the consultant's name, to be told that it was Professor Méhari. I could hardly believe it, and the hysterical laughter redoubled on all sides. First the camel, then the Méhari — the Arabic racing dromedary. I nearly fainted I was laughing so much. Finally I made such a scene that they had to let me go.

I was taken back to my flat on boulevard du Montparnasse, I went to bed and was told that a queue was forming downstairs at Jimmy's: with the radio report, everyone — including my son — thought that both my legs were broken. I also gathered that at Castel's certain people, among them Doelnitz and Bostel, were singing: 'Avoir un beau chameau ...' and 'C'est la fille du bédouin ...' I decided to call them: 'Well, darlings, how are you doing? Are you coming over for a glass of champagne with me?' Dead silence at the other end of the line. They must have thought I was in plaster up to my neck. 'But where are you?' 'I'm back home, drinking a toast to the camel.' A quarter of an hour later and the flat resembled an outpost of the circus, Jimmy's and Castel's rolled into one, with general uproar. They told me that Jacques Ary never did quite make it into the Armenonville pavilion, and that he was still at large in the Bois de Boulogne astride a headstrong dromedary! The day after this crazy episode, Professor Méhari came to visit me at home, partly out of professional concern, and partly to meet this person who had managed to create mayhem among his team. Opening the door of my room he looked at me, I looked at him, and the giggles started all over again ...

I later learnt, through Émilien Bouglione, of the death of the German camel. The very nice professor Méhari and Jacques Ary are no longer with us either, so I'm the only survivor of the catastrophic remake of *Lawrence of Arabia*.

I stayed in bed for ten days, because my hip still hurt, and because I was fairly shattered by it all. Luckily I was insured and, as the accident occurred while pursuing my professional career, I got quite a lot of money. When the insurance people got my claim for 'falling off a camel, and attendant major trauma', they must have been rather surprised. I imagine that they will have changed the wording on their policy to read: 'damage incurred while camel-riding is not covered by this policy ...'

My trip to Russia in 1963 was incredible too. A year before, Gilbert Bécaud had said to Georges Cravenne: 'I'm going to sing in Moscow. You should publicize it.' So Georges had the deceptively simple idea of inviting Paris to Moscow for Bécaud's first night. General de Gaulle had not as yet opted for a political 'rapprochement' with the Soviet Union, and Stalin had only been dead for ten years ... On every level, the arrangements proved difficult, expensive and risky. Cravenne made contact with the Russian embassy, with Air France, and after two trips to Moscow he managed to get it all organized. Not since royal progresses of the French court in the seventeenth century had a package holiday had greater snob value. One hundred people were invited, the quintessence of Paris society and the business world: Marcel Achard, Marcel Bleustein-Blanchet, Bernard and Annabel Buffet, Pierre Cardin, Jacques Chazot, Arnold de Contades, Pierre Daninos, Luc Fournol, Elsa Martinelli, Moustache, Jean Poniatowski, Alexis de Rédé, Jacqueline de Ribes, Hélène Rochas, Carmen Tessier, Roger Thérond, Paul-Louis Weiller ... and me.

Departure was from Le Bourget airport. I took a taxi on my own, arrived and asked for the special Moscow plane. 'Which plane?' they said. I then discovered we were flying from Orly airport. So, in a panic, I dived into another taxi, telling the driver to put his foot down. He didn't seem very happy and asked where I was going. I told him. He was outraged and started being extremely rude. I replied in kind and ... he dumped me and my luggage at the side of the road. I hailed another taxi and arrived at Orly where the private charter plane was waiting for me — when I say 'waiting for me' I mean it, because I was very very late. Certain individuals started haranguing me once I was on board, none of whom had been unlucky enough to hail a taxi with a White Russian driver.

A total surprise was our stopover in Warsaw! I said to Jean Poniatowski, who comes from a well-known Polish family: 'Aren't we lucky, going to Poland?' We stayed all of half an hour. A bit of airport and a waiting room was all I saw of Joseph's native land. But I did have time to lose my boarding card, and we had to run to get back on the plane. More scowls from the passengers.

Our programme was as follows: day one — evening at the Bolshoi; day two — Gilbert Bécaud concert at the Palace of Congresses: day three — Leningrad. From the word go, we all remarked how perfectly everything was organized.

However, I did notice that no one was doing anything about my enormous trunk, which was standing in the foyer of the Ukrainia Hotel, and out of the corner of my eye I could see Jacqueline de Ribes and Alexis de Rédé lugging their own bags up to their rooms ... There happened to be a group of young people observing our comings and goings with some curiosity. I asked if they spoke French. They were Czech, and said they did.

'Would you mind carrying my trunk up for me? It's too heavy for me to manage.'

'Yes!' — and they soon had it upstairs for me.

After coming down for breakfast in the dining room on the first morning, I wagered I'd get a tray brought up to my room the next day. 'Impossible,' Cravenne told me. The next morning, I stepped out into the corridor with my death's door look. The chambermaid helped me back into my room, and seeing what a bad state I was in from my open trunk, silk stockings scattered everywhere, and my Russian dictionary conspicuously open on the bed, she took pity on me and got my breakfast brought up to me. So I'd won my bet: two kilos of caviar.

In the evening, I wanted to call Jimmy's, like I do every evening when I'm not in Paris. 'Impossible!' again. Georges Cravenne and I pored over the hotel directory in my room, trying to discover which number might be the operator. It was all in Russian, and we couldn't make head or tail of it. Just for a laugh, I closed my eyes and dialled a number. By an incredible coincidence, we got through to the exchange. A young lady came on the line and asked me, a little surprised, where I was calling from. I told her, and asked for Paris. 'Impossible!' I talked to her, explaining a bit about Jimmy's, and eventually persuaded her to let me call Paris that same evening, and again the next. (Next day I met her near the hotel and gave her some stockings and perfume.)

After the meal that evening in a restaurant, a women's band played Russian folk-tunes and other songs which didn't sound the least bit American. The Czechs from the hotel — in Moscow for an agricultural conference — were with us too, including my four porters. People wanted to dance the twist, so I went over and asked the ladies if they didn't know a twist number. To my amazement, they did, and proceeded to play it! Everyone started dancing, even the Czechs, under the doubtful eye of the waiters, who were non-plussed. That night marked the debut of the twist in the Soviet Union.

But the most incredible thing happened in Leningrad the follow-ing day. After we'd visited the Hermitage museum (in two hours . . .) we were on the Neva Prospect when all of a sudden we saw an army of red flags marching towards us! Cravenne looked blank for a moment, then, ever 'au courant', said: 'It's 30 April today, it must be the rehearsal for the May Day parade.' So we gamely lined up and marched along in front of the others. A journalist took a photo of part of our group which, when it appeared in the French press three days later, did not go unremarked. Georges Pompidou, prime minister at the time, met Georges Cravenne at a dinner shortly afterwards and said: 'So it was you creating all the scandal?' (One newspaper even called it a 'shameful journey'!)

While I'm on festivities, I'll talk about 1968.

For two months, the kids in the streets went wild, and there was no stopping them as they set about pulling up the paving stones so laboriously laid by previous generations.

Jimmy's was right in the firing line. One evening, like every other evening for the past month, the area was in a state of siege, and at midnight it was almost impossible to get into the club. The place was crowded with people, each with his own analysis of the 'events'. Françoise Sagan, with her leanings to the left, was busy changing the world; Marc Bohan and Charlotte Aillaud still talked of the old order. All of a sudden a young Greek friend said slyly: 'I want to go out and see France at war!' I asked him not to. He insisted, and I let him go, shutting the door behind him and telling him I wasn't going to open it again. He had chosen a bad moment: at that instant a battalion of riot police were coming down from the Observatoire to rush the group of students near the Café du Dôme. In a matter of minutes, the no man's land which had previously existed round Jimmy's was transformed into a battle ground. Riot police poured in from all directions and the Greek, terrified, yelled for us to let him back in. I opened the door. He dived in, and I shut it again right in the faces of the police.

But during the three seconds the door had been open a policeman had lobbed a tear-gas cannister into the club! It hit a mirror just above Françoise Sagan's head.

The room was very quickly filled with smoke, and the sounds of choking, gasping, screaming. I was furious, but what could I do but evacuate the place? While the barmen (trained in panic procedures) were looking after the customers, and helping them out the back way into the rue Léopold-Robert, I took my friends up to the flat (via the kitchens where we usually prepared our breakfast-time spaghetti). Once we were 'above my means', we looked at ourselves and were rather horrified: no make-up, faces like sad clowns, no one laughing. War, as the Greek called it, had come to Jimmy's.

We got ourselves organized as best as we could, and called the ambulance for Marc Bohan and the door attendant whose eyes were injured. A vehicle came and took them away; the next day Marc Bohan made a formal complaint. I put the entrance banquette outside (to get rid of the smell) and decided to close Jimmy's down. Things had become too grave to carry on dancing. A cartoonist pictured me next day in one of the big American papers, standing up to the riot police, brandishing a champagne bottle, with the following caption: 'Régine defending her Jimmy's with Dom Pérignon'.

14

Joseph, Evelyne, Maurice and Lionel

I had no further contact with Joseph. I knew he was very proud of me, and that he made out that he saw me often. One day in 1965 I learnt that they had just removed a big toe after a bad attack of diabetes, which he had been treating with a drop of the hard stuff.

I went round to see him at the house. Ettie was there too. I had a sickening feeling that something was very wrong. A few months later, he was back in hospital. Arriving in his room I discovered a bedridden giant, appallingly wasted, naked beneath his sheet, with needles in his arm. I looked at him, frightened: it was hard to believe he could be so gravely ill. Casting a weary eye down at his arm, he said with his Yiddish accent: 'Régine, you, you understand, get them to take this away.'

But I didn't really know what he meant. I felt paralyzed, drained; I returned home and he died during the night. Back at the hospital, Maurice and I watched over his body for several hours. I was still embarrassed, painfully indifferent, my grief muzzled. I resented the emotional block which held my feelings back, and I felt that something important was escaping me, something that Joseph and I should have shared. Maurice and I had to make all the arrangements: the coffin, the burial. It was the first time I'd had to perform these rites of passage.

Before the funeral, cousin Prywes told us lots of things we didn't know about Joseph's childhood and youth. The bakery business in Poland, the defence of the ghetto, the refusal to do military service, the way he and my mother met, their flight from Poland, their

207

wedding ... He told me about my grandmother's ambition to be Poland's Madame Suchard, and the problems she'd had bringing up nine children. In the end, she disapproved of Joseph's marriage and disowned him ... Joseph had no photographs whatsoever of his brothers and sisters, not even of the American uncle, and remained alienated from the other members of his family, whose lives unfolded forever unseen, whether they struggled in exile, were thrown into concentration camps, or achieved great success in the world ...

Cousin Prywes said a strange thing to me, which has stuck in my mind: 'The Zylberberg family doesn't have memories, that's why they don't get old.'

On the day of the funeral, a man I didn't know, a great friend of Joseph's so they told me, made an extraordinary speech, saying lots of things about a Joseph I had never known, or had known only partially, and I began to wonder whether in fact this was the real Joseph. Many who attended the funeral seemed genuinely upset, and appeared unsurprised by this vibrant eulogy to Joseph's 'charisma' ... Jews in their hundreds from Saint-Paul, République and Belleville were demonstrating their loyalty to Joseph. Many non-Jews were there too, and for certain of them one could only speculate as to their possible connections with Joseph.

At one point a woman Joseph had never liked caught her feet in the wire which surrounded the grave, and nearly fell in: 'One of papa's little jokes!' I said to Maurice.

There was one big problem outstanding: how to pay off the debts Joseph had accumulated. Maurice and I judged that the money-lenders had fleeced him quite sufficiently already and we threatened to expose their practices and their interest rates. Panic-stricken, they tore up the IOUs there and then.

During the course of the next few months and years, I realized that Joseph knew many more, and more diverse, people than we would ever have believed, and that he himself was not what he seemed. 'Régine, you understand, get them to take this away.' Today I do understand: he knew we were alike, but I hadn't yet known it. In his hospital bed, he was feeling as I would have felt in his place: shame and disgust at all that paraphernalia which was contributing to his misery without alleviating his sufferings.

His taste for sparkle, for extravagance, for emotion, for parties and shows; his mania for spending money, his ability to give of himself, his fascination with the rich and famous, his desire to help people: Joseph was all this. Much of it is me too.

208

Three years after Joseph died, I got a phone call from a friend who said: 'Watch out, some strange things are going on at *France-Dimanche*. They're saying that your mother's in Paris, and eats lunch every day at a restaurant down in République.'

I could tell this was no joke and, sure enough, I got a call from a journalist wanting to interview me about it. I replied: 'Monsieur, I don't know my mother and I would ask you not to interfere.'

The woman who'd ditched us when I was five years old, and who had not shown any sign of life since, who hadn't answered a letter I'd written her while I was the barmaid at the rue de Beaujolais, here she was all of a sudden, turning up just when I was starting to make a bit of money and get myself known . . . (it was the year *Mazel Tov* came out).

I sent a detective round. He reported that she did indeed spend her afternoons doing just that, watching *Mazel Tov* in one of the cinemas near place de la République, and that she wept copiously during the programme saying: 'That's my daughter! My daughter!' I also learnt that a *France-Dimanche* journalist talked to her from time to time, trying to make her say that it was me who had forced her to leave France . . . He even tried to get her to swear that she'd been locked up in an attic for twenty years on my account!

I was so sick of it all, I phoned the director of *France-Dimanche* and said that unless the whole business was stopped there and then I'd take him to court on charges of libel and defamation. Panic at the newspaper office. They gave me their word. It all worked out in the end. Gradually, I understood what had happened. My mother had a sister living in rue Saint-Denis, whose son Léon (a gifted young harpist) and husband had both died after being deported. She was so scarred psychologically that she spent twenty years in the Sainte-Anne hospital (I had been to see her twice: in her long nightdress, with sparse hair, very calm, very gentle, she kept repeating that Arthur Rubinstein had just landed in the asylum courtyard to tell her that Léon would become a great musician . . .) When she went back home she started writing to my mother to tell her that I was very well known and that I had but one idea in my head: to see my mother return to Paris. The letters repeated the same thing over and over: 'Your children love you, they cry every day, they're waiting for you.' She had done the same thing to me one day, writing: 'Régine, your mother really does want to see you, she wants to return to France.' Of course, I hadn't replied. My mother, for her part, must have begun dreaming about the possible financial benefits.

Her journey was all the more peculiar — indeed incomprehensible — because she was a woman who lacked for nothing back in Argentina. She had married a violinist who earned a good living. Greed was the only possible motive for her journey from the other side of the globe. I had confirmation of this very soon: I was told that she needed twenty-five thousand dollars for some purpose or other, to buy clothes, etc. (There was ten thousand dollars in it for the helpful aunt!) I'd made my decision: there was no question of seeing her, or even writing to her. I arranged for her to be given some money and asked her to go back to Argentina. But, to my horror, I learnt that she'd left Argentina without a passport! With Joseph, she'd been so used to bizarre journeys and crossing frontiers without papers (all that time ago!) that she'd done the same again, for no particular reason, and without realizing quite what it meant nowadays.

So I had to make a fuss at the Argentine embassy in Paris to get her the necessary papers. Lionel was the only one to see her before her departure. She still lives in Argentina.

Évelyne, my half-sister (the daughter of Joseph and Thérèse) inherited her mother's beautifully delicate hands. As a teenager she was already quite ravishing and won beauty contests. We got on very well and when Jimmy's opened she started working at the club. She was intelligent and discreet (secretive even), with excellent taste, and the young men were very impressed with her looks; one of them told me one day: 'I only come to Jimmy's to look at your sister!' In addition she had a good sense of humour, which made her very much appreciated by my friends, in particular Jacques Chazot, who was something of a connoisseur. She was prone to bad luck (it seemed to dog her), and she often said: 'I need an iron constitution to cope with everything life throws at me!' When her mother died, she put on a lot of weight but kept the striking good looks so much appreciated by all who met her. She was still with me in New York, and she looked marvellous in Monte-Carlo in the summer presiding over the Maona, statuesque in the midst of all the movement and colour. With her chignon full of flowers, she was one of the most decorative and efficient things about the club. When I look at her today, I realize that she really is magnificent, and I'm a bit jealous of her figure and her superb eyes. Some people reckon she lives 'in my shadow'. But in fact she has neither the same tastes nor the same eccentric side as me. If she loathes me at times, it's because I'm very like Joseph and she isn't at all, apart from her passion for gambling, gin and poker.

I have already mentioned how while quite young Maurice found himself a family, and that the Biedermanns treated him like their own son. Business went well, and in time he replaced the workshops making traditional suits with a modern factory making fashion clothes. In 1968, the huge rise in wages among the lowest-paid forced him to think again: his profit margin dwindled nearly to nothing, and he had either to give up the business or to change direction and location. Without hesitating, he went international and left for New York where, though not speaking a word of the language, he set up a company. It was a flop, but it took more than that to discourage a Zylberberg. He came back to France, started all over again and, three years later, made another Atlantic crossing, this time with the Yves Saint Laurent franchise. And while the Saint Laurent ready-to-wear (and his imitators) sold like hot cakes, back in France he expanded the business to include women's wear, distribution, carpets, sportswear, military clothing, etc.

Our relationship remained 'frank': when we were children, we quarrelled and made it up repeatedly. Was it unpleasant to be called 'Régine's brother' sometimes? It annoyed him a bit. I told him one day: 'I don't mind being "Biedermann's sister" because I have the humility of the great!' (He wasn't very pleased.) Whatever, it was a constant source of teasing between us ... and for the press too. Sharp and intelligent, he had inherited Joseph's passion for gambling, but had transformed it into a passion for business: like me, Maurice knew nothing about cards. He liked speculating, taking risks, responsibility. He was a creator, a leader, and we were united on major decisions.

He may be more vulnerable to criticism and failure than I am, but he could still be my twin. Like me, he has the ability to carry people with him, thanks to exceptional physical strength. For him as for me, work is a drug. A hard drug. And while I multiplied my clubs worldwide, Maurice Zylberberg 'called Biedermann' built up a business empire in the United States, putting himself on equal terms with established French textile manufacturers, who had once looked down on this kid from Sentier.

Things weren't easy with Lionel. He was a shy, reserved boy who got on badly with his brusque, exuberant, temperamental, generous,

211

egotistic mother. In adolescence, he'd started (rather like I had) to try a bit of everything. Instead of continuing his studies, he turned sales representative, then credit collector (chez Biedermann), then hack, writing about dogs getting run over, at *Paris-Jour* ... At twenty, he joined the Communist Party for a year, and spouted left-wing ideas, though the logic of his behaviour escaped me. I badly wanted him to be successful, but it seemed to me he was going about it all the wrong way. Even his work with *Paris-Match* or *L'Observateur* (where he did some brilliant reporting on guerillas, in particular) didn't strike me as being heavyweight enough. And when he refused to do military service, I was furious ... By contrast, when in 1972-1973 he became interested in jeans and started importing denim from all over the world, I said 'Bravo!' But it didn't last, and he slipped back into yet other vague and often-changing occupations. I reproached him for wasting his intelligence and his flair, and for his lack of ambition. Our quarrels were frequent, and the reconciliations short-lived. He despised osten-tation, luxury, seductiveness, and very few of his employers or colleagues knew that he was Régine's son. My friends came from a world which did not interest him — except for Françoise Sagan, whom he loved dearly, and who thought highly of him. He criticized me for not having confidence in what he was doing, for not being able to cope with his life-style, his way of thinking, his style of dress ... These last remarks were particularly hard for me to take, and I told him angrily: 'You're charging down a blind alley!' And so, while on a trip to India (the hippy Mecca), he sent me a drawing of someone running headlong into a brick wall ... which really made me think.

I was less than enthusiastic about his first marriage, but I was over the moon when, in 1971, his son was born. I became a doting grandmother, substituting my grandson for the second son I never had (I'd been married to Roger for two years at this time, and had recently had a miscarriage which left me totally exhausted). Family life seemed to be becoming a reality at last when a tragedy occurred, changing everything.

Lionel, his wife and their five-month-old son were driving to Deauville when, eighty kilometres from Paris, they had an accident. The car skidded, and turned over several times. Lionel had three crushed vertebrae and was in a semi-coma. At the hospital in Vernon, two weeks later, he was to learn that his son had died. His wife was suffering from shock, but had no serious injuries.

I was in Monte-Carlo at the time of the accident, getting very anxious. I couldn't understand why Lionel wasn't in Deauville; I'd been trying, in vain, to contact him by telephone. (Having refused to stay at Le Presbytère, he'd rented a room in a widower's villa.) When I got back to Paris, there was a message from Paul's secretary, asking me to call her as soon as possible. That's when I learnt about the accident; Roger and I left for Vernon immediately. At the hospital, Paul took me in his arms, and we cried. Lionel was still unconscious. I went to the police station and made the necessary arrangements for the baby's burial. I was in a dreadful state of shock. I thought about that child, and what he represented for all of us, a shield which had now been snatched away; I thought about Lionel, so seriously injured, and wondered what effect this tragedy would have on one so principled, with such respect for others . . . It was the worst blow fate had dealt me since the war, since my childhood. I gritted my teeth. But our misfortunes weren't over.

I was with Roger in the hospital foyer the next day. He was reading the local paper. Suddenly, he went off saying he was going to see Paul, who was in Lionel's room. In fact, he'd just read the most awful thing in the paper: as it turned over, Lionel's car had run over two young people of Polish origin who were lying on the verge. They were hitch-hiking from the north of France to Deauville, and were resting for a few minutes behind the signpost for Vernon. They had both died in the same hospital. Roger, thinking that Paul hadn't wanted to tell me, had gone to speak to him about it. Paul looked at the article, the colour drained out of him, he started shaking, and then began crying. He had known nothing about it! No one at the police station or at the hospital had mentioned it to him, or to me. Roger came to explain what had happened. Now I understood why Lionel's wife had said there were other people injured (we had thought she was suffering from shock and had been mistaken), and also why Paul had found the hospital staff so unfriendly, and why they had been seeming to say: 'We've got other people to look after too.'

Clearly, Lionel would have to be sheltered from all this. He would have to know about the child, but we decided not to expose him to a further shock by telling him about the two boys. We made contact with the unfortunate families of the two victims, who had not even tried to meet us, and asked our insurance company to do all the necessary business for us. After a month in hospital, and devastated by his son's death, though still unaware of the rest,

213

Lionel left for three months' convalescence in Saint-Raphaël. He was recovering from his injuries when my lawyer Maître Lombard's secretary phoned him to ask for some information concerning the insurance policy and mentioned the two dead boys. 'What are you talking about?' Lionel asked, baffled. He called his father straight away, who had to tell him the whole story. Then he phoned me, yelling like a madman that it was monstrous to have left him in his cocoon while two families mourned the loss of their children. He was right, we should never have kept the truth from him. I heard him shouting: 'I'm a murderer, you realize, a murderer!'

Once he had recovered, he picked up the threads of his life, and our quarrels began all over again. We remained on bad terms for several years. I told him one day that there is a certain 'emptiness which one never fills'. I was referring to children I'd never had; he thought I meant the years we hadn't spoken to each other: yet another misunderstanding, another row ... Just as Maurice had sometimes refused to be my brother, so he refused to be my son. But little by little, almost imperceptibly, we have grown closer together, and have come to understand that far from being each other's opposites we are actually very similar. And I like my new daughter-in-law very much; she's English. They met while working on a script together. The first time they went out together, he took her to ... a hospital where he was involved with a physically handicapped group.

Lionel mainly works for *Libération* these days, writing articles on music, cinema, social issues. But he does lots of other things too, in particular writing scenarios. I've realized that despite appearances to the contrary he has, like me, method in his madness, and quite a clear idea of what his life and his career should be. Obstinate, disciplined, he is a workaholic too. He gets on well with Roger and life goes on: we each do our own thing, but have had some wonderful times together, some real discoveries. With him (as with others), my relationship will never be calm: but at least it's on a more even keel nowadays. We are getting to know each other a bit better, and I dream of becoming a grandmother again one day.

15

Roger

One July Sunday in 1968, I was eating in the restaurant at La Coupole, as I did nearly every Sunday evening. It was always a difficult time of the week for me because it reminded me of boarding school, having to go back and let them shut us in again. I could never stay at home that evening: I absolutely had to go out somewhere — it took me years to get over it. After dinner I went to Jimmy's as usual. That evening Jean Poniatowski was sitting on the banquette in the hall with an Italian actress called Sylvia Monti and a dark, Mediterranean-looking boy. Jean introduced me to Roger, and told me that he was an old friend of his, a Frenchman from Morocco whom he'd met in Rabat. I joined them, we started laughing and the evening really took off. We were all on form and amused ourselves casting a critical eye over everyone who came in or went out.

Being Sunday, I was casually dressed, un-made-up. Régine 'au naturel' among friends. I had a dance, then came back to join them, went off to dance again; the hours went by. Jean and I sat reminiscing: particularly about the last holiday we'd spent together in Saint-Tropez. From time to time Jean's friend said something which made us laugh: he had a dry sense of humour, quick, unaggressive. The disc jockey kept putting on a Bérichon record, 'T'as un talisman, mon frère', sung with the *pied noir* accent from North Africa: we loved it and all joined in.

About three in the morning, Jean's friend leant over and asked me to dance. It was a slow one. I never dance to slows, yet found myself on the dance floor. He didn't dance very well, but he held me very tight. When we sat down he asked if he could come again. 'Of course!' I told him. Half an hour later, our little gathering broke up and I went up to bed. Three-quarters of an hour after that, they phoned through from Jimmy's.

'A gentleman wants to speak to you. He says you've got a rendezvous.'

'A rendezvous?'

He came to the phone.

'You told me I could come back. So I've come back.'

I laughed and said: 'But not tonight! Call me tomorrow.'

The next day, my secretary said a Monsieur Choukroun wanted to speak to me.

'Who?'

'Monsieur Choukroun.'

I didn't know who they meant. I picked up the phone. It was him again. He said: 'It wasn't very nice of you not to wait for me.'

The cheek of it coming from such a shy boy irritated me a bit and I said: 'But I never said I would wait for you!'

'Have you got time for a cup of coffee?'

'No, I'm just off to Cannes.'

'Listen, I only want a few minutes. I work in Montparnasse, I can be with you in no time.'

I don't know why but I said yes, and asked him to come round at half-past three.

When he arrived, the flat was full of people, as it often was, and I didn't know where to put him. So I took him into my bedroom-bathroom corner. He came up to me, very close. It surprised me, unnerved me, and I put out my hand as if to stop him. He seemed embarrassed and said: 'I want to get to know you, to talk to you.'

We spoke, but not for long: I had to get to Orly airport. In Cannes, at the Hotel Majestic, a telegram and flowers, from Roger, awaited me. A nice touch. Roger Choukroun . . . I was getting used to the name, the shape, the smile.

He called me as soon as I got back to Paris, and invited me to dinner. We went to L'Orangerie, Jean-Claude Brialy's extremely elegant restaurant on the Île Saint-Louis. Every time I dined there alone with a man, Jean-Claude would make a good-humoured assessment of the new boy and report back to me: Roger scored top marks. After dinner, we squeezed back into Roger's little tin can of a car (a Fiat 500 on the verge of a major breakdown) and went round to Jimmy's. By two in the morning he had told me he was a

216

computer engineer with Philips and that he'd studied in Toulouse and Nîmes. I thought him both subtle and charming, brilliant and reserved: everything I liked in a man. Did all this add up to falling in love? No ... But then again ...

Between 10 July and 5 August we saw each other almost every evening, alone or in a group, and spent our first nights together. He was due to go off on a holiday to Crete with two female friends at the beginning of August. I teased him about this apparently well organized trip. He protested that it really was a holiday with 'pals'. While he was off looking at the Minotaur, I was commuting from Deauville, where I spent my weekends. After a week, I got a long letter from him telling me he was bored and was planning to come back very soon and join me in Deauville. I realized that I'd been waiting for this letter ... He missed the Saturday flight and arrived in Paris on Sunday morning, leapt straight into his tin can and turned up in Deauville about midday, having fully expected the car to break down at any moment during the journey. It was that Sunday, after cutting short his holiday, that Roger really became part of my life, and permanently so.

One morning a few months later, before he left for work, he said he wanted to talk to me seriously and suggested we eat lunch together. Over dessert he announced that he had just made a major decision. He wanted to go into music publishing, and to work with me. I already knew that, before he met me, it was my songs he liked, and not so much my 'public persona': he'd seen me on the beach at Saint-Tropez one day, swathed in voluminous black veils, and he said I'd 'frightened' him a bit ... But he was mad about the songs. And I wasn't really surprised at his decision. He'd always liked show business and seemed to have all the qualities necessary for success in the field. It was his way of getting closer to me, and of living at the same pace. I felt he was making me a great gift, and that at the same time he showed a certain taste for adventure: life in the music business is very different from life as a Philips engineer ... But his thirst for adventure went further still because after announcing this news he asked me to marry him!

I was overcome, frightened, and didn't know what to say. For a few moments I felt utterly cut adrift, then I said yes. We'd known each other for nine months.

The engagement (unofficial) was one of the happiest times of my life. I introduced Roger to all my friends. He was at ease with all of them, and was immediately 'accepted'. We lived together at my flat, where he kept some of his clothes, to the great annoyance of Suzanne, who was jealous, and detested him. Whenever she found a shirt of his she'd say to him: 'Here, you've forgotten something.' Roger just gave her a broad smile.

Just before our wedding I was the mystery guest on Catherine Anglade and Jean Bertho's Sunday night television programme 'L'inconnu du dimanche'. They interviewed me, I told them a bit about my life, and I sang. They also questioned some close friends about me, including Suzanne. She wasn't going to miss out on her scoop, and announced that I was going to marry . . . my secretary! But this time Roger let his smile drop, and took it rather badly — especially when she added: 'We used to have one secretary, now we have two.' I wrote to the papers to clarify the matter. (But I really couldn't get angry with Suzanne. Seventeen years later, in 1985, she was helping me move house yet again, and proved more energetic than anyone else.)

The wedding was to take place in a Normandy village whose mayor was André-Louis Dubois, Carmen Tessier's husband. He was to tie the knot. We'd planned a big lunch party at the Dubois's house, with the witnesses (Jean Poniatowski and Claude Davy for Roger, Françoise Sagan and Suzanne for me) and the guests: Lionel, the Giannolis, the Guerrand-Hermèses, Maurice, Évelyne, the Bénichous, Suzanne . . .

6 December 1969, ten o'clock, I was ready. Marc Bohan had made me a bordeaux coloured woollen suit, with a full length coat (that was the fashion) complete with fox-fur collar. We picked up Françoise Sagan on the way, wearing a little toque. En route for Boncourt! It was very cloudy, but not too cold. But then, at half-past eleven fine snow began to fall. Gradually, the flakes grew larger until we were in the thick of a real blizzard.

Ten miles outside Anet, and progress slowed to a miserable three miles an hour. Roger, looking very elegant in his Prince of Wales check suit (with a bordeaux thread to complement my outfit . . .) got out of the car to assist other drivers in difficulty and to help clear the road. In the car behind was Jean Bertho and a camera crew who were coming along to film this 'follow-up' to 'L'inconnu du dimanche' . . . Jean came to interview me in the car, asking me for my impressions. They were all rather anxious ones. Françoise Sagan suggested that I could always get married the following day. But I wouldn't hear of it. I told Roger that it was bad luck to get married too late.

Having left Paris at eleven o'clock, we finally got to Boncourt at four in the afternoon. An absolute record. Everyone was very tense and the lunch had been a write-off — except for the journalists and those of the guests who had managed, I've no idea how, to arrive on time. They'd all gone down to the local café and were in much better shape than we were .....

The ceremony began. I heard André-Louis Dubois, doubtless a bit tired and having missed his siesta, ask: 'Régine Zylbergé, do you take this man Roger Choukroun to be your lawful wedded husband?' I was so nervous that his getting my name wrong like that made me splutter with laughter. I said 'I do', and could feel Françoise pinching my arm as if to say: 'This is not the moment to laugh.' Then I could hear one of the Europe Numéro 1 reporters telling his radio audience: 'Régine is crying, she's so overcome with emotion.' That set me off again and I had to bite my lip. As if that wasn't enough, André-Louis Dubois, clearly even more tired than I thought he was, then said: 'Roger Choukroun, do you take Régine Zylbergé to be your lawful wedded husband? ... At 'husband' I was off again.

After the ceremony, thirty of the guests were supposed to come on with us to Deauville. The others, who'd for the most part abandoned their cars, took the train. They told me there was a man on the train (who hadn't been at the wedding) who wouldn't stop talking. It was none other than Marcel Marceau, the mime artist. Roger and I went to Le Presbytère (no problems on the road; ten miles further on and there was virtually no snow) and the others stayed at the hotel where we'd reserved rooms. Lucien Barrière had let us have the use of his restaurant at the winter casino, where we had a Russian meal (blinis, caviar, violins) and Frédéric Botton sang and played piano with Françoise Sagan. Bénichou never tired of making us all laugh. Ingrid and Pierre Smadja were there too. It was a fantastic party, and afterwards Roger and I left for our real honeymoon at Le Presbytère. Next day we had a big lunch at L'Excelsior with prawns in pastis and more than a few rounds of drinks .....

Over the next few days I got my first letters addressed to 'Madame Régine Choukroun' or 'Madame Roger Choukroun'. To others, as to myself, I immediately became Madame Choukroun, and Roger never got called 'Monsieur Régine'. Proving just how expertly he'd played a role which had not been clear at the outset.

The problems arose after the wedding. Previously, Roger had

been firm, funny, intelligent and good-humoured. He was to remain firm, funny and intelligent, but began to lack a little good-humour. I discovered that he was very jealous. The hubbub around me made him nervous and jumpy. I couldn't stand being treated with suspicion and got very angry. The past is the past, and as I don't like to look back I wanted him to do likewise and to stop asking questions. It took us five or six years to reach a real equilibrium. But now we have.

I often tease him about how I prefer tall blond blue-eyed boys: but of course, Roger couldn't be more my type. Gradually, as the need arose, he stood in for the people who went missing from my life: the unfaithful friends, lovers of yore, my brother or my son when we became too distant. Our characters are very different, but we share the same love of activity and the same sense of pride. He is not daunted by things, and he's always there when times are bad. And whenever I phone my lawyer or my friends to tell them I'm going to get a divorce, they only half listen, and no one believes me. Our crises are superficial: our story is one of hearts and minds. The only two things which last.

In spite of his expectations, the way music publishing worked irritated Roger a bit after a while. He was a successful editor, but when he saw that I needed someone I could trust to help me put my projects into action, he decided to work with me in the club business. He took on the difficult aspects, allowing me a freer creative rein; with his managerial ability, and my preference for the creative side we made a good team. He is obsessive, scrupulous, careful; he loves paperwork, full stops, commas and graphs. I work more instinctively and we usually arrive at the same conclusions by different routes. I often get there first, which never ceases to amaze him.

My 'instincts' do have their disadvantages. I admit to being difficult to live with and unpredictable. I have fixed ideas, pet hates, and moods. And if I might sometimes appear in an unsympathetic light in this story, it's because frankness is my one defect. Here I am in my true colours, speaking plainly, not hiding my temper or my tenderness, my passions or my let-downs. If I seem hard, it's because I've always had to be in order to live, and sometimes even to survive. I have a long memory, I hate lies and I don't know how to cry. But I do know how to be warm and generous in response to warmth and generosity. Roger knows that, and so, I believe, do my friends. I love anything which lives, which sparkles, reacts, fights and forces you to take notice. I love real things, uncontrived things. I also love decoration, games, the immediate. I love anger and madness. And I love Roger. I am Régine of the night, with chiaroscuro in plenty. To quote Prévert: 'I am what I am and I can't do anything about it!'

Roger and I were both made for the single life; our marriage is a triumph over fate by the strong-arm tactics of love.

16

Songs and films

One day in 1963, Renée Lebas (a singer I used to enjoy listening to in the old days at the Folies-Belleville) said to me: 'You've got a great voice, you should be a singer.' My childish fantasies came racing back, the concerts in Aix, singing on the boulevards, the Yves Montand records ... Of course, I had thought about it from time to time, and now, after the success of Jimmy's, perhaps this was indeed the 'right moment'? I had nothing to lose, and everything to gain.

Over the weeks which followed, the idea took off. I talked to Charles Aznavour, and he gave me several songs to learn ('Tel qu'il est', 'La Javanaise', 'La Cuisine'). I bought a piano (not easy to squeeze into the flat), and I took lessons, from a lady of Russian origins called Tosca Marmor (easier to squeeze in, but a bit thunderous). The charming, deliciously 'musical' name belied the joviality of the lady herself who told me her whole life story over cups of tea. We drank plenty of tea, but practised very few scales ... I went back to see Renée Lebas, but her formula, not to be rude about it, was hardly any more helpful: she just wanted me to sing like she did, in the realistic style, full stop. I found realism pure and simple rather sad. About the same time, I met Emile Stern. The first time he heard me he shook his head and said: 'You really want to sing?'

'Well ... yes. Why shouldn't I?'

'Yes, indeed, you're quite right: judging by what you hear these days, why shouldn't you?'

Getting down to business wasn't much fun, but we started work and gradually came to like each other. I made a couple of test tapes, which I got Charles Aznavour to listen to. He told me I had three quite distinct singing styles — which might be a good thing or a bad thing: realistic, humorous, and sad. It was this particular cocktail which later got dubbed 'sophisticated', although it was nothing more than realism with a touch of irony, in the traditional 'Edith Piaf' style. Then Aznavour wrote me two songs, 'Nounours' and 'Tu m'bats plus', which I was able to record almost immediately on a contract with Bel-Air.

Just before my first record came out, Maurice Chevalier (whom I'd heard in Aix during the Occupation) asked me to help with a fund-raising party he was arranging for a home for aged actors in Ris-Orangis. He asked me to invite friends and clients and to sing three songs: two birds with one stone. He'd never heard me sing, but he had faith in the rumours he'd heard ... I assembled the most sparkling array of guests I could muster, and prepared myself for the big day.

The party was to take place on 19 January 1965 at Maxim's. My first public performance. Maxim's is on rue Royale, so I wasn't too far from home. But I wouldn't say I was over-fond of Maxim's at the time. Its occupation from 1940 to 1944 didn't endear me, and since Liberation, the clientèle hadn't been up to its pre-war standard: the invasion by the Vaudables and Suzanne Luling hadn't yet started. The décor was sublimely filthy (or filthily sublime) and bore too many stigmata of a rotten era. But then, I wasn't going to snub Ris-Orangis for the sake of the threadbare carpets at Maxim's and I threw myself wholeheartedly into the adventure.

In actual fact, it all went off very well — except that the 'wings' were stuffed full of pots of mustard and having to go through the decrepit kitchens was enough to make you feel physically sick. (Thank you, Cardin! He it was who bought it and made Maxim's resplendent once more.)

The single I made with Bel-Air was well received, and on 8 February I appeared on television in 'Musicorama'. The producer Denise Glaser had chosen Jacques Chazot to interview me, and introduce me to the world at large.

Shortly afterwards I made the valuable acquaintance of Serge Gainsbourg, someone I had admired ever since I heard him sing 'La Petite Rousse' at the Milord l'Arsouille. He didn't get on very well with Émile Stern, who had by now become my friend, composer and accompanist (Serge Lama and I were the colts in the Lebas-

223

Stern stable). But that didn't matter: my dream was that he would write songs for me and the dream was about to come true. The snag was that I didn't know him very well: he had come to the club two or three times, but each time he'd been feeling a bit maudlin, which didn't make for easy conversation. The next time I talked to him more seriously and explained what I was after. A week later he called me: 'Well, I've written you a song.'

I asked him to come over and he turned up at the flat one afternoon with his wife, who I had heard was a very jealous woman (pre-Jane Birkin). She sat herself down in an armchair, got out her work and started knitting, watching me out of the corner of her eye. I played Gainsbourg my record. He liked it. On the occasion of their second visit (they both came that time, too ...) I deliberately hadn't had my hair done and had just pulled on any old clothes. I thought it better not to make much of an effort, given the wife's jealous nature. She seemed much reassured, because she didn't knit quite so furiously this time. She must have been thinking: 'There's not much chance of her pinching him!' because the next time she didn't bother to come at all.

During the course of our second meeting Serge, adopting a rather vague expression, presented me with a song entitled 'J'te prête Charlie mais il s'appelle reviens'. I read it through; it was perfectly in character and made me laugh too. Three minutes later, still apparently unconvinced, he pulled another screwed-up ball of paper out of his pocket: 'I've got this too, another song, you never know ...'

I read it: it was 'Les Petits Papiers' ... The words were quite wonderful; I was thrilled. I swiftly recorded both songs and the press started referring to me as a singer — not without 'arrière-pensées', as if to say: 'She's already in all the gossip columns, now we'll have to talk about her on the entertainment pages too.'

In friendship and by mutual choice, at least I believe so, first Serge Gainsbourg and then Eddy Marnay became my personal song writers: being a late starter in the 'business' I wanted super-gifted song writers to create a proper repertoire of songs for me rapidly. Thanks to the talents of these two (and others whom I shall mention later) I managed to build up a very respectable one. At the time, nearly everyone else was singing adaptations of English or American songs, but given my unstoppable dancing feet and my street looks, I preferred to sing French. I didn't care about the hit parade. I simply hoped that the songs I sang, which came from the streets and which were for the streets, would find their way back there some day.

I was also keen to have Francis Lai, whom I greatly admired, write songs for me. People said: 'You must be mad; he hasn't written anything for years.' So what? It's just a question of getting back into it again. He came round with his accordion and in collaboration with Françoise Dorin wrote me: 'Qu'est-ce que vous voulez que j'en fasse?'

I have some remarkable memories of shows I sang in at the start of my career, in all four corners of France, mainly because of Émile Stern, my accompanist. As he hated flying and I couldn't stand long car journeys, I tried to reach a compromise by hiring light aircraft. Whether we made any money out of the shows was a moot point, but that was too bad. The first time I suggested this means of transport to Émile he protested vehemently, but I explained to him how this particular plane was the 'nec plus ultra', safe, silent, comfortable. I assured him that in flight it hardly moved — so to speak. He started to believe me, and was much impressed, as people tend to be when I want to persuade them of something. We climbed aboard the splendid machine in question and between Paris and Montpellier everything went smoothly until we hit the biggest air pocket I've ever come across in my life! Émile turned distinctly green, and that's the way he stayed for the rest of the flight. Once we got there he announced that there was absolutely no question of him playing that night! Nothing I could do would change his mind, and I just had to watch while Émile took himself calmly off to bed! I would have to go on without him. On other occasions, as he was very sensitive and got upset when he heard people laughing (he always thought they were laughing at him), he threatened not to play or else played crossly and uncomfortably ... If the piano did not meet with his approval, he used to tinkle a few notes with an air of disdain, get up and declare: 'I never play on an out-of-tune piano. I have never, in all my life, played on a piano which is out of tune, you understand, Régine ...' So everyone had to sit down and wait while the piano tuner was summoned.

On another occasion, we were starting our rehearsal and Émile sat down at his instrument in an excellent mood. Suddenly, we saw him look alarmed and begin searching desperately for the pedals with his feet! No pedals! Émile bent down, poked about under the piano, and pulled them out from underneath, quite stupefied. With pedals in his hands his whole world was topsy-turvy! That night we played on a piano with no pedals.

He was also very good at 'placing' songs, and getting himself 'well-placed' too: 'I think we could move the piano forward a little, don't you? Like that, you see? Perhaps a little more? Wait, it would be perfect about two feet further forward ...' Some evenings I ended up behind the piano. And I couldn't help laughing at his little navy blue suits, apparently so understated. The discreet silver flecks which ran through the material and were almost invisible by daylight would suddenly sparkle into life under the spotlight. When the lights went up, pow! All you could see was Emile's suit glittering! He had five musicians playing with him (rumour had it they were one of the most expensive bands in Paris), Armand Molinetti on drums, Freddie Vendair on the accordion and the arranger Alain Goraguer. They were the best, of course. If I was going to be a singer, I had to do it properly.

Apart form Gainsbourg ('Mallo-Mallory', 'Ouvre la bouche et ferme les yeux') and Francis Lai and Eddie Marnay ('Patchouli-Chinchilla', 'Okazou'), my other lyricists were Patrick Modiano ('L'Aspire-à-cœur'), Serge Lama ('Les Maisons grandes'), Jean Cau ('Je veux être celle'), Jean-Loup Dabadie ('L'Accident'), Michel Magne ('Un jour je quitterai tout'), Michel Grisolia ('Kafka c'est dansant'), Charles Level ('Azoy'), Joe Dassin ('M. Lapin'), Vahé Katcha, Françoise Sagan, Dutronc and Lanzmann. Frédéric Botton wrote the words and music for 'La Grande Zoa', and it was Emile Stern who wrote the music for 'Okazou' and 'Patchouli-Chinchilla'.

I soon left Bel-Air for Pathé-Marconi, the top record company at the time. They gave me a big contract, and with the proceeds I bought a house in Saint-Tropez, a one-time pottery which belonged to Vincent Roux. (Vincent was an old friend of Paul Lombard, who became my lawyer.) Ever since the garage I'd had in Saint-Tropez during the crazy years I'd dreamt of having a proper house, and I started doing it up rather luxuriously. This time, too, I was living 'above my means': like Joseph and his jam, I borrowed money, making the house about as ruinous, with all the interest I was paying, as the paternal factory had been.

At Pathé they found me eccentric. I had my own ideas about everything and I was set on changing the system. I wrote to them about sales, demanded fifty musicians for my albums, etc. They didn't dare say too much, but they thought plenty! In 1967 I won the Grand Prix du Disque from the Académie Charles-Cros, and the following year I starred in Musicorama at the Olympia with Joe

Dassin, in conjunction with Europe Numéro 1. Rapturous applause: seventeen curtain calls which wasn't bad considering I was still a newcomer. That same evening, Coquatrix offered me another concert at the same venue. *France-Dimanche* re-issued the photos of me and the Duke of Windsor dancing at the rue du Four. A journalist quoted something I'd said during the course of the interview: 'When I'm fed up, I open my wardrobe and count my shoes and soon I'm back on top!' I had also told him all about my childhood and what a 'little old lady' I had been, surrounded by octogenarians in the Lyon old people's home during the war.

At the end of 1968, I co-starred with Raymond Devos at the Olympia. I had terrible stagefright, which turned me into a live wire, but it went very well. Barbara had written a superb song for me: 'Gueule de nuit'. It was then that Jacques Brel, whom I'd met in Deauville two years before, gave me this advice: 'When you sing sad songs, you must hold yourself a little stiffly, with your feet together. When you sing happy songs, stand with your feet slightly apart and bend a knee.' One evening while we were in Deauville, enjoying one of those walks he was so fond of along the beach, I asked him why he never came back on stage to do encores. He said: 'You'll see; afterwards, it's never the same as it was before.'

I felt the same way, too, and followed his example.

In October 1969, I played the Carnegie Hall in New York. Roger came with me. He also arranged all my recording sessions in Paris. He is a perfectionist and will not tolerate anything less than the best. I won't either, I hasten to add, and if I felt he was holding back from telling me that something still wasn't right (after several attempts), I'd say: 'Okay, I understand, let's start again.'

The preparations for the Carnegie Hall show were complete madness. Because I couldn't find a producer, I had hired the Hall myself. The show was to be on 16 January 1969. As *Mazel Tov* had been such a success in New York (under its English title, *Marry me, Marry me*), I bought lots of advertizing space in the papers and filled them with 'Régine, the star of *Mazel Tov*'. The effect was immediate. But on the organizational side it was utter chaos. The musicians themselves only arrived the evening before and we couldn't really rehearse. Fortunately, Mort. Schumann had written some jokes for me to tell between songs and with the generally buoyant mood that prevailed everything went well. Our insouciance must have cheered up the heavens too, because the blizzard which had brought traffic to a standstill in New York the previous night, gave way to brilliant sunshine.

In 1973, I sang at the Bobino. I used the same format, on a grander scale, that had been so successful in Monte-Carlo: a multi-faceted show with songs and different acts which linked together.

The curtain went up on a spectacular samurai sword and dagger fight (by two French stuntmen). To finish, one of the blades cut a circle out of a paper screen, to reveal me standing on a fluffy cloud with a very authentic boa round my neck ... I sang 'La Grande Zoa', then handed over to Philippe Genty with the feather boa which, many impersonations later, magically became three extremely facetious ostriches. Then I came back on stage with another of Philippe's puppets. After me came Yves Duteil, then a Brazilian group dancing the samba and bossa-nova. One of them was called Touka, plump, brilliant and very funny. I joined in their stunning carnival performance. After the interval came the Ivanovitch gypsies and their balalaïkas, then Claude Vega with his crushing caricatures and dolly-bird impersonations. I came back on stage once more to round off the show with ten new songs, including 'Bilbao'. For this show, directed by Nicolas Bataille, we wanted to break the music-hall mould. We got rid of the traditional boring old compère who usually announced each act, so everything was much more fluid and lively. The audience at the Bobino, who were expecting the time-honoured ritual (curtain up, English act, American act, yet another act, etc.) were a little disconcerted at first, but took it in their stride. The reviews were excellent. *Le Nouvel Observateur*, after commenting on the type of 'friendship' on offer at Jimmy's ('part whisky, part vendetta: only Régine herself isn't fooled by it'), decided that my repertoire was, like me, 'popular, sophisticated, sharp'. *L'Express* talked of 'sophisticated ribaldry', while *L'Aurore* thought I came over on stage 'just like I did at my club'. The critic added: 'She and her boa know each other well and she launched into her first song, "La Grande Zoa", in admirably relaxed fashion.' He also commented, to my delight, on the fact that I wore 'half a dozen different dresses' (all by Levasseur) for my ten songs. *Combat* thought highly of 'Azoy' and 'La Rue des Rosiers', a song which was 'bloody complicated and difficult to put over for someone trying to be a popular singer'. Galant, the critic from *Combat*, added: 'She manages to maintain a tradition without looking as though she's stepped out of the waxworks museum!' As for *Le Monde*, I'll be speaking about that paper later on in my chapter on

228

the 'living dead'.

After a series of broadcasts on Europe Numéro 1, in which I told my life story, without excessive embellishments, I appeared in 1969 on 'La Tête de l'art', with a comic, Jean Rigaud. In my Dior dress (red, with stripes and big pompons), I was finding it hard to concentrate, not because of the dress, but because of the audience: there were several gentlemen there with their ladyfriends who were more interested in kissing and cuddling than in watching the show.

One night in the bar I was talking to Fernand Raynaud, who told me: 'I've just been to see an incredible guy at Don Camillo. He's only eighteen. He knows the lot.' I asked who he was: Thierry Le Luron. As Fernand Raynaud was not known to be free in his praise, I decided I had to meet this young prodigy. I called him up and invited him to come over to Jimmy's whenever he liked. I'll never forget the day he came, this boy who stood knee-high to a grasshopper, who could barely reach the spy-hole in the door, yet who was destined for the heights and was to become the darling of all France, a Napoleon among comics and impersonators. He had a heart, talent, honesty, and an incredible gift for improvisation. He had everything going for him, and great generosity towards others. As for his 'targets', they had to laugh at themselves because, when all's said and done, it's always better to be talked about than not. (A propos Régine, he often told me that I have a melancholic look when I sing which is difficult to copy. That's just what other female impersonators have told me too.)

My boa from the Bobino was not the first snake I'd held in my arms. The year before, I'd chosen to do a snake-charmer act for the Union des Artistes show. 'Chosen' isn't quite the right word: all the other options had been taken. I felt rather revolted when they showed me the animal in question during rehearsals at the Cirque d'Hiver (where I met up with Émilien Bouglione again). I looked at it, it looked at me, and I felt very uncomfortable.

'I can't do it,' I said, 'they'll have to do without my song.'

Then what do I see but Roger brandishing the snake and murmuring sweet nothings to it! I could already hear the comments he'd be making: 'Who was afraid of the snake then?' And my pride got the better of me.

'All right, put it on me, then!'

I felt the colour drain from me as soon as the creature was placed on my shoulders. However, I did realize that 'it' was neither cold nor slimy, but warm and dry. I was beginning to feel a little more confident when all of a sudden the beast raised its head.

'Take it away! Take it away!'

The boa's keeper didn't exactly jump to it, and I started to panic, flailing my arms about. The snake tightened its grip even more and curled up lovingly on my breast. He had me surrounded! Everyone agreed: this boa adored me. So I adopted it, but obviously didn't look all that happy because I could see Fellini in the audience laughing at me. The gala evening went off very well and my boa was much applauded.

For the Bobino show I needed some help from Émilien Bouglione, who'd got me my camel for the Barclay ball. He sent me over a rather strange man who brought amazing creatures back from Africa three times a year — snakes, donkeys, camels and even ... scorpions. You need all sorts of things for a circus. When he came round, he took three snakes out of a cloth bag, and quite calmly put them on the floor. Suzanne walked in at that moment, cast an anxious eye over them, but merely said: 'Those things don't wee on the carpet, do they?'

I didn't have quite the same perspective as Suzon, but I was beginning to wonder whether I really could carry it off, this idea of appearing on stage every night with a live boa. The salesman, a little disappointed by my reaction, said; 'But they're so nice, they're so friendly!'

'Yes, they're friendly, but from a distance!'

All things considered, I decided not to give up my plan, and set about selecting my serpent. I eliminated one of them straight away: he was big, black and horrible, all lumps and bumps.

'What's the matter with that one?'

'Nothing ... He's just eaten his rabbit, that's all.'

Feeling quite sick, I told him to say no more, and chose one of the other two, lighter in colour, quite sweet-looking, and of apparently tranquil disposition.

The night of the première, I arrived on stage with my boa. We'd had time to get to know each other a bit. He could tell that he'd got a good owner, and I could tell that my boa was mad on music: he adored it, and even liked popping flashbulbs too. Nothing seemed to make him bad-tempered and on stage he'd wag his head about with pleasure, rather like a dog wags his tail. I told the audience that my boa had no name, and that we'd have to find him one. Someone shouted out: 'Philibert!'

So we called him Philibert.

For a whole year, and long after the show at the Bobino, Philibert lived with me in Paris, and in Monte-Carlo, where I took him for shows. One day at boulevard du Montparnasse, he vanished. We searched the whole flat. The rumour spread through the block, and within an hour the entire place had emptied onto the street. I carried on with my search, and was just about to call the fire brigade when I found him, up on the bookshelf, quietly digesting behind the Grande Encyclopédie Larousse. An intellectual boa!

If I had to get him down to the Côte or back to Paris again I dragooned my friends into helping. Once Luc Fournol took him by train, very nervously. Jacques Clément, my make-up artist, and Diego, my hairdresser, were also given charge of him. One day Jacques came through the police control at Nice airport with Philibert in a bag.

'Open up!' said the policeman.

'No, I can't,' said Jacques, who was terrified of the snake.

Just then the bag moved! The policeman (already a little surprised by the amount of make-up in Jacques suitcase) asked: 'Have you got a cat in there?'

'No, it's not a cat.'

'A dog? But he can't possibly breathe in there!'

'No, it's not a dog. And you certainly mustn't touch it.'

'But what is it?'

'I can't tell you.'

'What do you mean, you can't tell me? You might have a bomb in there!'

Clément, who couldn't have looked less like a terrorist, said: 'Do I look like the kind of guy who'd carry bombs?'

The man decided he'd still have to look, and after a stomach-turning moment let the make-up man and his monster through.

Scenes like this were always happening. Philibert had a tummy-ache and I asked Diego (who loved him dearly) to take him down to the vet. The waiting room was full of ladies with little lapdogs and old gentlemen with Persian cats. One old lady felt sorry for him: 'Have you got a cat in there? You must be mad, he'll suffocate.'

So Diego went to explain to the receptionist. Suddenly, the vet could see him straight away.

One day, alas, Diego bought a big juicy rat for Philibert from the

Paris docks (as he did every three weeks). But this particular rat can't have been a very healthy one, because Philibert never managed to digest it. It killed him.

I carried on singing 'La Grande Zoa', but without him I felt almost undressed. Something which didn't improve from year to year, with or without the boa, was stagefright, and how unbearable I was before going on. I couldn't stand flowers in the dressing room: it reminded me of funerals. I would arrive on stage, the words sticking in my throat, overcome with the deepest gloom. Once I got started everything went fine, as it does for everyone. But the preparations for going on stage were exhausting, and especially for other people. I really needed star treatment and the reassurance of court followers, to defuse my nervousness. At the Bobino, I had to have Roger beside me while I was being made up. When he'd had enough he used to go over to the café opposite, La Belle Polonaise. He returned rather late one evening, only to hear me shout: 'Hey, I'm the belle Polonaise around here!'

It was different with records, but I used to get so excited that I made everyone listen to them at the flat before they were released: my friends knew each one by heart before ever hearing them on the radio. Jacques Chazot assured me that each time a new album came out I used to ask people: 'Don't you love my new record?' There must have been rather a lot of that sort of thing!

Since the fame of 'La Grande Zoa' had spread beyond France, I decided to appear with a live boa again at the Union des Artistes gala performance in Los Angeles in 1976. The Americans had especially asked to have the gala in their country that year. (After that they held one every year, with American artistes ...) This time I changed the act a bit and came on as a snake charmer. I undulated, was very sultry, sang, danced, and when my number was over I went calmly into the audience and sat myself down ... on Paul Newman's knee. It was a promise I'd made one day, and my boa seemed a good way of making sure I fulfilled it. Paul Newman went a bit cross-eyed, but remained impassive, unlike his neighbour Liza Minnelli, who screamed in panic.

Apart from the Carnegie Hall, my next biggest hit was at the Persian Room, in the Plaza Hotel on the corner of Fifth Avenue and Central Park. The fifteen musicians were directed by Raymond Bernard, who was once Bécaud's arranger and accompanist. Nothing could make you feel more like a star than those vast suites of rooms big enough to rollerskate in, and the chauffer-driven limousines they put at your disposal. The last show took place on a Saturday, and on Monday before leaving I was supposed to visit my manager Sol Hurok's newly opened New York offices. But I wanted to get home, and took a flight for Paris on the Sunday evening. At eleven o'clock on Monday morning, a bomb went off in Sol's office, killing his secretary. Before I left Paris at the start of the trip, my medium had said to me: 'When you return from New York, you will learn that you have narrowly escaped death.' Roger had said jokingly: 'The Plaza will probably burn down after you've left.' But it wasn't the Plaza.

But I've had failures in my singing career, as elsewhere — and notably with the musical called *La Neige en été*, which was staged at the Porte Saint-Martin, based on an idea by Carmon, a young Israeli, and scripted by Jacques Lanzmann. From the very start of rehearsals I felt something was wrong. The dialogue wasn't much good, but Lanzmann absolutely refused to change anything. But that wasn't all. Mouloudji (whom I greatly admired) and Nicole Croisille, who were my co-stars, kept fooling around, and I didn't understand why. When I was rehearsing at home in the evening with Francis Perrin and Jean-Claude Brialy, they advised me not to let them mess me about: 'If they do,' Brialy said, 'just walk to the back of the stage, fold your arms and wait.' Not so easy for a novice to do ... The director, a Jew who spoke very good English and Yiddish, but alas not such excellent French, didn't really help. The costumes (gypsy) were atrocious, and on top of everything the pills I was taking to help me slim were making me feel giddy. It was doomed, and on the night of the première, I saw deep consternation written on the faces of Michèle Morgan, Gérard Oury and Philippe Labro, who were among the first to see it in all its awfulness. Their sympathetic hearing and kind words were no consolation. My medium was right when he told me: 'You think you'll produce a beautiful baby, but it'll be a monster.' The reality was every bit as bad as his prediction.

Once the show stopped running (it didn't last long), I left for a holiday at the Club Méditerranée in Dakar. There was one good thing about it: during the course of the show, I'd reached an all-time low in weight: eight and a half stone. Beautifully skeletal beneath the coconut palms, I forgot about the failure of the Porte Saint-Martin.

I have other, much more pleasant memories, though, like the times I spent with Charles Aznavour. For a long period while he

233

was single, we used to go off in his Rolls-Royce for weekends in Deauville. He's a good, generous, sensitive person whom it's impossible not to enjoy being with. After his exhausting tours, he liked to relax in Saint-Tropez. One day when we were down at the harbour, he started telling me how fed up he was, living alone. A lovely blonde girl in shorts and a cap was walking along just ahead of us, and in a sudden flash of inspiration I said to him, only half joking: 'There's your future wife!' My prediction turned out better than I could possibly have imagined. Her name was Ulla, they were to meet a couple of hours later, and they are still together.

Michel Sardou is another singer whose strength and talent I admire. During the summer of 1984 he celebrated his wife Babette's thirty-fourth birthday at my club in Monte-Carlo: it was the only time during their holiday that they left the boat they were living on, day and night, with their children. In an interview I did with him that summer for *Paris-Match*, I asked him this question: 'As a child, what did you think when you saw your father (Fernand Sardou) acting?' He answered: 'I didn't think my father was working, I thought he was just having a good time. I used to say to myself, "He's dressing up". One day I thought he looked really ridiculous: he was in a bear costume for a play. When he came back into the wings he caught sight of my mocking expression and said: "Don't you take the piss, this is what pays for your bread and butter!"'

It's no surprise that I've got such a sharp memory for my stage appearances. In my real job, at the club, I perform constantly. From nine o'clock in the evening onwards I have to forget my own concerns. Daytime preoccupations get put under wraps, especially if they have been less than cheerful. In the evenings I'm like a clown, like an artist, like someone else, but I'm still me. It's neither 'put on' nor 'acted': it's both a necessity and a trait in my character. I don't put on an act in my clubs, and when I smile it's first and foremost because I'm happy to be there. I've made each club just how I want it to be; it's like having my own personal theatre complete with repertoire, usherettes, barmen and clientèle. Even with several clubs, they would still always be made to measure, with special attention paid to the finer points of detail. And the atmosphere created would be the same in each club. My physical presence could only be there at certain precise moments. With

Régine's International, I would still be there in spirit, but from a distance, rather like a medium ...

But before we get to that bit, I want to talk about films. In 1968, I made the transition from stage to screen with *Mazel Tov* or *Le Mariage*. The film was directed by Claude Berri, who also appeared in the film, and who had achieved some fame the year before with *Le Vieil Homme et l'Enfant*, starring Michel Simon. I accepted enthusiastically, but on two small conditions: my scenes would have to be filmed in the afternoon and I wanted to be able to change one or two lines. I also added a line which people found funny: 'Men like to go out with thin girls, but they come home with fat ones.'

During one stage of the filming (five days in an Antwerp apartment) my mind was not always on the job because I had to make sure I didn't miss the evening train to get to Jimmy's in Paris by opening time. But for the most part the filming went very well, except for a few tiffs with Elisabeth Wiener and some bitter-sweet comments from the assistant, Berri's brother-in-law, Jean-Pierre Rassam (the future producer of *La Grande Bouffe*), who said to Berri: 'She'll steal the film.' I was delighted at the success of *Mazel Tov* and proud of the review by Jean-Louis Bory in *Le Nouvel Observateur*: 'Amongst a discreetly effective cast walks a star, one might say, about to be born, who plays herself, a foreigner fascinated by Paris, who ends up opening a club there.' Robert Chazal in *France-Soir* described my part, that of a tempestuous woman, as small but well acted.

In this first film, and after, I appreciated playing what I call cameo parts, minor character roles which give a film a realistic 'feel' and a rather 'strange' atmosphere. From *Mazel Tov* to *Les Ripoux*, directors have let me play parts which were very 'me'.

In Pierre Granier-Defferre's *Le Train*, with Jean-Louis Trintignant and Romy Schneider, I played a tart-with-a-heart. Was it because I look like a nocturnal creature, because of the job that I do, because I'm a working-class *femme fatale*? Whatever the reason, I got more and more offers to play tender, humorous, down-to-earth parts. They were filming *Le Train* near Nevers. It coincided with the opening of the Sporting d'été in Monte-Carlo, and a big party hosted by Their Serene Highnesses Prince Rainier and Princess Grace of Monaco. That day I had to leave Nevers in the afternoon by private plane, fly to Nice, drive to Monte-Carlo, organize and supervise everything at the Maona and Jimmy's, spend the night dancing and doing the hostess bit ... then at six in the morning I took the plane back and by nine I was in my caravan in a field near Nevers, half into my dressing gown and greatly in need of sleep. But it was out of the question: they were shooting at ten, out of doors. Grass and mud substituted for the diamonds and fountains of the night before.

My next film was *Robert and Robert* by Claude Lelouch, with Jacques Villeret. Lelouch had 'explained' the story (I rarely read the script right through) and then, every morning when I arrived, he gave me a piece of paper with my lines. I came in my own chauffeur-driven car, and Germaine Montero (who was also in the film) was convinced that Lelouch was paying for it ... There was a very good atmosphere during filming, we all had a lot of freedom, and I felt quite in my element.

I also appeared in Roger Kahn's *Sortie de Secours*, produced by Alain Delon, with screenplay by Michèle Perrein and script by Pascal Jardin (excellent reviews, small audiences ...), and in Herbert Ross's *Seven per cent solution*, from the book by Nicholas Meyer: I played a Vienna brothel-keeper, and sang the Stephen Sondheim song 'I never do anything twice'. The film was a great success in the United States.

I continued seeing all my film world friends at the club, among whom Philippe de Broca. It was in one of his films that I had made my screen début, for a laugh (*Un Monsieur de Compagnie*, 1964, with Jean-Pierre Cassel and Jean-Pierre Marielle), and Philippe met his wife Michèle at my flat at the Porte Dorée one Sunday afternoon, at one of my meatball lunches.

In 1984, while filming *Les Ripoux* (showing as *Le Cop*), I read Roman Polanski's autobiography (called *Roman*), and was deeply affected by it. I recognized myself in his book (as in *Hannah* by Paul-Loup Sulitzer). The war had been the same for both of us, though in different countries and in different languages. I know Roman well and was struck by the number of phrases which I could have written myself, for example: 'As a child, I never doubted for a moment that my dreams would come true one day.' This child who, at ten years old, loved to make people laugh but got upset over trifles, who adored the cinema but who, in the Cracow ghetto, saw slogans on the screen which read 'Jews = lice = typhoid!', who had to leave his parents and flee the Germans to live with a Catholic couple where the sign of the cross punctuated every mealtime; who as an adolescent nearly died of hunger and then got rations from Russian soldiers (who were 'liberators'); and who, after the war, behaved like a delinquent in class (convinced that he would have a different future, different teachers ...); and who, after the tragic death of his mother, was once again sent to boarding school because his stepmother didn't want him (and who offered him presents instead ...); who had to profess to being a Catholic in order to continue his studies; and whose first girlfriend, a 'tender and stimulating' young lady, knew how to remedy some of the gaps in his education; the young man who discovered, in wonderment, jazz music, Juliette Gréco, the Voice of America, and for whom 'shoes were more important than anything'; this man who discovered Paris, the 'heart of the civilized world', who decided to conquer it, and who haunted the discotheques around Saint-Germain-des-Prés, making everyone laugh with his Marlon Brando and James Dean impersonations, and who came gradually to be accepted as one of the greats of the cinema; from boyhood through adolescence to adulthood it was impossible not to recognize parts of myself in his story: the problematic childhood, the lice, the antisemitic schoolfriends, the Occupation, running away, boarding schools, the convent, Joseph and his presents, stepmothers, Claude, who in the silence of Lyon introduced me to literature, the Liberation, the Americans, discovering night clubs, music and pairs of shoes, my little world-shaking dance routines, and above all the certainty of 'winning through' one day, by working hard and having faith in myself ...

My latest film is Claude Zidi's *Les Ripoux*, with Philippe Noiret and Thierry Lhermitte. The atmosphere on set was exactly the same as in the film: lighthearted, funny, natural, intimate − in a word, great. When *Les Ripoux* came out, no one concealed their pleasure and the film thoroughly merited its success. Zidi really had a big hit (he got a César for the best film of 1985). The role of mistress-confidante who knows all about life and men amused me a lot. I only wish it had been a bigger part.

Meeting actors in a club and living and working with them are two quite different things. Among those who have greatly impressed me − I can't mention them all − are Romy Schneider, Françoise Dorléac, Alain Delon, Yves Montand, Philippe Noiret, Gérard Depardieu, Catherine Deneuve − who met Marcello Mastroianni at my house.

Romy Schneider was fascinating, even when she seemed anxious or even, some days, rather lost or absent. Sometimes she was there with us, sometimes she was elsewhere. Françoise Dorléac was 'beautiful inside and out'. She was dynamite, with a gorgeous figure, smouldering eyes, enormous talent; she had what it takes to become a great star, but death decided otherwise. And I feel Alain Delon and I are somewhat kindred spirits. We both like to do and to prove things, and are wary of being soft-hearted. He hates failure; so do I. Beneath what is sometimes a fragile exterior, and intermittently (because he goes out very little), I believe our friendship is genuine. At least, I hope so.

I'm still great friends with Mireille Darc. For me, she is femininity and tenderness personified. She is calm, reserved, and her smile is one of the most magical things in the world. Even though she's not an actress, I include here Sylvie Vartan, who is always there when I need her, and with whom I have cemented a solid and intimate friendship. And Simone Signoret, one of the greatest actresses of the century, is intelligence itself, and as sure of herself as a star should be. And furthermore, she's now a writer as well. (She told me one day I should play Helena Rubinstein in her life story. I'm ready and willing.)

On the borderline between the night and the cinema, there is also Pascal Jardin, avid partygoer and brilliant scriptwriter. Well before his marvellous little book *La Guerre à neuf ans* came out, he had told me all about his life in Vichy, and I had compared it, silently, with my own. Two very different childhoods, one and the same experience transforming everything, linking, in their dreams and their innocence, the little Jewish girl from Lyon with the son of a French statesman ... In his case, too, death won the battle against youth, laughter, imagination and talent. Pascal Jardin was taken from us in 1982, at the age of forty-eight.

Among foreign actors, one in particular struck me. When Jimmy's first opened, Jean Poniatowski, then public relations director of 'Télé 7-Jours', told me that his paper was bringing Steve McQueen to Paris; his series 'Au nom de la loi' (Wanted: Dead or Alive) was doing incredibly well on French television. I met him and we clicked. Inexplicable, more or less, as things like that often are. He had a reputation for being a bit of a rough diamond; his smile was quite disarming. A year later, I was staying at the Connaught Hotel in London, and having dinner one night with my agent Caroline

Pfeiffer. We were at Aretusa's, a big Italian restaurant, very much à la mode. Caroline told me that Steve McQueen had just flown in from the States. I called him right away.

'Steve, hello. It's Régine. It would be good to see you. We could have dinner, if you like.'

He told me he was having dinner that night with three friends.

'Come to Aretusa's! It's wonderful!'

'Okay. We're coming.'

The evening was well lubricated; me drinking lemon tea, he was on vodka. It was as though we'd known each other for a thousand years.

The day after, I arranged a lunch party for him at Les Ambassadeurs. This was a very smart gaming club restaurant belonging to John Mills, an English businessman of Polish origins who looked very like Joseph. His son and Lionel had been great friends at their Swiss school, and I got on with John the instant Lionel introduced us. Les Ambassadeurs was part of a sumptuous town house which had once belonged to the Rothschilds, and consisted of a vast lounge, a large bar and a dining room where, depending on the time of day and the mood, either violinists or a pianist would be playing. I had invited Mort Schumann to lunch, still unknown in France but a celebrity in the United States. And as a treat for Steve McQueen, I'd ordered a very sophisticated meal, with 'pommes de terre-caviar'. He seemed to like both.

Two years later, he came to spend a fortnight's holiday with me in Saint-Tropez. The news spread rapidly round the village, and I was bombarded with phone calls and invitations. But he wanted to rest, and so did I. So we spent most of our time quietly at home, or else taking long walks along the beach. It was June, so the place was quite quiet. At the harbour he bought me two straw hats which I've still got, like little relics, and which never get worn in the sun. He met Ali MacGraw shortly afterwards and that was the start of a real love story. I went to the twenty-four hour race at Le Mans with him, and that was the last time I saw him. His illness and death hit me very hard, and I felt immense grief at the loss of such a special person.

It was during the songs and films phase that I began to pay constant (and almost guilty) attention to my toilette. In a night club you have to be elegant; on stage and on the screen, you must try to be unforgettable. But it seemed that my figure, except on a few notable but brilliant occasions, had decided to stay quite rounded, so I tried to forget about it by buying lots of dresses: with each new dress I felt thinner. My figure was the couturier's delight: there was no question of hiring their dresses, they had to be made to measure and bought!

So began a kind of clothes mania, compared with which my purchases of the rue du Four era (Scherrer, Carvil, Maud Frizon, Rossetti in Venice) paled into insignificance. Without abandoning the classics, I had a field day with Sonia Rykiel, Laroche, Ungaro, Dior, Saint Laurent and Cardin. André Oliver, at Cardin, made my dress for Musicorama in 1969. His dress was as lively as the dancers who accompanied me, the unforgettable Jeannot, Fufu, Skippy and Gello ... Marc Bohan created my dress for the Olympia show, black with coquettish fringes.

Like all good customers, I pay late, it's a habit of mine. People do forgive me, but nothing ever quite equalled my first mink, which I had to pay for in six instalments — by necessity rather than by choice ... Over the years, the madness continued; although I remained faithful to my 'ex's', I bought some quite exceptional dresses from Karl Lagerfeld (who took my measurements one time sitting on the edge of my bathtub), from Paco Rabanne, Montana, Chantal Thomass ... My five hundred dresses, religiously preserved, provide a comprehensive history of fashion over the last twenty-five years. Together with the shoes, which fill an entire room, they form a stunning collection, a real costume museum. People know me as Régine, but I know myself as pairs of shoes.

My triple 'career', clubs, singing and cinema, caused me to be cited at length in 1969 as an 'example', during a conference, by a woman then little known, but who became famous a few years later: Alice Saunier-Séité. At the time she was the only female head of a literature faculty and had been invited to address a general meeting of the Rotary Club in Great Britain. Her theme: successful women. She began by declaring straight away (without levelling accusations at anyone) that successful women were a rare commodity ... It was very rare indeed, she said, for a woman on her own, that's to say without a personal or family fortune, and without a well placed husband or lover, to get to the top. Régine, she went on, has managed to construct her own train, carriages, engines, station and rails too. At the time, she had never met me, and she used me as an example because she (modestly) said she couldn't think of another one: in fact her own success, already in evidence, was to become more striking when she was named Secretary of State for universities.

At the time I didn't know about this particular conference, but two or three years later Jean Bertho, who happens to be her brother-in-law, told me there was a text floating around about me which was quite fun. That's when I met Alice Saunier-Séité, and was delighted. We got on immediately. She saw in me the spirit of fun and a good dose of 'common sense'; I saw in her that freedom of thought and consistency in action without which one can do nothing of value. As for our faults, shared or respective, let our critics draw up the list. Alice Saunier-Séité has been savagely attacked, but has continued her work at the Ministry and rightly so: she is not one of those women — or more usually those men — who can be accused of fishing in troubled waters and compromising their ideas. It's no more than you would expect: when you've made yourself into someone, you can't change or the whole edifice collapses.

And since I was mentioning critics, I will now turn to my dear 'living dead', the people who have wished to harm me, and who think they have done so. You'll be able to judge for yourselves.

17

The Living Dead and Court Cases

I expect an awful lot of my friends and the people I love, but of people in general all I ask is a little elegance, good manners, some intelligence and humour if possible. I like people to be direct and I'll never forget how the very distinguished Professor Pasteur Vallery-Radot thumped his fist on the bar at the rue du Four, when they put on something soft after a whole hour of uninterrupted twist music, and said: 'Mademoiselle, I haven't come here to dance a smooch!'

But there are some sorts of people I will not tolerate, racists to start with. I am intransigent on that point, whether we're talking about the past or the present. You can understand my fury when André Harris's film *Le Chagrin et la Pitié* came out in 1971. After seeing a preview, a friend warned me that at the end of the interview with Christian de La Mazière (an SS officer during the war) the gentleman declared: 'It was so wonderful living in Paris in those days; Maxim's was full of people, it was just the same as it is today, only Régine was missing.' I do feel that a Frenchman who happily donned Nazi uniform could have found a name other than mine to encapsulate high society collaboration in occupied Paris. I threatened to take them to court, and the company who had sponsored the film (made incidentally especially for television) promised to cut that bit. Once the film was released, I was told that they hadn't in fact cut it at all. I informed my lawyer, who assured me that it was unintelligible and that you couldn't actually make out my name any more ... Apart from that, he explained:

(1) that the fact of having led the good life (or been associated with it) in 1944 did not constitute a crime in the court's eyes;

242

(2) that to say for example 'only General de Gaulle was missing from the military Circle' would not constitute an insult to General de Gaulle ...;

(3) that the reference was more of a compliment in the sense that it meant simply that I was a somebody in Paris society.

So there was no case to answer. I just told myself that the initial antipathy I had felt towards La Mazière when Juliette Gréco introduced us had been wholly justified. I didn't know at the time that he had fought on the German side (neither that he would make use of my name one day), but perhaps I just felt that he could never be one of my friends.

There are less delicate people, like those I sometimes hear remarking in my clubs: 'Lots of Arabs here'. I don't know whether to laugh or cry about it sometimes, especially when they're looking at a table full of ... Brazilians! Of course, people like that would be the first to ask for complimentary tickets for any new Arab friends.

In similar vein, I took Michel Clerc to court after a passage from one of his books was reproduced in a daily paper on 11 July 1978. Monsieur Clerc went a bit too far calling me 'Rasputin in skirts' and 'Polish Juno brought up by the banks of Saint-Martin canal'. He wrote that I had been 'string-pulling in the Fifth Republic for a long time, providing the most diverse services'. (The crudity of the allusion needs no comment.) The only law I knew, according to him, was 'the law of the jungle', and I was constantly 'grovelling to petro-dollars'. There was plenty more.

Of course I won my case (both author and editor had to pay one hundred thousand francs), and the paper which gave Monsieur Clerc the column space had to publish the judgement and my reply, for which they used this discreet headline: 'Régine writes'. It was a real rap over the knuckles for Monsieur Clerc, finding that his so-called 'Polish Juno' was far from tongue-tied.

Monsieur de Vilallonga was another one who couldn't leave me alone. One day he described my clubs as 'leper colonies for the over-privileged', which must be about the most snobbish inverted snobbery there could be. All the evidence suggested that this society chronicler was criticizing me for having created a 'ghetto' which was sufficiently elegant to have excluded him on several occasions. In another book he moderated his disapproval and talked of the 'monkey cage which Madame Zylberberg runs so frenetically'. Not a very nice thing to say about lepers.

The latest person I've had to throw out for this kind of thing is

Gérard de Villiers, who can't stop saying unpleasant things about people he considers (and I don't know why) to be his inferiors. He overstepped the mark when he made this comment to Bobby Barriet at the end of 1984: 'You've really sunk to the depths letting all these Arabs in.' Bobby was furious, and reported it to me. I got up and told Gérard de Villiers never to darken my door again.

I took it much further with someone else, less well known maybe, but particularly dangerous: Alain Naulin. He started off as a gossip columnist in the Midi, then came to Paris to work as Edgar Schneider's assistant at *Paris-Presse*. Several times I was told that he was in the habit of referring to me as a 'dirty yid', or when really drunk as a 'fat yid'. I wrote to his boss, Max Corre, asking him to keep better tabs on his subordinate. Max Corre said: 'I'll send him over to see you.' Naulin and I did some straight talking.

A few months later, and he started all over again. I decided that this abscess by the name of Naulin should be drained once and for all. Naulin needed the Naulin treatment. I thought I would take advantage of an occasion that Cravenne was organizing at the Moulin-Rouge. Everyone was to go in black tie, women included: Yves Saint Laurent had just started the fashion. That evening, I warned the friends who were to be at my table (Éric de Rothschild, Hubert Rosenthal and the Guerrand-Hermèses) that something was going to happen. Cravenne was worried and asked me not to make a scene during the show, and had taken the precaution of putting Naulin at the other end of the room. With great restraint, I waited till the end, when I caught sight of Naulin loaded down with the little handouts, perfumes, etc, which get given away at gala events. He must have been round collecting them up from other tables, because he was staggering beneath the weight of them: so he pours filth on others, but dowses himself in eau de toilette.

I went straight up and slapped him.

'Cow!' he screamed.

Since he seemed to be so fond of free gifts, I gave him a couple more slaps for good measure.

Of course, everyone was watching us, him with his free samples and me pale with rage. He ran over to Edgar Schneider, who comforted him and then wrote in his paper next day: 'Régine meted out punishment to my colleague Alain Naulin last night, much as she does to her songs.'

It was an even more curious comparison considering that I had not at that point yet appeared publicly as a singer. Naulin decided to bring action for assault. I too decided to bring action for incitement to racial hatred. For some time now, I had been asking people who heard him call me a 'dirty yid' to confirm it in writing, and earlier that same evening I had sent the following missive by express post to the chief editors of the Paris papers: 'I hit Monsieur Naulin the man last night, and not Monsieur Naulin the journalist. Otherwise I would have picked on Monsieur Schneider, who is his boss. I took advantage of my masculine attire to do something which a husband, had I had one, would normally have done for me. Monsieur Naulin has the bad grace to forget my correct name and prefers to call me "dirty yid".'

With such a letter, Monsieur Naulin would be able to plead premeditation ... The paper's owner, Lazareff, embarrassed, called me up and asked: 'What do you want me to do to sort this one out?' I answered: 'Nothing at all. I just don't want Naulin making use of his profession as a cover for his antisemitic views.'

The two 'parties' found a way to an amicable agreement. I asked Naulin to make a formal apology before a judge, which he did, and I only had to pay a thirty-three franc fine for the slap. After this, I asked Max Corre to make sure that neither Naulin nor Schneider mentioned me again ... (I'm glad to say that Edgar Schneider and I patched things up.)

Philippe Bouvard and I had our ups and downs, with the latter more frequent than the former. In the early sixties, my close friendship with Georges Cravenne, the great organizer of parties in Cannes and Paris, meant that I often went in to premières and gala evenings ahead of certain other people, which did not please our little friend very much. One day he wrote: 'There is one lady who has worked her way forward from the twentieth to the front row. She occupies two whole seats, and her name is Régine (Zylberberg).' I sent him a swift reply: 'Dear friend, Not wanting to appear impolite, I am sending you three telephone directories so that you won't miss the show from the back row.' Did he ever receive them? Either way, I didn't hear from him for some time. Then his nature got the better of him and I was on the receiving end of a few more snide remarks. He certainly had a sense of humour of some sort, but not always a good one. He would keep making remarks about my body, and one day my anger erupted. It was on the beach at Saint-Tropez: I caught sight of him in his swimming trunks, large, fat and white. The very idea that this man could criticize other people's bodies seemed an absurd joke, I went up to him and said: 'You've got a nerve making remarks about other people's bodies ...'

'But ...'

'My name is Régine Zylberberg, without the brackets. I'm a Polish Jew and it doesn't bother me.'

And then, curiously, we started talking, about something else altogether. We even became quite good friends and did some broadcasts on RTL together. Then we quarrelled again, but made it up one day in Deauville. I'm still not convinced that we have reached an equilibrium ...

I have a reputation for reacting strongly to any aggressive or unjust remarks, in the press or elsewhere. I never let anything slip through, and everyone knows that when attacked I fight back. But the spiciest story, and the longest-drawn-out court case I've been involved in, was with Émilien Amaury, the director and owner of *Le Parisien libéré*. On 10 March 1972 he printed a picture of the Roman starlet Lily Moon on the front page of his paper (at the time the biggest circulation daily paper), together with a picture of a group of Romans dancing with me. The two pictures had the following caption:

'The ripples created by the huge police investigation being carried out among Roman "dolce vita" circles are far from subsiding ... One scandal among others which has attracted the attention of Italian public opinion is the "Lily Moon Affair". The young starlet has accused the film producer Luigi Torri of having kidnapped and drugged her and handed her over to his friends. She then retracted her accusations and Luigi lodged a complaint. As the photograph taken at the famous Number One club in Rome, featuring Régine, Elsa Martinelli, Gigi Rizzi (ex-boyfriend of Brigitte Bardot), Prince Dado Ruspoli and Luigi Torri, shows, the showbiz world often gets together to forget the vicissitudes of life, in pleasure houses where drugs are rife. But it does not mean that everyone is implicated: indeed, no one can be considered guilty until proven.'

A real masterpiece of the underhand. What's more, the photo had been taken four years previously: I was in Rome for the release of my first Italian record, and had gone to the opening of Number One along with the others.

I asked for the right of reply, but this was refused, and I immediately lodged a complaint. On 22 June 1973 Monsieur Amaury was brought before the Criminal Court of First Instance. He dragged the proceedings out for as long as possible but on 21 June 1974 the tribunal rejected his plea for non-suit. My lawyers based their argument on two principal points: there was insult — suggesting that I often go to 'pleasure houses where drugs are rife' — and defamation — making out (by association of pictures and text) that I was mixed up in the 'huge police investigation being carried out among Roman "dolce vita" circles'. The last sentence of the article, with its unpleasant innuendoes, only served to make the case against *Le Parisien libéré* all the stronger.

However, unexpectedly, the tribunal held on 21 March 1975:

'With regard to the insult: that the presence of Madame Choukroun in a Roman night club was entirely in character, without there being any need to attach any injurious sense to her presence, or to infer that she takes drugs;

With regard to the defamation: that the first part of the article, supposedly defamatory, did not mention the name of the plaintiff, and was clearly a caption to the photograph showing Lily Moon and not to the other which showed among others Madame Choukroun; that nothing in the text could lead the reader to think that the plaintiff might be "mixed up in the huge police investigation being carried out among Roman 'dolce vita' circles ...";

For these reasons, Amaury is found not guilty.'

Understandably, I appealed against this judgement through my lawyers, Maîtres Alexandre and Lombard, and on 22 October 1975 it was overturned and I obtained complete satisfaction: the court recognized that there had been both insult and defamation, and sentenced Émilien Amaury to a fine of two thousand francs, plus three thousand francs for damages and costs, which I donated to the Curie Foundation Radium Institute. The court also ordered the publication of the judgement in *Le Parisien libéré*.

For Monsieur Amaury, who appealed, the affair was far from over. It didn't finish until three years later (six and a half years after the publication of the article): the Criminal Chamber of the Supreme Court of Appeal rejected his appeal and the judgement against him was final. I had battled for six and a half years to stop a certain newspaper from making shabby allegations. Can you imagine Monsieur Amaury's reaction if a picture of him appeared eating lunch with one of the numerous famous personalities who might have been involved in some legal wrangle dating back forty years, with the caption: 'As the photo above shows, Monsieur Amaury frequents establishments where vice is rife. But it does not mean that he is implicated: indeed, no one can be considered guilty until proven'?

Here is another example, much less serious, but characteristic of the kind of thing which has to be stamped on before it gets out of hand. On 31 May 1980 *Le Matin Magazine* published a picture of me under this headline: 'Régine, the worst dressed.' I see. Three days later *Le Matin de Paris* (the same paper) published another article this time entitled: 'London: *Régine*, it's all over.' If it was a coincidence, it was unfortunate. But if it marked the start of a campaign, it had to be stopped. That's what I did. My lawyers got in touch with Monsieur Perdriel, the director, and obtained the following:

'On 8 June 1980, *Le Matin de Paris* will publish an article on the entertainments page under the title 'Régine, the businesswoman with plans for an empire', with the subtitle: 'After music, films and night clubs, Régine expands her empire into luxury hotels.' It will consist of an interview given by Madame Régine Choukroun to a journalist from *Le Matin de Paris*, a copy of which is here attached.'

There was also to be a photo of me in the same format as the one which appeared with the first article. It's what they call an agreed statement.

I've already talked about my show at the Bobino. The day after the première, Claude Fléouter, the *Monde* critic, wrote an article about me which, while avoiding personal remarks, made much of the 'Madame Rochas's hat' and the 'jet-set' side of things, which was guaranteed to alienate a good many *Monde* readers. Of course I don't mean that critics should be prevented from expressing their opinions, but they should, on such occasions, try to tell the whole story. The anti-high-society aspect of his piece had nothing at all to do with my qualities as a singer. If Monsieur Fléouter's sensibilities are offended by premières, which I can understand, then why didn't he wait a couple of days before going to the show? Madame Rochas would not have been there, and he would have been able to breathe more freely. I sent him a sharp letter, together with a pot of Herbezan, an effective laxative. *Minute*, the following week, reported the incident thus: 'Régine, displeased with an article written about her by a colleague on *Le Monde*, has sent him some powerful laxatives. He'll probably be more forthcoming next time.'

The food writers are another group who've done me no favours. Réginskaïa's was an excellent restaurant: the current one at Régine's in rue de Ponthieu is exceptional. I am allowed to say so, because I don't do the cooking. Under the pretext that it's a private club, they all refuse to mention it! And when they do break their silence, it's to talk about anything but the cooking ... the distasteful Monsieur Courtine (known as La Reynière) who, column after column, bores his readers in *Le Monde* with his hatred of snobs and so-called 'nouvelle' cuisine, has also described me (in Yves Mourousi's book *Les 300 inévitables*) as one of the three people he would 'never have at his table'. I didn't know that Monsieur Courtine gave dinner parties and, even if he does, there is no reason for our paths to cross. (I am in good company since the other two people on his list are Jean-Paul Sartre and Jacques Chaban-Delmas!) And to the question 'To which restaurant would you not accept an invitation?' he replied: 'Réginscaca ...' People like him may have fine palates, but they use foul language.

You have to react on all fronts or else people try to put one over. Witness the pretensions of Madame Sukarno, widow of the Indonesian president. On the pretext that she had been turned away from Régine's Paris one day because she wasn't suitably dressed (all clubs have their own code of dress, which is adhered to), she took me to court on a trumped-up charge, mixing up, in her fury, things and people which, in the eyes of the law, were not connected. Her one supporter in the press: Monsieur Michel Clerc, who congratulated her for wanting to defend her 'position in society'!

Madame Sukarno, trembling with calculated indignation, demanded jointly from me and the director of Régine's the sum of fifty thousand francs. Her claim was rejected. She claimed the same sum from Régine's Paris Club. Her claim was rejected. She demanded ten thousand francs from SOCR (Sociéte de l'Organisation de Cabarets et de Restaurants). She got one franc. Even after this judgement, serious papers said that Régine's was not to be regarded as a private club, but as an ordinary bar, open to all. That's what Madame Sukarno had said; but that's not what the judgement said. *La Gazette de Paris* wrote, when commenting on the decision of the tribunal (23, 24, 25 March 1980): 'When a restaurant or bar is made available to an association founded in accordance with the 1901 Act, and is reserved for its members, it goes without saying that such an establishment is private and reserved for the members of that organization.

'Numerous sporting, literary or professional associations make use of this time-honoured procedure to ensure that only their members are allowed into their bar or restaurant.

'A club where dancing takes place, would not seem to be an exception to these legal provisions.'

I hope this will put paid to the notion that a person cannot *legally* be forbidden to enter my clubs. This idea surfaces from time to time in the press or elsewhere, like a monster from the deep, but is totally contradicted by the laws. Thus when *L'Aurore* wrote on 18 January 1980: 'Madame Sukarno will be able to return to Régine's Paris', they were wrong.

18

From Régines's
rue de Ponthieu
to Régine's
International

In 1973 I opened Régine's in rue de Ponthieu — and kept Jimmy's Montparnasse going until 1977. Changing from one side of the river to the other didn't make me change my ideas. With the help of Roger (and François de Lamothe, my interior designer) I worked out the décor of what was to be, after Jimmy's Montparnasse, the new temple of luxury and elegance.

As you come in, a mirrored lift connects the outside world with the party world inside (which in Paris rarely mix), the day with the night. I kept the thirties décor; it's the only style which creates a real impression of comfort at the same time as being natural yet sophisticated. Everything is as far removed as possible from the aggressiveness of laser-beams, high-tech plastic upholstery and migraine-inducing music. The lighting is gentle and diffused, brought to life by dancing candle flames reflected in the mirrors. The ceiling, copied from a fragment of genuine thirties ceiling found in an antique shop, is made up of thousands of pieces of mirrored glass. (The Italians have since copied this, selling it by the square metre.) The illusion begins the moment you enter; landmarks disappear and the space becomes distorted. People can move and experience things freely.

There is a whole story behind the ashtrays. I don't smoke myself and I've always hated half-extinguished fag-ends. They stink and make your mascara run. And it's irritating too when the waiter has to reach past you to put a clean ashtray on top of the full one, remove both and then replace the clean one. It may be smart, but it's tiresome, and time-consuming for the waiter who can't be serving drinks at the same time. When Jimmy's opened, I designed a special table with a chrome ashtray twenty inches deep, full of water, set into the middle, which could easily be removed for cleaning. Above it, an arm supports a large candle. When you throw cigarettes in, they fall into the water. When I put similar tables into the rue de Ponthieu I took out a patent. So everyone who copies the idea has to pay me royalties.

When dancers have finished gyrating on the dance floor, they can seek refuge on comfortable low-backed pouffes or banquettes at low, solid, heavy tables. The carpet's imaginative geometrical design, thirties also, invites them back into that period

I invested the same love and care in the creation of Régine's Ponthieu as I did in Jimmy's Montparnasse, and had the same desire for perfection. I benefited from having more space, from previous experience and the constantly renewed will to do better. Having learnt from my experience with Réginskaïa's, I decided to make the club restaurant one of the best in Paris. I managed it, too, thanks to one of the greatest French chefs, Michel Guérard. His light, sophisticated, fresh and beautiful style of cuisine and presentation corresponded to my own taste perfectly. We got on extremely well, and one day he was to say: 'Our relationship was as delicate and elegant as that needed to create exquisite sauces.' That's what makes for perfection: time taken, and depth of flavour.

The dining room was particularly carefully designed, with paintings by Jouve, Ruhlmann wall-lights from the Normandie hotel, and of course, as in the club itself, the sparkling of candles, lacquer and ivory. Both business entertaining and more intimate occasions took place in the most welcoming environment possible, and by all accounts business deals went well, friendships were cemented, and love declared. Numerous 'first meetings' continued to occur at my clubs, and why not: people have always met at parties, and what is Régine's if not a big worldwide party?

But even before creating Régine's Ponthieu (at the same time as I set up in Monte-Carlo, of which more later), I had decided to go 'international' and I founded the chain Régine's International. What existed in Paris had to be provided elsewhere, so I had to expand, if not throughout the world, then at least to a few key cities in the western hemisphere. So marketing went ahead on a grander scale, and I was to anticipate people's needs rather than sit and wait for them. (In songs you always have to wait for the phone to ring, but I decided once and for all that I'd be the one making the calls.) For this international offensive, I asked forty 'key' women, chosen for their energy, their skills as hostesses, and their international contacts: 'Who would be on your list of four hundred guests?' I sent this questionnaire to Belgium, Switzerland, France (ten to Paris, five to the provinces), to Brazil, England and of course the United States. There was a lot of overlap in the responses I was sent, but I ended up with a core of about ten thousand people that I'd like to invite to the clubs, either in big cities like New York, Rio, São Paulo, London and Geneva, or in holiday resorts like Marbella and of course Monte-Carlo.

Slowly but surely I opened clubs in all these places; finely tuned environments always 1930s-inspired, 'Régine style' the world over. My dream has come true: I have built a rock-solid French image, like the great French couturiers. It has taken considerable mental and physical input, great force of character (when a club is about to open there is at least one serious problem per day and one minor irritation per minute), and therefore a longing for speed and efficiency which can often − which almost has to − reach shouting point. Five minutes later and it will all be sorted out, all forgotten. If you slip up on the tiniest detail, then your whole house of cards collapses. When I'm having a party I put 'see you soon' on my invitation cards, and one day I said that's what I'd like inscribed on my gravestone.

Some people say it's a job like any other. But it isn't; it's not like a factory or a market where you have to be punctual; each time, there's a real 'baby' which has to be conceived, given birth to, fed, nurtured and kept warm. Some of them are born pink and plump; others have to go in an incubator because the 'climate' in the outside world might damage them; still others look normal enough, but the nurse on the spot turns out not to be quite up to scratch ... I don't finance the clubs myself: I create, I provide the 'know-how', the décor, the style, the marketing; I give my name, and I 'animate' − in the true sense of the word: I give it a soul, my own. In my contract, it always says I have to be present a certain number of days per year. Of course I choose the days when something's happening, a cultural event, or some society 'do', or a sporting occasion (tennis championships or motor racing ...) Whenever I organize a party, the information is sent to all the members of Régine's throughout the world, and each time I work out how I can adapt the idea for use elsewhere: when I work for Rio or Paris, I also work for New York and Monte-Carlo.

In each city, I increase the number of business lunches and dinners with friends (or vice versa), I make multiple contacts when I get a new idea; I ask questions, I take stock of the problem, I make decisions; I send twenty telexes and make fifty phone calls per day; I surround myself with the minimum number of people working with maximum efficiency; and I listen to Roger, who helps me enormously, especially concerning the United States, which he knows like the back of his hand.

And good luck to the American, Japanese or other show business 'spies' who come and spend evenings at the rue de Ponthieu to discover the 'secret' of my success. My secret is me, my childhood, my desires, my dreams and my nightmares. The night is a second home, and people can grill their computers as much as they like; they'll only get trick answers or inanities out of them – never the final word on the story, on *my* story. The night has been my destiny, my place of refuge and my bewitcher. Chemistry is more subtle than any calculated effect can ever be, and my 'magic', simple though it might be, is intangible, like everything that comes from the soul.

The first Régine's for export went to Rio and Bahia. The Méridien group had decided to set up in these two cities and I signed a contract with them to create two Régine's in the hotels themselves. The first to open was Rio in 1970. I've been mad on Brazilian music for years (and re-introduced it to France) and to my mind Brazil is where they really know how to celebrate.

The club's décor was by Alberto Pinto, inspired by François de Lamothe's design for New Jimmy's (Régine's rui de Ponthieu was not yet open). The launch was brilliant, wild, with three samba schools and the cream of Rio society, a little surprised at this Frenchwoman who dared to throw parties as good as theirs. My 'godfather' in Brazil was Adolfo Bloch, boss of the publishing group Manchete, who had just created *RedeManchete*. He was a legendary figure, a Russian Jew who had come to Brazil at thirteen and started life as a bill poster. Today he heads a huge empire. He marked the official inauguration of *RedeManchete* (coinciding more or less with my launch) with a big lunch party, during which he declared: 'This occasion is to celebrate not only the birth of *Rede-Manchete*, but also the presence among us of Régine, who has tirelessly been telling the whole world about Brazil and its music. I also want to pay my deepest respects to her cousin Maurice Prywes, one of the great supporters of the state of Israel, and to her brother Maurice Biedermann.' When I first arrived in Brazil, Adolfo Bloch had been quite amazed to learn that I was the cousin of that same Maurice Prywes who had been instrumental in setting up the Ben Gurion University, raising funds for it throughout the world.

After Rio and Bahia came São Paulo (the most important industrial city in South America), with a Régine's which is even more spectacular than the others. For fifteen years now in these three cities, but more so in Rio, I've had a 'nucleus' of people whom I go out with, and who of course come to my club — the 'smart set' — 'my' set; Luciano christened the Rio group 'the beautiful people'.

Brazilian high society is incredible; for every one or two Adolfo Blochs there are dozens of descendants of the Portuguese, all extremely wealthy. Cariocas — inhabitants of Rio — love gossip, as do people from Bahia and São Paulo, and the columnists positively churn the stuff out: they call their particular brand of gossip *fofoca* (a cocktail of honey and poison, with the poison predominating). The *fofoca* got quite out of hand when I made a black Frenchwoman director of my club in Rio! Being 'hosted' by a black was already quite something for the Cariocas. But to be refused such and such a table (or even entry) by the same person really threw them.

But the press — without doubt the most 'sensationalist' in the world — was more damaging. The tabloids, full of scandal, are very widely read and terribly powerful, and they are virtually untouchable.

Despite these minor irritations, I've thrown some of the best parties in the world in Rio over the last fifteen years. During Carnival, my dance-school (called the Circo Fantastico) is probably the most sought-after, and if I call on two thousand people to dress up as sirens and Neptunes, they will. Of course, many of them aren't actually natives of Rio, but that's the spirit of Carnival, and it is precisely because of that mixture of the 'cream' of Rio and the international jet-set that every evening is a triumph.

The most prestigious step in the development of Régine's International was New York. I opened it in 1976, at a time when — all America agreed — New York was all but drowning in debts, a housing crisis and security problems. In the course of a press

255

conference, I gave this answer to a journalist who asked me why I was setting up in a city suffering its death-throes: 'If New York's going under, I'll give it the kiss of life.' And when they said: 'All the night clubs are closing down one after the other,' I replied: 'That's great, the rent will be cheaper.' Mind you, I did get a good deal of moral support from the mayor and other city chiefs and politicians, who gave cocktail parties at the club.

With my sister Évelyne's help, and Roger's of course (this one was very much 'his' club, though he deals with all the administrative side of Régine's International), I launched Régine's complete with restaurant, discotheque, reception room for sumptuous private parties, and Réginette's, a very up-market lunch venue. Réginette's was always full to bursting point, and made the New Yorker's lunch break into a real occasion. It was the classiest 'canteen' in Manhattan, and not the most expensive by any means. For dinner I served food which was both sophisticated and satisfying, with prices no higher than in good restaurants.

In the evenings, the ritual is identical whether I'm in New York or at Jimmy's in Paris. I arrive perfectly made up, with my hair immaculate, wearing something wonderful or so I hope. I greet everyone, I say a few words to each, I make people laugh, I laugh. I have a duty not to forget anyone. I am working but it doesn't look like it. The night is my domain, to work magic in for others, and to make plans for the nights to come.

In 1977, my launch in the United States merited the cover story in *New York Magazine,* with a nine page article by Julie Baumgold — who remarked that I was one of the few people in the world who could walk down grand hotel corridors in a bathtowel with perfect ease. She quoted the words of someone who worked with me: 'If she loves you, she kills you. Like a Florentine prince, she's surrounded by rather masochistic admirers, who remain her disciples for life.' And she also quoted something I'd said: 'At the dinner table I always get up after ten minutes because after fifteen minutes people start telling you their problems. I can't stand intimate confessions. I just like working, playing the fool and having a good time.' A curious mixture of truth and fable ... But that's how legends are created.

The most curious thing is that I often don't need to be on the spot to know that something's gone wrong. To remedy the situation, yes, you do have to get your hands dirty; but to understand the problems a telephone call suffices, as long as you're on the ball and really listening to what people are saying. I sometimes have a clearer picture of the difficulties from a distance. It's what I call 'instinctive management', and it's not in the least bit electronic. Like Hercule Poirot, I've got my 'little grey cells', which crackle when something's wrong. On the rare occasions that there have been real problems, it's always been because the people I've associated with have thought the battle was won, once and for all, and have stopped trying, which is not 'Régine's way' . . .

Marbella is a place particularly close to my heart. I have two clubs there: the older of the two, Régine's at Puerte Romano, was opened in 1979 (with a big five-year anniversary party last year, all white and gold), and the newer, opened in 1984 at the Marbella Club. For a change, this smaller club is . . . a pagoda, lacquered red and black. As usual the night before the opening nothing was finished, and at the last minute we had to replace the tables, which weren't heavy enough, polish up some object which looked too rustic, darken down the colour of one of the walls, move a huge green plant, change the front doors, block up an opening, check the lighting for the dance floor, re-do the bar . . . the usual performance. And as little as two hours before the guests arrived, the floor was still thick with rubble and my hair covered with plaster dust . . .

In Marbella, as elsewhere, I've got a group of very close friends who spearhead the summer — and winter — season. Régine's attracts all the 'happy few' from the Costa del Sol, Madrid and Barcelona. As in New York, my setting up in Marbella coincided with the end of a somewhat slack period at the resort: I had guessed that, there too, it wasn't terminal. I did what I could to get the place going again, and I think it worked. I had to tread gently but also do a bit of shaking up. But you can't please everyone — and it's a very bad sign if you do.

As elsewhere, I do my best for my clientèle, inviting them to dinner parties and making myself part of things by being interested in what counts. It's only by being everywhere at once and continually on the lookout that you can possibly regenerate a resort or, as others might prefer to put it, keep up its reputation. If you just sit in your ivory tower waiting for things to happen, they never will. You must be on the qui vive, making things happen, shaking people up. As everything goes on in my head at top speed all the time there's always something to show at the end of it: you have to turn over lots of stones before you find the diamond. If you really want things to get going, then you need to work at it day and night.

As my friend Paul Giannoli said: 'Régine's only failure is not to have found a way to make more hours in the day and more days in the year.'

It's certainly no miracle: my job is all about keeping one step ahead: stealing a march on time, and leaving fashion behind by creating my own. It was true at the rue de Four; it's true now, in quite a different way, on New York's Park Avenue, on quai du Mont-Blanc in Geneva, on Avenida Atlantica in Rio, and Miami's Grand Hotel Bay. (In Miami, a lady journalist once asked me: 'Your name is familiar throughout the world, and it seems that to make it so, you haven't minded hitting certain famous people?' I thought she was exaggerating rather, and that there was no point in disabusing her: 'It's true that it has cost me dear.')

In April 1980 we opened a club in Santiago, Chile, making the Brazil — Argentina — Chile connection. Someone said: 'You've got a cheek.' I told them: 'Saint Laurent, Cardin and Guy Laroche are all in Chile, I don't see why Régine shouldn't be too!' The club duly opened, with a splendid restaurant which gave onto gardens. We had two associates; one was great, the other proved to be catastrophic. What happened was that, at the end of the first year, he decided that the club hadn't made enough profit (although you always have to allow two years before you start to recoup your investment and make a profit in this sort of business) and he thought he'd explode a bomb in the restaurant and get the insurance money! Thank God the club was empty.

There have also been clubs which we've put together for special occasions, for one particular party, and then dismantled again. One such was at the British Embassy in Paris, for a reception in honour of Prince Charles. John Mills had introduced me to the Prince in London, during a charity dinner, given in aid of the Worldwide College, founded by his uncle Lord Mountbatten. I saw him again in the grill at the Hotel de Paris in Monte-Carlo, where he asked me: 'Will we have the pleasure of hearing you sing?' I was astounded that the Prince knew I sang. (A lot of French people don't know!) And then in 1981 I got to know him better. It was Whit Monday, just after the presidential elections. After being Daniel Wildenstein's guest of honour at the Deauville races, the Prince was to attend a banquet at the British Embassy, again in aid of the Worldwide College. The Embassy asked me to set up a disco. I set to work and Monsieur Sanchez, my sound man, created a luminous dance floor. After the banquet (to which I was not invited) the party guests arrived. Karim Aga Khan, who had been at dinner came in to see what the club was like and told me: 'Prince Charles is really keen to come, he talked about it over dinner.' After dancing to an English band in one of the other rooms, he decided to try Régine, and his aide-de-camp came to announce his impending arrival. I turned up the music, and the lights, and the Prince made his entrance.

He greeted me, and then a general came over to me telling me that he loved my songs and that he also enjoyed dancing. It was General Lemaire, whom the Prince had invited because he was his commanding officer while he was with the parachute regiment in Toulouse. I danced with the general, then with the Prince. The Prince seemed particularly to enjoy the Brazilian sambas, and danced for two hours. He asked if we had a Rita Lee record. We put her latest on the turntable: he already knew the words by heart. At four in the morning, the Prince having gone, the ambassador came to ask me: 'Can we close now?' I had tried to get the Prince to come to Régine's Ponthieu, but only got the aide-de-camp. While we danced, the Prince asked me: 'What happened to your club in London?'

I told him and he said: 'I hope you'll be back very soon.'

'I will be.'

Another 'one-off' 'Régine': the one in Los Angeles, after I'd done my snake charmer number for the Artistes Gala. Mixing usefulness with pleasure, I organized a one-night-only party in a swiftly christened Régine's, and gave the proceeds to charity. In Los Angeles you can't sell alcohol after two in the morning (the time varies from state to state), and I insisted that the law be scrupulously respected.

After the oil boom of 1974 the various different 'circles' of which Paris society is made up (jet-set, café society, etc.) were joined by another, that of the oil-rich Arabs who were beginning to travel. Those among them who travelled the world prior to this were never 'remarked upon', and no one, as far as I know, ever made much of King Hussein of Jordan's visit to Jimmy's in Montparnasse (where there were always quite a lot of Lebanese and Iranians). But from the moment they started coming to Paris in greater numbers, and bringing their friends and relations, people cried invasion. Right from the start, I asked them to leave their bodyguards in the cloakroom, and once people had got used to them they felt quite comfortable. Needless to say there were some royal backhanders distributed to ensure the best tables, but I put a stop to that, asking waiters to return very valuable watches and things they'd been given. Arabs got precisely the same treatment as everyone else: there is a sense of proportion which has to be respected, and anyone stepping out of line, be he Arab or French, is shown the door.

Régine's Ponthieu all comes down to Bobby Barriet, my manager and one of my oldest friends. He used to come to the rue de Beaujolais every night with a group of pals, among them Pierre Baton (who later bought Fouquet's and opened 33 on avenue Foch). I was patroness and adviser to this group and ever since Bobby started working with me (at Réginskaïa's in the early 1970s) I've remained his friend as well as his boss.

On the till there's Gina, who's been with me since the beginning of Jimmy's Montparnasse. Before that she was part of the team at the Vénus and the Jockey, as dancer-acrobat, and wanted to change jobs. When I set up Jimmy's, the owner, who was also the proprietor of the Jockey, had strongly advised her to come and work for me, because he knew I was looking for a cashier like her. She didn't want to, though: clients like mine weren't her type. But she came nevertheless, and has stayed for twenty-years so far! She has just the kind of firmness needed, and no one gets by without paying!

Bobby and Gina, plus barmen Bernard and Giovanni (twenty-two years we've been together) and Yvon (fifteen years) are the cornerstones of Régine's Ponthieu. Each waiter has 'his' tables; I've often told them that their tables are their fortune. We make a solid, trusty team, I will always be the boss, but also their friend, and I can ask anything of them.

With trump cards like these, let people be nostalgic for the fifties at the rue du Four, or for the sixties at Jimmy's, and for the seventies wherever they want ... I'll never stop (I'm much too scared to), and I intend to carry on creating things to be nostalgic about for a hundred years yet.

As Yves Navarre wrote: 'Those men and women who have sought to imitate Régine are limited by what they know about her: nothing at all.' The readers of this book will know a little more.

One day I said: 'I'm not saying I won't have my Waterloo. But if I do, I shall win.' Someone said it was a good definition of optimism. While waiting, on 29 April 1985 I celebrated thirty years' worth of friends and thirty years in the business with an Erté ball.

Success is an uphill struggle and it's normal to feel anxious sometimes. It's even a good sign. I've always slept with my jaws clenched, but some nights they're even more clenched than usual. Like when I was a kid, I'm afraid of missing out on something while I'm asleep: I sleep little, but life goes past so quickly ... I had bitter pills to swallow as a child, as an adolescent, during the first years of my marriage, and afterwards as a representative. The tears of rage, crying because of having to endure the cold and hunger at boarding school, my heart so empty. Today, there's no question of having to swallow anything. Everything has to work, and history has to become destiny. A friend once said it would be better to pick a fight with the Minister of the Interior than with me. That's because, generally speaking, ministers don't have bitter pills to swallow as children, but they do as ministers. With me it's the opposite. As Jean-Marie Rivière, a friend from way back, said: 'She has a need to shock, to do the impossible. She's extreme, loud, always the first to laugh at her excesses, and not easily upset. But she's always there when you've got a problem.'

With fourteen clubs all over the world I travel a lot, and whenever I leave a place I always feel I'll be away a long time. Exile is an everyday occurence for me. Perhaps that's partly what being 'international' means ...

19

Monte-Carlo

Monte-Carlo first caught my imagination as a child when a photograph arrived in Aix showing Joseph, Maurice and Évelyne on the steps of the Hôtel de Paris. I hadn't been there with them, and when I saw the picture I became dreadfully jealous.

And then, at the beginning of the fifties, I spent a marvellous weekend there at the Old Beach Hotel. The little barmaid from the Whisky-à-gogo had been invited to that new and ultra chic place by a friend and another couple, and had discovered Monte-Carlo, danced at the Sea-Club to the Aimé Barelli orchestra and Sacha Distel, and had promised herself that she'd come back 'properly' one day.

The opportunity arose in 1966 when the centenary celebrations, under the auspices of Her Serene Highness Princess Grace, were scheduled to go on throughout the year. Georges Cravenne was in charge of public relations for all these sumptuous artistic and society events. One of the high spots was to be the 'Centenary Ball' given by Hélène Rochas. The theme of the ball was to be '1800', the era of the *Incroyables* and the *Merveilleuses,* Benjamin Constant and Madame de Staël ...

I was tremendously excited about returning to Monte-Carlo, and at Jimmy's Montparnasse Françoise Sagan, Marc Doelnitz and I talked about it endlessly. Françoise gave me an idea: why don't we go together and arrive by balloon? 1800 was the era of the heroic 'aerostats', and in 1966 a new craze for ballooning was just starting (there was much talk that year of a balloon specialist called Dollfus). I instantly pictured a superb balloon landing on the Casino terrace, and being the centrepiece of the celebrations ... I got in touch with this Monsieur Dollfus, we cobbled some plans together, I reserved a balloon, and paid a deposit.

A few days later, I told Françoise it was all arranged. She said: 'Not so fast, not so fast! Have you really booked the balloon?'

'Yes.'

'Listen, I don't know whether I really want to disappear off like that, up into the air ... I must have been rather tired when I suggested it. It's cold up there. And where will we fly from?'

'From a boat, because of the wind.'

She looked at me, utterly amazed. She didn't need to say another word: I could tell, I'd be going up on my own, with a professional.

Cravenne, who had thought the idea tremendous to start with, phoned me and said: 'Régine, this balloon thing is out of the question. I've been speaking to people here and it's just too dangerous, you might hurt yourself, or someone else, when you land.'

I told him: 'You're afraid I'll completely steal the show, aren't you? If I hurt myself, the press will be full of it, and if it all goes to plan, then my co-pilot and I will be the stars of the show anyway!'

'No, no, that's not it at all. It's because of Monte-Carlo, the people, they're really terrified. No one's ever done it before.'

I sulked and said: 'I'm going to come by balloon or not at all.'

Then Hélène Rochas called me too: 'Régine, you can't do it! You absolutely must come, but not by balloon. It's much too risky. You're full of good ideas, think up something else.'

Seeing as the world was against me and my balloon, I decided to abandon it. Marc Doelnitz and I dreamed up another grandiose entrance: in a carriage, as Queen of the Night 1800. Marc rapidly sketched my costume, right out of a fairy tale: layers of transparent veils, midnight-blue tights, midnight-blue kid boots with diamond-studded heels, and a vast tulle cloak covered with moons, stars, entire galaxies.

Costume-makers started work on it, while Alexandre made me tons of plaits and ringlets. It was going to be 'inc'oyable', as the *Merveilleuses* used to say.

I phoned some carnival float specialists in Nice to explain my requirements: 'To match my Queen of the Night 1800 costume, I shall need a shell-shaped carriage, all covered in silver sequins, from the wheels up. I need four white horses, with long silver streamers flying out behind them. It's got to be very light, very fairy-tale.'

263

'That's no problem, we can do that for you. But have you driven a carriage before?'

'No.'

'Okay, we'll provide a driver.'

'Yes, but listen, he must be just as beautiful as the carriage. A sort of Ben-Hur, Roman-looking, young and impressive.'

'Right. No problem.'

Evidently, nothing was going to be too much trouble. A dream. I could already see the carriage gleaming in the moonlight, me whipping the horses to get to the Casino all the faster, and to the sound of wild applause. Wanting to leave nothing to chance I phoned Nice again: 'Don't forget, it's all got to be silvered: the wheels, the shell, the horses, the driver, everything!'

'Don't worry, I understand perfectly.'

'How much will it all cost?'

'I can't say exactly. About five hundred thousand (old) francs. But it will be incredible.'

The night before the great departure for Monte-Carlo, I did try to get to bed early, but it was impossible. I got home at six in the morning, after predicting a spectacular arrival to all my friends. They told me they did not doubt it would be.

The next day we arrived in Nice on a charter flight. There were about a hundred guests. Once we got to Monte-Carlo, I kept well away from the beach, the pool and the sun, and stayed in my room at the marvellous Old Beach, which was now completely renovated and had become the Monte-Carlo Beach Hotel. It's an extraordinary place: no restaurants, no reception rooms, just the desk and a bar, and three floors of magnificent bedrooms with superb views over the sea and the Beach. Immediately to the right of the hotel is the pool and the seashore, and to the left a little green peninsula with, at the top end, a sort of hanging restaurant called La Vigie, where you can eat over the water.

I rang Alexandre's two hairdressers, who had come specially to do the guests' hair. They were obviously totally swamped. I told them I didn't mind being last. At a quarter past seven they finally arrived and started work. There were so many knots, pins and false bits that the operation lasted more than an hour. At eight fifteen Cravenne rang through: 'Hurry up or you won't be there before the Prince and Princess.'

'Yes, I'm coming!'

I was terribly on edge and excited at the thought of my imminent carriage ride. I hadn't seen it yet but was as sure of it as I was of myself. The finishing touches with the comb, and it was half past eight ... Various friends (two of whom were to ride in the coach with me) appeared at the door laughing and saying: 'Madame's carriage awaits.'

'Is it wonderful, my carriage?'

'We've never seen anything like it!'

I left the hotel, all made up, star-spangled, with my silver and midnight-blue veils, I couldn't have tried harder. In front of the hotel I saw a bizarre old jalopy, a battered carnival float shaped like the bottom half of a stagecoach, with four rickety steps and a roof which had once been painted silver. The final touch, yards of yellowing tulle! I recoiled in horror. Was this the sublime carriage? But the surprises weren't over: the coachman, dressed in 1800 costume, must have been born around the same time himself. And as for the horses, they were strong working animals, and there were no silver bits remotely visible. 'This can't be my carriage!' But it was.

I screamed out in anger: 'I'm certainly not getting into that thing. I'll walk!'

The friends who were supposed to be riding on the ancient vehicle with me kept saying that it didn't matter: the most important thing was to have fun. Horribly vexed, I got in and we departed.

A few yards past the Beach, where the trees are very low, we heard a sinister crack above our heads. We looked up: the roof which had been simply resting on the coach, rather than attached to it, had got caught in a tree!

Decapitated, discomfited, we sat there not knowing what to do next. My friends began roaring with laughter. I just got more and more furious, not finding it the least bit funny, and started yelling at the coachman, who couldn't do a thing about it anyway. The two hairdressers from the hotel were following in a taxi, so I said to them: 'You get in here, I'm taking the taxi.'

And off I went. We hit a red light a few yards further along. The coach caught us up and my friends shouted down at me: 'Régine! Régine! Come on! You must arrive in your carriage!'

Stoically, I got back into the contraption and we finally arrived at the Casino, where we were a huge success! Not so much the coach as the costumes ... The coachman asked if he should wait for me.

'On no account. You must go back and congratulate your boss on his exquisite taste.'

The party began, and I forgot all about the float and the coach-man. André Levasseur's décor was fantastic. And so were the costumes, so extravagant. Everyone was there: the stars, the jet-set, the international aristocracy ... Diamonds sparkled, champagne flowed freely, everywhere people danced, and laughed, and cel-ebrated. I got completely carried away by the fairy-tale atmosphere, the incredible costumes and the supreme elegance of it all. All that is best and rarest in the world seemed to have been gathered together that night, in a profusion of great names and crazy clothes. When I left at dawn, it was to carry on partying at the Tip-Top with the milkmen, the other party-goers who weren't ready for bed, and the croupiers from the Casino. At ten in the morning I finally went home, only sorry that the party was over so soon.

They never sent me the bill for the carriage and I never asked for it.

I went back to Monte-Carlo in 1970. This time André Levasseur persuaded me to do a sort of mini-revue, just for a week. People said it was about as risky as arriving by balloon: people hardly even applauded at the Red Cross charity galas, so what would they do for a whole week ... I would have to be very sure of myself. I was.

André Levasseur designed my dresses. Mini Vergez made them for me (as for Guy Lux's shows and the Carpentiers'), Diego did my hair and Jacques Clémente my make-up ... It all had to be perfect. André worked out a spectacular entrance for me. Wearing a black dress with artificial roses round the bottom, I was to join my ten superb boys and girls on stage in a balloon basket which was to be lowered down from the gallery of the old Sporting Club. The basket was manœuvred by two men, not by motor, and depending on how the mood took them, they would swing me to the left or the right. It was fairly precarious, but the effect was stunning.

On the first night, a trumpeter from the Aimé Barelli band said to me: 'Yes, tonight there are plenty of people, but what about tomorrow!'

I looked at him and answered a bit sharply: 'Don't hassle me, there'll be people every night!'

And there *were* plenty of people on the second night, and the third, right through till the end. André Levasseur was thrilled. And so was I.

One afternoon I was by the pool at the Old Beach when I bumped into a friend, Guy de Brignac. When I asked him what he was doing here he looked at me in amazement and said, laughing: 'You obviously don't read your contracts very thoroughly. I'm from the Société des Bains de Mer, and I signed you up!'

I explained that when I know everything's organized I leave it up to my agent, and don't read the small print. As I was with Roger, he invited us both over to lunch the following day, with his wife. At the end of the meal he asked me what I thought of Monte-Carlo and whether I might not have one or two ideas to make the Principality just that bit more attractive. I told him that I'd had a lot of fun during my stay but that I hardly knew Monte-Carlo at all apart from the Casino and the other famous places ... like the Tip-Top, where all kinds of people gathered at the end of an evening for croque-monsieur and spaghetti; tables spreading out along the pavement according to the numbers, with cars almost brushing them as they drove past up and down the steep hill ... The whole town had a cheerful feel to it, bags of joie de vivre, and my only regret was that the average age of the holidaymakers was so advanced: there were plenty of Rolls-Royces, but a fair number of wheelchairs, too ... Guy de Brignac asked me whether I could suggest some ways of making the night life more appealing to younger people, and a bit less 'formal'.

I had a think about it when I got back to Paris. Monte-Carlo had a fantastic tradition: of concerts, gambling, theatre, opera, balls, the Red Cross galas so dreaded by the performers but popular with everyone else ... It was vital to keep all the established attractions, but a little more emphasis on youth and modernity was needed. I put some proposals in writing and sent them to Monte-Carlo. They were accepted, but not without real (and quite understandable) scepticism in certain quarters.

My plan was to make the Maona disco (a contraction of Maria Onassis) into a Polynesian restaurant and to use the lovely piece of open ground next to it, bordering the lagoon, just below the Sporting Club, to build a Jimmy's which would reach the water's edge and would be separated from it only by fountains. I went down to the site to assess the feasibility, and when everyone was in agreement I started work. André Levasseur did the décor, which I wanted to be quite similar to Jimmy's in Paris. I planned the menu for the restaurant with the Food and Beverage people (who dealt with all the catering in Monte-Carlo). The menu had to be vetted by Their Serene Highnesses, and over a private dinner at the Hôtel de Paris they gave their seal of approval. The Maona was all set to embark on its new career.

To get the club (called Jimmy'z de la Mer, with a z in honour of 'la Grande Zoa' off the ground I used the same tactics as in Deauville to attract the young, the dynamic and the fashionable, and hence the media too. This time though I had very superior means of doing so, because of my contract with the Société des Bains de Mer, whose president was Prince Louis de Polignac. Because the contract also covered the public relations side, I planned to invite 'key' young people and fashionable young couples very much in the public eye, and have them stay at the Hermitage. This was one of the component parts of the launch scheme which little by little made Jimmy'z de la Mer a magnet for everyone on the Côte d'Azur − everyone in the world.

The opening took place in July 1971. It goes without saying that there was a gala evening at the Sporting Club to celebrate the event, and that all the guests came over to the club afterwards. But plenty of others were queueing up outside the door trying to get in, and I had to spend a good part of the evening keeping an eye on the situation in case anything untoward happened.

Many people thought Jimmy'z de la Mer the 'most beautiful club in the world'. It's certainly the most 'glamorous' of all my clubs. There's a fabulous view and the fountains give a magical touch to the whole place. The smells wafting up from the lagoon aren't exactly Guerlain but they liven up the atmosphere a bit and give people something to talk about.

In hotels, my cards with a special welcome in French, English and Italian await personalities when they arrive. Now people come from Saint-Tropez, Cannes and Nice to meet at Jimmy'z de la Mer and the Maona, and the Italians who had rather deserted the French Riviera in favour of Spain or Sardinia are now back in droves.

The little personal messages I leave for stars when they come to Monte-Carlo, Paris or New York (depending on where I am) are more important than people might think. Either because their friends aren't in town, or because they don't happen to have any there, even big stars might spend evenings all alone with nothing but stacks of telexes, business letters and telegrams to plough through. And then there's the intimidation factor, which stops people talking to them, be it in the hotel, or in restaurants, or even at work.

Régine's International means that any star will be welcome at my club in the evenings: I will introduce them to friends, or organize dinner parties, and it's only rarely that they won't come across someone they know.

A propos solitary evenings in hotels, Marcello Mastroianni told me this anecdote. He was in Florence one night, where he didn't know a soul. Tired out, fed up, with no idea where to go, he decided to eat in the hotel restaurant with his secretary, a very nice, efficient person, but ordinary. The dining room was empty, but for two other gentlemen (it was very late): one of them was quite old, very dignified, with extraordinary presence, the other man younger and very reserved. Towards the end of their meal, the younger man got up and came over to Mastroianni and said: 'Monsieur, the person with whom I am dining, Monsieur X., would like the pleasure of your company.'

'Monsieur X?' said Mastroianni.'The Nobel prizewinner?'

'Yes.'

'The pleasure will be mine.'

Mastroianni went to sit at the learned man's table, and began talking with him. But he caught snatches of the conversation going on between the two secretaries, who were sitting together at the other table. And just when the distinguished man was telling him a marvellous story full of humour and poetry, Mastroianni overheard his own secretary saying: 'How many prizes has your boss won?'

'One,' replied the other secretary, a little astonished. 'The Nobel Prize.'

Upon which his man retorted, disdainfully: 'Mine's won seven Oscars!'

One day, Fred Chandon said to me in Monte-Carlo: 'How could we sell more champagne in a place like this?'

I told him I really didn't know: we had never managed to sell much. But then, one evening, on my way to the club, I had a flash of inspiration. I asked them to remove all the bottles of whisky with people's names on, and to replace them with magnums of champagne, sticking out of ice-buckets. We sold thirty-eight that night and carried on at the same rate ... Without entirely blacklisting whisky, I put all the different makes of champagne back on the map (Dom Pérignon, Krystal Roederer, Taittinger ...). I agree it's not as economical (you can't keep your bottle or put your name on it ...)

but it was much more fun and much more attractive for women to drink! As Madame de Pompadour put it: 'Only champagne can keep a woman beautiful while she drinks.'

As for mixing people, I reached a high spot. One evening, Mick Jagger trod on Francis Blanche's toe. Francis said: 'I see, so you're letting in all these pasty-faced hippies now, are you? He didn't even say sorry, that one. Who was it?'

'Mick Jagger.'

'Oh really? I didn't even recognize him.'

I called Mick over and introduced them. They spent the rest of the evening together, laughing like maniacs!

Frank Sinatra was one of the first regulars. He used to eat at the Maona and then come to Jimmy'z with a lovely woman, Barbara Marx, whom he later married, and her son. I'd known him for fifteen years, ever since Rubirosa introduced us. He was a great friend, but not easy to get along with: he couldn't stand photographers, and I always had to be very careful about whom I sat him next to. And he adored crackers and fireworks of any kind. He always had his pockets stuffed full of them, and his friends would forever be giving him the latest, most sophisticated types. Whenever you heard, even far away from the club, the sound of fireworks, you'd know it was Frank Sinatra having fun with his friends (and sometimes my barmen, too). They would throw jumping jacks into the water where they exploded and jumped, creating showers of sparks and an appalling noise.

One summer evening in 1973 I was at the Sporting Club rehearsing a show when the unmistakable sound of Sinatra's firecrackers started up. They were going off at such a rate that we had difficulty getting the sound system adjusted, and everyone was getting a bit uptight. We were trying our best when suddenly my sister Évelyne rushed in to tell me that a fight had broken out between the 'Sinatra table' and the 'Hélène Rochas table'. That was the first I heard of the story which was to run and run in the press, relegating the rest of the news to the back page.

I went down to the club straight away and found the place in turmoil. Sinatra looked extremely angry and I was amazed to hear the usually unruffled and elegant Hélène Rochas shouting: 'I regret I cannot speak better English, then I would tell you what I think of you!'

Vilallonga was there too, delighted to be adding a bit of fuel to the fire. The 'celebrated Polishwoman', the 'tough cookie' (as

Vilallonga called me when describing the incident in one of his books) calmed everyone down and Jimmy'z rapidly returned to its normal self. When I went back to the Sporting Club, Kim d'Estainville and Évelyne told me what had happened.

Hélène Rochas and Charlotte Aillaud had been sitting with Kim at his table. The noise of the firecrackers got on their nerves so badly that both started to feel unwell, one of them even beginning to tremble. The two tables were very close together, and Kim d'Estainville, in full view of everyone, requested Sinatra and his friends to stop, banging his glass, full of ice cubes, down on their table in an angry gesture. Unfortunately, one of the ice cubes shot out of the glass, landing on Barbara Marx. Sinatra's bodyguards marched over to the reckless Kim and began to pick a fight. They didn't come to blows, thanks to Giovanni and Bernard, my two barmen, who jumped on the most aggressive-looking bodyguard ... The only person who was really hurt was Madame Bacardi (of rum fame), whose leg got hit by a stool ... That's when I walked in.

That episode seemed to have been forgotten when a second incident occurred. When he first arrived at Jimmy'z at the start of the evening, that's to say long before the 'row', Sinatra had been unpleasantly surprised by two Americans at the club who took a picture of him. Irate, he had snatched the camera from the amateur photographer and thrown it in the lagoon! But the man, with his (boy-) friend in tow, didn't just leave it at that: he had gone back to his hotel (the Hermitage) and called a press agency and the police, telling them that Sinatra had given chase in a car and had tried to strangle him. To substantiate this rip-roaring tale he had also called a doctor, to examine the 'marks' he had on his neck − marks he had without doubt put there himself! A police officer arrived at the club, and Évelyne, who had been there right from the start, explained that Sinatra could not possibly have pursued the American because he had not left the club after the incident occurred. The officer departed, but then the reporters duly started arriving.

To cap it all, a third incident, which I did not hear about till much later at the Tip-Top, had taken place in a nearby bar. The Sinatra party were all there, including Madame Bacardi ... Seeing the bodyguard who had kicked the stool over in the first place, she started complaining and showed him her wounded leg. By way of an answer, he got heavy again! This time she made a formal complaint at the police station.

It was rather excessive for one night, and having probably been warned that the police were about to come round to his hotel, Sinatra checked out at half past six in the morning and left the principality by private plane ...

Two months later in Paris, someone told me that Sinatra was cross with me and was telling everyone so. Rather surprised, I didn't make the connection with the previous events in Monte-Carlo, which I had totally forgotten about. I then discovered that he held me responsible for the articles which had appeared in the papers at the time! I just couldn't believe it, especially as I always try to play down any incident which might occur in my clubs, which is precisely what I had done in this case. I generate a lot of publicity about myself, but I am always discreet in the extreme when it comes to my customers. I also gathered that Sinatra had asked all his friends, including Gregory Peck and Paul Anka, not to come to my club any more. I begged Paul Anka to tell Sinatra that I had nothing at all to do with it, but it was wasted breath: he still shuns me.

Two years later, he did a show at Caesar's Palace, one of the casinos in Las Vegas. Paul Anka, who was appearing after him, made one of my dreams come true by having me in his show with him. When Sinatra saw my picture in the hotel foyer, he asked the show's director to have it removed! He was told that it was in the contract and that there was nothing they could do about it. And another thing, it's traditional that when a performer does his last show, he announces the forthcoming celebrities. 'This time,' I said to myself, 'he can't ignore me.' But no. He announced every single one ... except me! He even said: 'I don't think I've forgotten anyone.'

I wanted to get up and shout: 'What about me!'

But for once my courage failed me.

And then again, it's also normal practice to send flowers to the stars who follow, the women anyway. Since he didn't send *me* any, I had a superb bouquet delivered to him! Next day we bumped into each other in the hotel lift. He kept to his side, I to mine. When the lift stopped he did say, 'Good evening!' I returned his greeting ...

So I'm on bad terms with a tremendous entertainer, all because of something stupid, and I deeply regret it. He has been back to Monte-Carlo since, but I haven't seen him. In 1985, however, he seemed to have decided that it was time to patch things up, because he turned up at the club. Sadly, I was in Villefranche for the first gala in aid of S.O.S. Drogue International, and I just missed him. The reconciliation I so badly hoped for hasn't happened. But at the next opportunity it will.

In 1974 we created a Jimmy'z d'hiver; then, while they were building the much talked-about new Sporting Club, the Société des Bains de Mer and I re-did Jimmy'z d'été and the Maona.

The new club, designed by François de Lamothe along similar lines to Régine's in Paris, was much larger. With a roof which opened to the skies like its predecessor, it was even more beautiful and also spared us the odours wafting up from the lagoon ... It gave onto a splendid Japanese garden, an idea of His Serene Highness Prince Rainier's. As I couldn't resist fountains, the garden was embellished with jets and cascades which almost made people feel they were actually on the water. The gigantic spherical fountain, which I had briefly intended to site close to the club, now greets people at the entrance of the Sporting Club, and the effect is superb.

The Maona restaurant gives the impression of being an immense flower placed above the lagoon. Exotic trees, rare plants, Gauguin-style paintings, fountains, illuminations: you feel as if you're floating in a dream world. It's a multicoloured grotto, open to the sky, a secret garden in which five hundred people a night can imagine themselves in some far-flung corner of the earth. This time, the cuisine at the Maona was part-Polynesian, part-Brazilian.

The party to mark the opening of the new Sporting Club, Maona and Jimmy'z was fantastic, despite a misunderstanding which sadddened everyone. Sammy Davis Junior was supposed to be singing at the Sporting Club, but by a complete oversight he was not included on the guest list for a little unofficial welcoming party for celebrities to which Her Serene Highness Princess Grace paid a flying visit. He decided not to sing after all and disappeared off on a boat hired for him by the Société des Bains de Mer ... I tried in vain to contact him. The Sporting Club party coincided with the professional tennis championships, which attracted numerous international stars, and several of them said they would each perform a little number to make up for Sammy Davis Junior. So the evening at the Sporting Club went off very well, and luckily the misunderstanding did not permanently sour the good relations between Sammy Davis and the Principality of Monaco. He came back to sing there again soon, to my great delight.

The Prince and Princess were to make an appearance before the guests left the Sporting Club to go on to the Maona and Jimmy'z.

Up till then they had only seen the plans, so I was rather nervous (more so because I had just come straight down from filming *Le Train* and hadn't slept for forty-eight hours). But everything went without a hitch, and on his way out the Prince turned to me with a smile and said: 'It's very good.'

All the guests from the Sporting Club and all the American stars like Gregory Peck, Bob Wagner, David Niven, came on down to Jimmy'z. Of course there were also lots of Italian and Greek businessmen, including Agnelli, Niarchos and Onassis ... At the start of the evening I was surprised to see lots of young men in white jackets and black bow ties dancing, apparently uninvited, with my female guests. They were the waiters and extras from the gala! I requested that they return to their posts — sadly for the ladies, who seemed delighted with their company.

The new Jimmy'z and the new Maona were a tremendous success. One evening in 1974, Jean Prouvost (the press baron, owner of *Paris-Match* among others) said to me: 'I haven't been to Monte-Carlo for ten years. It's incredible. How on earth did you manage to attract all those people?'

I explained how I'd done it, and he carried on asking me more questions, including this one: 'What else would you like to do?'

'Make the front cover of *Paris-Match* without having to die first.'

And two weeks later there I was.

In Monte-Carlo, as elsewhere, I am particularly attentive to the young, though that's not to say I favour the younger element exclusively in my clubs. Indeed, you get the most fun by mixing different generations, and anyway the most energetic, the most spirited, are often the older group. And I mix types in the same way as I mix age groups. For fifteen years now all sorts of people have been gathering in Monte-Carlo: the beautiful-but-not-so-rich, the very-rich-but-not-so-beautiful, the elegant and the talented, the unavoidable and the geniuses, café society with a sprinkling of kitsch, designers, fashion people and interior decorators. And jewellers have been having such a field day in Monte-Carlo, and their exhibitions are so terrific that it almost makes you want to wear fakes ...

I go down to my favourite haunt, the Old Beach, every summer. Tent M. is mine, and it's the obligatory meeting place: it's both the focal point and voyeurs' corner, where people do anything and say anything, in between iced teas, the mozzarella and tomato salads, and the phone calls that I make next door at the massage parlour.

Then there's also the solarium, and the swimming lessons (I got my first certificate two years ago: *Chi va piano va sano*). Another strategic spot is the hairdressing salon, right on the Beach, a venerable 1950s establishment where nothing has changed except the gossip. That's where they swap tittle-tattle about the two or three big parties that get thrown per night, and gossip about the new arrivals.

I feel very at home in this apparently sheltered little world. And the financial microclimate is attractive, because there is a completely international atmosphere: you breathe the air of Paris, New York, Palm Beach, Milan, London and Marbella. And each year (or every two years) when I organize a concert, and start to get nervous, I remember what the evenings were like during my tours of the provinces, when you *had* to go to bed at midnight because the place was dead, all shut up and fast asleep. It's quite the opposite in Monte-Carlo: it feels as though the whole town stays awake until I go to bed. There's no such thing as solitude, which is great, because like all real loners I don't like being alone.

I was in Monte-Carlo again in August 1984, exhausted but delighted to be there, after spending three days in Cairo getting my next club ready (opened in May 1985). In the afternoon I had to go to Toulon for a show which was being recorded before a live audience, to be broadcast two days later. It starred Enrico Macias. I took the helicopter at half past midday and touched down ... thirty kilometres away from Toulon (a top-secret military zone). I did finally reach the concert hall where I found Enrico Macias and asked him if he would come and perform at my gala on 7 August, in aid of S.O.S. Drogue International, for which I needed the help of all my friends. He said yes. Then the mayor of a town near Toulon came over to me and said: 'Do you know, my wife thinks she knew you a long time ago. She read an interview in which you talked about a convent in Aix in 1941. She was there too!'

He told me her maiden name, and it rang a bell. I asked if I could see her.

'Yes, of course, she's in the auditorium.'

He went and found her, and we greeted each other as long-lost friends. We reminisced, and she told me lots of things about the convent, bringing back details I'd completely forgotten, not least my dislike of tapioca, and making it all come brutally back to the surface for me.

She told me something which the Mother Superior had said

about me: 'Régine is an orphan, you must be kind to her.'

And then she added: 'Do you remember when we baptized you?'

'Baptized me?'

'Yes, don't you remember? Because you didn't take communion, we thought you had no religion and, the night before you left, another girl and I baptized you secretly, in the dormitory, with a face flannel.'

Not a very Catholic baptism, but as moving as immersion in the river Jordan.

She also said that, because they had no news of me for two years, she and the sisters had thought I must have died under deportation.

That evening, on my way back from Toulon, I dropped in at the hairdressers on the Beach, where I sat watching the rich and famous of Monte-Carlo pass by. No, I wasn't dead, and in just two hours the big Red Cross ball was due to start at the Sporting Club.

Cairo, Monte-Carlo, Toulon ... The future, the present, the past. Everything had become confused over the last twenty-four hours; it would have made a good song title: 'Sphinx, diamonds and tapioca'. My head was spinning and when I got back (very late) I said to Roger: 'I think I've short-circuited! I need to sleep.'

That night, I slept so well, happy to be alive.

20

Politics and me

The man who, one evening in 1961, came down the steps of the rue du Four, was not well known to the general public. The well-informed knew him to be a friend and colleague of General de Gaulle, a director of the Rothschild bank and a member of the Council of State. He and his wife had been launched on the Paris social scene by the Rothschilds, and never missed a première or an important dinner. They spent weekends at their house in Orvilliers or at Pierre Lazareff's house at Louveciennes. That particular evening, the respectable bank director, sharp-eyed and with something of the peasant about him, was having a go at the twist: 'A little patience, and I'll get the hang of it, you'll see,' he shouted to me on the dance floor.

I don't know whether he got it or not, but whatever, a year later this serious man, by the name of Georges Pompidou, replaced Michel Debré in the Hôtel Matignon as Prime Minister.

Eight years later, while he was between Matignon (which he left in 1968) and the Élysée Palace (where he moved in 1969), we met at dinner. It was the worst period in his life, politically and personally: he had broken with General de Gaulle only to have calumnies heaped on him, and on his wife. But a true politician is never mortally wounded, and the following year he got his revenge.

We talked politics a little over dinner and he told me that he had heard it said that he would be the next President of the Republic, something which my medium had told me, and which I had already been telling all my friends for six months.

'If it's true,' he went on, 'then your medium will have been very clever to guess, because at the moment there can't be more than thirty people who still count me as a friend.'

We continued our conversation. I asked him, knowing that he loved poetry, whether he had sometimes written poetry himself.

'In my young days, yes. But it's difficult to write poetry when you know that it's you who will have to tell them when to shoot ...'

When he was President, he did not invite me to the Elysée Palace, perhaps because the left-wing press already criticized him quite enough for having worked for the Rothschilds: there was no point in providing extra ammunition by saying that he'd also danced the twist 'chez Régine'.

One of Georges Pompidou's ministers and close friends, Olivier Guichard, became a good friend of mine, and it was he who helped me, in 1969, obtain my French nationality (at last!). During my divorce from Paul, I had taken the necessary steps, but the fact that I was divorced hadn't helped and they had refused me. It had made me think of Joseph, who had met similar opposition but because of his diabetes. When I started travelling abroad, I realized that my Polish passport was more of a hindrance than a help: I always needed a special authorization and was constantly filling in forms. So I got myself a stateless passport (which meant I got longer visas than anyone else). When I went back to the Préfecture de Police in 1969, I saw the same official who had been dealing with my problems for twenty years, who exclaimed: 'Are you only just becoming French?'

I don't understand much about politics but I do have hunches. I have never rendered any 'services' to any of the leaders of the Fifth Republic (as Monsieur Clerc once insinuated), but I have sometimes surprised them by my 'intuition'. I have that good womanly sense which comes from listening to all sorts of people talking about all sorts of things: love, money, morals, politics. In politics, chit-chat is of prime importance. I make a mental note of everything that interests me and I'm often able to get a feeling about what's going to happen.

In 1972 (Pompidou was then president), I met Valéry Giscard d'Estaing through friends. At Jean Poniatowski's wedding lunch party at the Ritz, I was sitting next to Jean's brother and the (then) Finance Minister was sitting at the high table behind us. Before dessert Valéry Giscard d'Estaing turned to Jean's brother and said: 'You should introduce me to your neighbour; I listened to her for a whole week on the radio while crossing the desert.'

He was referring to a series of interviews I'd given to Jacques Ourevitch (the Michel Drucker of the day) early in 1969. At the time Valéry Giscard d'Estaing had not been a minister. Turning right round to speak to me, he said: 'I really liked your frankness, and the way you spoke, you were very natural.'

I replied perhaps rather too quickly: 'Talking comes very easy when you're telling the truth.'

'Yes, that is indeed very true.'

That was the sum total of our conversation, and when my interviews came out on record, I sent him a copy with an unpretentious message. He never did thank me for it.

Then Valéry Giscard d'Estaing was elected President and one night I was invited to the Élysée Palace, not by him but by the general secretary, François de Combret, on duty that night. We ate in the flat which was reserved for the officers on duty. Albin Chalandon was there. The President was not at home. Suddenly at the end of dinner, François de Combret was called to the telephone. When he came back, he said to me with a smile: 'The President has just returned. He saw the Mercedes in the drive and asked me whose it was. I told him it was yours and he requested me to ask you on his behalf to buy French next time.'

That rather diconcerted me and I said: 'I attract plenty of foreign exchange, and isn't Germany part of the Common Market? And you can ask him from me why he doesn't buy his guns from Manufrance!'

Subsequently I was told that it was just his sense of humour and that he said things like that, without really meaning it, just for the effect.

This episode took place during the second half of his seven-year term, when Raymond Barre was Prime Minister.

My introduction to Raymond Barre was certainly not lacking in piquancy. I'd been invited to a reception at the Élysée (for the first time) in honour of the President, or the Prime Minister, or the First Secretary of Poland, a young woman attaché of the Prime Minister presented me to Monsieur Barre like this: 'Monsieur Prime Minister, let me introduce you to Régine ... Régine Crespin.'

I thought: 'This just can't be true! I hope she'll correct herself ...' But no, she didn't realize her mistake, and I heard Monsieur Barre saying:

'Madame, I hope you might sing us a little song ...'

Not quite knowing what to do, I looked at the Republican Guard

Band standing close by and said with a laugh: 'If the band feel like playing "La Grande Zoa" and "Patchouli-Chinchilla", that'll be fine . . .'

I saw the Prime Minister's eyes open wide. The President's brother, Olivier Giscard d'Estaing, came up to talk to him and said hello. I left them and, very embarrassed at this incident, told François de Combret about it, who soon cleared up the misunderstanding. The following morning, Monsieur Barre had laughed when he told his family the anecdote over breakfast. His son Olivier told me about it a couple of days later.

During the 1981 presidential campaign, I supported Valéry Giscard d'Estaing. But it was certainly not my weight which tipped the balance, because I'd been slimming.

On 1 April 1982, we were celebrating Thierry Le Luron's birthday at Régine's. The club was full of politicians, show business people and socialites. Thierry was sitting between Serge Dassault and Alice Saunier-Séité but was called away to the phone for a moment. When he came back, he said to me: 'Président Giscard would like to talk to you.'

It was April Fool's day, so I didn't hurry.

'I promise you it's him!'

So off I went.

'My dear madame, I didn't want to congratulate Thierry Le Luron without paying my respects to his hostess. It would be a pleasure to dine together one evening.'

'Monsieur le Président, why not come tonight and surprise Thierry?'

He replied good humouredly: 'No, I don't want to steal his thunder.'

The dinner in question took place in May at a mutual friend's house. I sat on Valéry Giscard d'Estaing's right. We began by exchanging small talk about night life and my clubs. I answered the Prince de Beauvau-Craon rather curtly when asked how my 'houses' were doing: 'You've been there often enough to know they're called Régine's.' And they're doing fine.'

As nothing very interesting was happening, I took the initiative and addressed my neighbour.

'Monsieur le Président, I am very honoured to be sitting on your right. I presume I am here because you wished to meet me. Was this perhaps to deepen your knowledge of the night and its inhabitants?'

He laughed and we talked in more detail about the way people communicate, what I call word of mouth, publicity and public relations.

'Do you really believe,' he said sounding unconvinced, 'that word of mouth is an important means of communication?'

'Yes, I do. And what's more, Monsieur le Président, that's what lost it for you.'

'Ah really? You think so?'

'Yes. Part word of mouth, part non-action, and part politics.'

'So for you it really is important.'

'Yes.'

And I added, half-serious, half-joking: 'Tell me something nasty about someone you know, and within a fortnight that someone will come and talk to you about what you said!'

The conversation lapsed a little after that but livened up when I talked about the forthcoming presidential elections. I said to him: 'There will be three right-wing candidates: Monsieur Chirac, Monsieur Barre, and you.'

'No question of Monsieur Barre standing.'

The French, however, are quite versatile enough to recall someone they've already chucked out once before.

As for Monsieur Le Pen, he could get into the Élysée Palace more easily than into one of my clubs.

21

S.O.S. Drogue
International

At Carol's during the fifties there was a wonderfully funny and beautiful woman. She was elegant, she was rich, she was a princess. Yet despite all these advantages, her life was a trauma: she took drugs. And died as a result. It was my first contact with drugs: having once seen the effects I have never forgotten them.

At the Vieux-Colombier too, in Juan-les-Pins there was a woman I greatly admired, who was the hostess of the club, the life and soul. To begin with I couldn't make head or tail of her mood swings, the alternating silence and agitation, cheerfulness and gloom which marked her personality. When I finally understood the root cause I could only ask myself: why? Why do such beautiful and talented people have recourse to such artifice?

And as the years went by and drugs invaded en masse, I watched as more and more wonderful people destroyed themselves. I remember certain dinner parties in the early seventies when, of the eight original guests, only four (including me) would be left, the others having disappeared temporarily we knew not where . . . .

As I have always systematically rejected drugs, persistent users don't come to my club: they know where I stand and that they won't find anyone in the club to sell them drugs. I demand the greatest reserve of people, and to accept anything less would go completely against my 'system'.

Everyone needs a 'drug': be it love, sex, work, little pink pills, alcohol. But you have to be stronger than your drug or else it's the beginning of the end. But with real drugs the fight is unequal. One

282

day, my doctor said: 'I can't understand why you are still so well with all the pills you swallow.'

It's because I'm stronger than my pills. I would not have been stronger than real drugs.

When I opened the club in New York, I let it be used from time to time for the benefit of anti-drug groups (some of which enjoy the patronage of Mrs Reagan). And then I also started visiting treatment centres (including the Anti-Drogue Abuse run by the Serotas, who are friends of mine) and came to grasp the full horror of it: I saw what unimaginable damage this scourge can cause, and now even to our youngest children, and also how very harmful it can be when a family maintains a conspiracy of silence about the problem in its midst. I came to feel personally concerned and involved, and decided to make use of my public image to set up *S.O.S Drogue International* in France, to alert thousands more people to the problems and win them over to the cause.

Today I am involved in the campaign body and soul. It has been a good way of bringing together the 'caring' people around me, those who are prepared to think of others, of the disinherited and the lost. I have always had many friends, but until now I have never asked anything of them. Today they are standing up to be counted, and I am happy to say they are no less numerous than before.

S.O.S. Drogue International, founded in 1984, is a completely apolitical organization comprising a scientific committee and a great number of celebrities from the worlds of show business, sport, the press, and business. I am able to count on the support of Monsieur Laurent Fabius, Prime Minister, Monsieur Jacques Chirac, Mayor of Paris, Monsieur Jack Lang, Minister of Culture, Monsieur Chaban-Delmas (whose wife has worked in this field for many years) and Monsieur Gaston Deferre. These last two have given S.O.S. Drogue International the use of properties of theirs, one near Bordeaux and the other near Marseille. The serious aims of S.O.S. Drogue International (which works in close collaboration with the interministerial committee for the drug problem, and is in touch with sister organizations in America) are universally recognized.

To raise funds, I first spoke to people around me — and when I say 'spoke to people' I don't mean in vague terms or to the world at large. This is a grave matter. The people without much money can give a little; the rich must give generously.

I know where the money is; I can find sponsors. It's not dilettant-
ism on my part, I'm not playing at it, and I certainly don't just take
pot luck. The offensive is planned in the minutest detail.

I become the leader of an army on the march. Michel Sardou
dubbed me 'Patton' on one occasion, because like Patton I get stuck
in, but only when the battle-plan has been thought through to the
last detail.

I organize gala performances for which stars offer to perform free
of charge, setting an example for others to follow, rich or not so
rich.

The two big stars who have given me the most wholehearted and
generous support are Thierry Le Luron (28 November 1984 at the
Gymnase Marie-Bell) and Julio Iglesias (14 January 1985 at the
Rex).

I have already mentioned Thierry Le Luron, and I must say a
word here about Julio Iglesias. We have been close friends for years
and have spent some marvellously happy times together.

Neither his fifty-eight albums in fifteen years, nor his tens of
millions of fans (especially female fans) have spoiled him, hardened
him, or made him lose any of his great integrity — quite the
opposite. I often see him in Miami, where he has been living for the
last five years. I love that city: gateway as it is to both the Americas,
North and South, and turned towards Europe too. Julio's brand of
success is akin to Régine's brand of success. In moving from one
country to another, he — like me — has not sought to change his
style, but has simply made minor alterations to suit the needs of his
audience, rather like a painter who, as Julio put it, 'changes the
frame round his picture'. He too puts his success partly down to
luck, but mainly down to hard work and self-discipline. Something
he said about the rhythm of 'the crooner' has much in common with
the rhythm in my own professional life, which is based on the length
of the day, not the exploitation of that day: 'The crooner is never in
too much of a hurry, he stops if he needs to, takes it easy. Some
performers are always in a hurry and then one day, they take a song
slowly and get through it just the same: then they start wondering
whether that wasn't their best performance yet.' This charming
man is happy to admit:'Some days I don't like myself at all. But
any complexes I might have had I've got firmly under control'.
Complexes we control or use to our advantage, that rings a bell for
me ... To say nothing of another comment of his which might
pass as my own credo: 'First and foremost I'm a fighter, and I like

people who want to win. The competitive spirit is the most attractive thing in the world, it's what makes me tick . . .'

I'm still a fighter today, but first and foremost for the cause of S.O.S. Drogue International.

22

São Paulo

26 September 1982. A hairdresser's salon in São Paulo, Brazil. Mirrors everywhere, bright lights, a jumble of scissors, combs, brushes, beauty products, jewelled clips and white silk bows... While manicurists and pedicurists were bent over the smartest hands and feet in town, the hairdressers, all affectation and make-up, laughed, squealed and twirled about like marionettes. The occasion? Not the big Carnival ball: wrong time of year, and anyway they don't make so much of Carnival in São Paulo. No, it was 'simply' the first Julio Iglesias concert in Brazil. And it was being held at Régine's ...

While Angelo worked on my hair, I pondered over all the problems I'd had making this show happen. All the authorities in the city had been against me, and Julio's Brazilian tour promoters too ... On my side I had Julio, who had said: 'You can have my first concert for charity, before I start my Brazilian tour proper.'

And come hell and high water, and despite all the telexes from people wanting to make him change his mind, he had held fast: 'I have promised my first concert to Régine, and I'll sing in the street if she asks me to.'

And united by a strong bond, and having total confidence in each other, we won the day. The concert was to be in aid of handicapped children, whose patron was the wife of the Brazilian President.

It was also the evening before Yom Kippur, the Jewish Day of Atonement, their day of fasting and expiation. Roger and I had promised we would spend the following evening, Monday, at the synagogue. Fasting was normal for us at Yom Kippur, but we hadn't set foot in the synagogue except for weddings and barmitzvahs for a very long time ...

Angelo wouldn't stop asking me questions, and when he did stop wittering (in the nicest possible way of course) for a minute, assorted Brazilian ladies would come over with gushing hellos and pleasantries they generally didn't mean.

I was thinking about Nagi Nohas, my partner in Brazil: a very handsome man of thirty-eight, who has succeeded in everything he's tried to do. Régine's is built on some of his land, it cost three million dollars and is with Monte-Carlo the most beautiful of all. He and his wife Soula had bought numerous tickets for the soirée.

Three hours later, and all São Paulo arrived at the club. Together with every single white flower to be found in the city (lilies and orchids): the effect was striking, and I'd never seen a Régine's looking more luxurious. I was talking with Julio in his dressing room (a caravan parked behind Régine's ...). Guy Laroche had made me a wonderful sequinned dress, with a fox-fur edging. I had lost weight, felt great, and was ready to go.

The evening went brilliantly. Julio gave a stunning performance and then the President's wife led the dancing. She danced very elegantly, for a long time, and the party finished very late, as so often in Brazil.

Roger and I woke happy next morning. We were to meet at the Nassers' house at five o'clock, to be joined by the Safra family. The Nassers and the Safras are both extremely rich banking and business families. They have strong ties between them and are like one family, with many members, whose hospitality and generosity are legendary. Before going to the synagogue together, Madame Nasser senior had made us a marvellous meal, after which we would fast through until sunset the following day. The tables were covered with white cloth, as for the Sabbath, and they had lit dozens of candles.

We went on foot from the house to the synagogue (which had been built by the Safras, their relatives and friends), like I had once done in Lyon.

Women sit upstairs in the synagogue, in the tribune which faces the sanctuary. The men remain downstairs. We all wear white because *it is not downcast and in sombre apparel, like that worn by those who plead before a judge or an earthly ruler, that the Israelites should appear before the Supreme Judge, but joyful and clad in white raiment.* That's why men wear a white silk prayer shawl over

287

their dark suits. Jacky Nasser lent Roger his grandfather's skullcap and prayer shawl, and he sat among the Nassers and Safras in their family pews.

The rabbis, both young and old, looked most handsome with their majestic beards. The children were all in party clothes, running about gleefully, their skullcaps held on with hairgrips.

The ceremony began, and we recited the general confession of sins, those we had committed *under compulsion and of free will, wilfully and unknowingly, by utterance of the lips, openly and secretly, unchastely, by violence, by evil speech, by scoffing, by our haughty eyes, by our impiety*.

As we confess our sins only once a year in our religion, there is a long list to be forgiven by the Eternal One. The chanting moved me deeply; watching the ancient rabbis, in whose eyes shone all the goodness of the world. Then came the moment for the families to make their gifts to the Temple. The bidding went up, the women murmured, everyone competing in their generosity. I thought of Joseph ...

Then, as Roger stepped forward to kiss the books of Moses, I suddenly saw, through my tears, the rabbi from Lyon, Benjamin Dreyfus.

It was wartime. Claude was sitting in the front row. It was his last Yom Kippur before the extermination. The Heymanns were there, looking lovingly at their son. And I could see other faces too, Maurice, Évelyne, Lionel. As I looked at Roger, his image fused with Claude's.

I think I have spent my whole life searching for the meaning in these ceremonies, and in that brief moment I felt the sacred enter me. The little girl from Lyon, who seemed so distant, had never been so close. I was all alone with my past, that deep wound which has made me so strong, and I cried. While a voice, terrible but gentle, told me that my past had perhaps been the best thing that ever happened to me ...

And tomorrow, when the fast is broken, the celebrations will start up all over again, profane and not sacred this time, the party which, I know, will continue until such time as God decides it's His turn to call me Régine.